THE X FILES ™

SEASON 11 • VOLUME 1

Cover by **Brian Miller**

Collection Edits by **Justin Eisinger** and **Alonzo Simon**

Published by **Ted Adams**

Collection Design by **Ron Estevez**

The X-Files created by **Chris Carter**

Special thanks to Joshua Izzo and Nicole Spiegel
at Twentieth Century Fox and Gabe Rotter
at Ten Thirteen Productions.

ISBN: 978-1-63140-527-3

19 18 17 16   1 2 3 4

www.IDWPUBLISHING.com
IDW founded by Ted Adams, Alex Garner, Kris Oprisko, and Robbie Robbins

Ted Adams, CEO & Publisher
Greg Goldstein, President & COO
Robbie Robbins, EVP/Sr. Graphic Artist
Chris Ryall, Chief Creative Officer/Editor-in-Chief
Matthew Ruzicka, CPA, Chief Financial Officer
Dirk Wood, VP of Marketing
Lorelei Bunjes, VP of Digital Services
Jeff Webber, VP of Licensing, Digital and Subsidiary Rights
Jerry Bennington, VP of New Product Development

Facebook: **facebook.com/idwpublishing**
Twitter: **@idwpublishing**
YouTube: **youtube.com/idwpublishing**
Tumblr: **tumblr.idwpublishing.com**
Instagram: **instagram.com/idwpublishing**

Originally published as THE X-FILES: SEASON 11 issues #1–5.

Written by **Joe Harris**

Art by **Matthew Dow Smith**

Colors by **Jordie Bellaire**

Letters by **Chris Mowry**

Series Edits by **Denton J. Tipton**

Executive Producer: **Chris Carter**

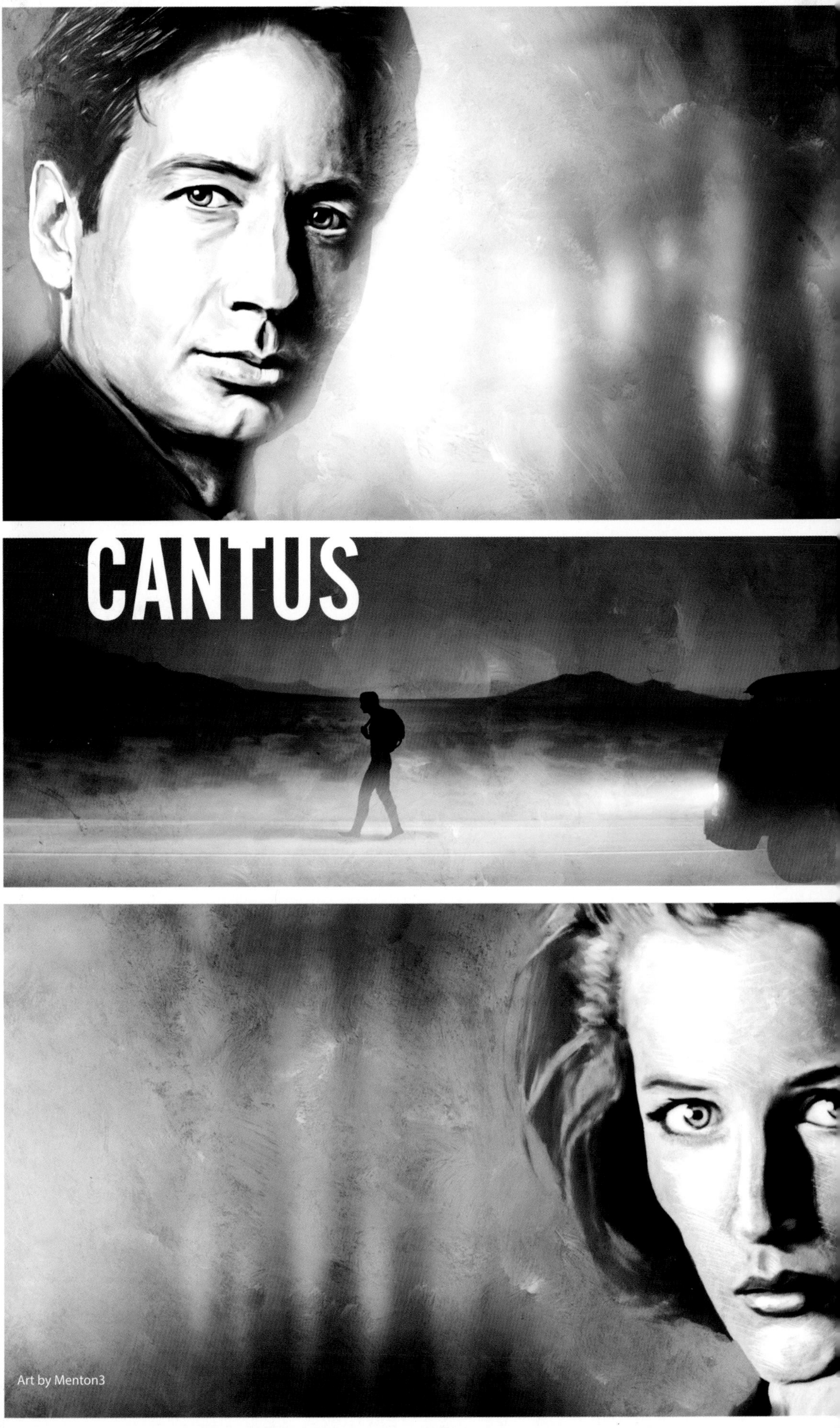
CANTUS
Art by Menton3

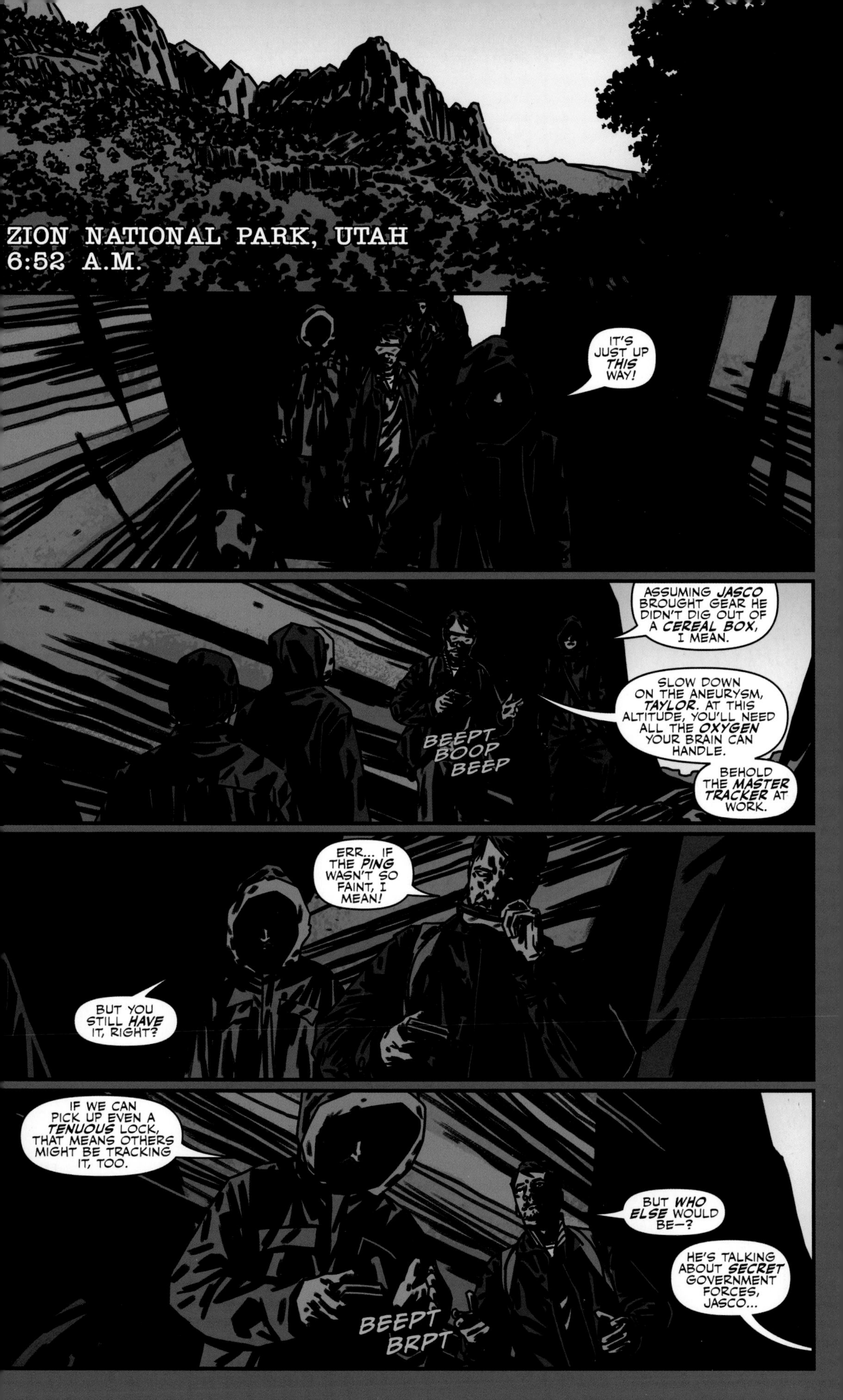
ZION NATIONAL PARK, UTAH
6:52 A.M.
IT'S JUST UP *THIS* WAY!
ASSUMING *JASCO* BROUGHT GEAR HE DIDN'T DIG OUT OF A *CEREAL BOX*, I MEAN.
SLOW DOWN ON THE ANEURYSM, *TAYLOR*. AT THIS ALTITUDE, YOU'LL NEED ALL THE *OXYGEN* YOUR BRAIN CAN HANDLE.
BEEPT BOOP BEEP
BEHOLD THE *MASTER TRACKER* AT WORK.
ERR... IF THE *PING* WASN'T SO FAINT, I MEAN!
BUT YOU STILL *HAVE* IT, RIGHT?
IF WE CAN PICK UP EVEN A *TENUOUS* LOCK, THAT MEANS OTHERS MIGHT BE TRACKING IT, TOO.
BUT *WHO ELSE* WOULD BE—?
HE'S TALKING ABOUT *SECRET* GOVERNMENT FORCES, JASCO...
BEEPT BRPT

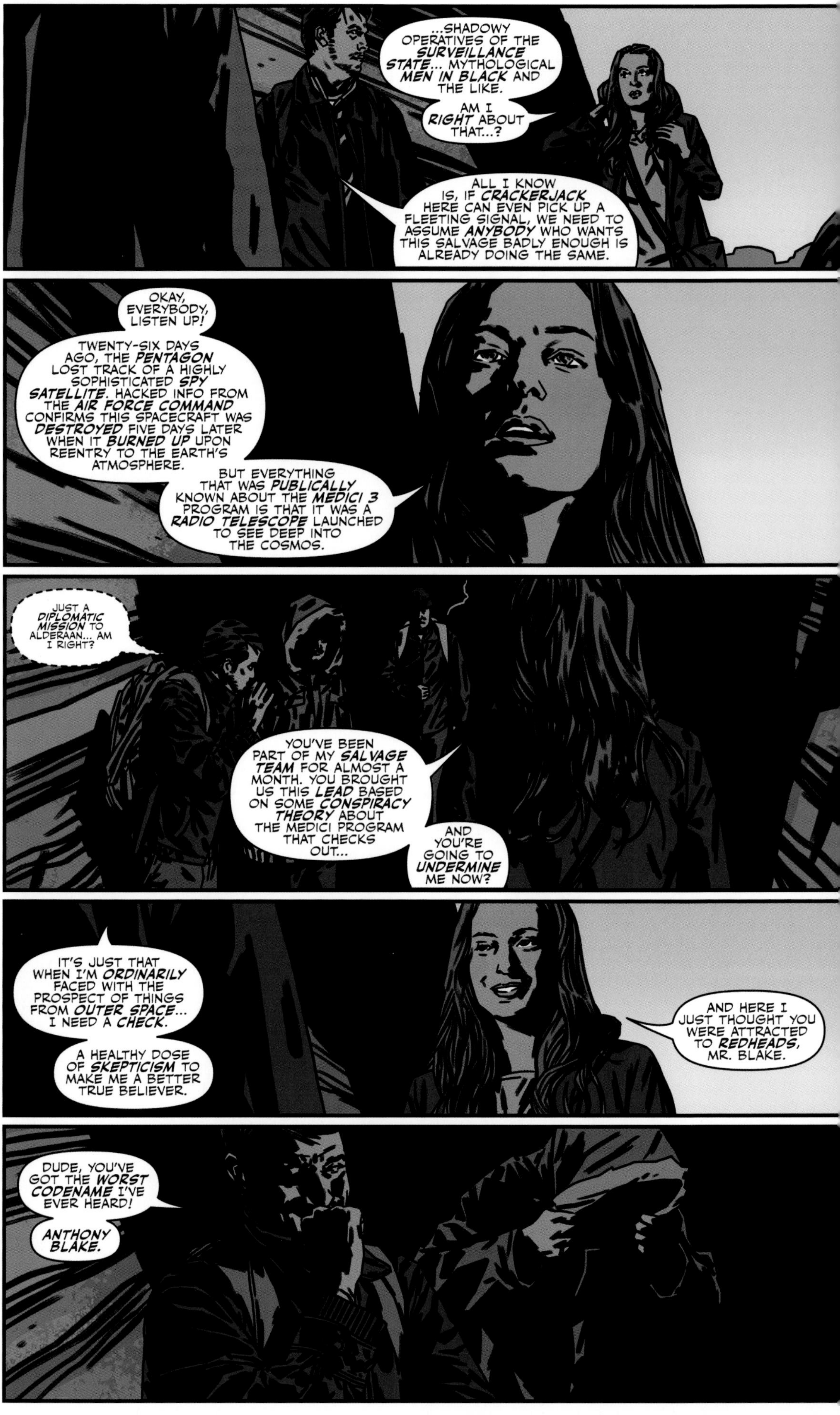
...SHADOWY OPERATIVES OF THE SURVEILLANCE STATE... MYTHOLOGICAL MEN IN BLACK AND THE LIKE.
AM I RIGHT ABOUT THAT...?
ALL I KNOW IS, IF CRACKERJACK HERE CAN EVEN PICK UP A FLEETING SIGNAL, WE NEED TO ASSUME ANYBODY WHO WANTS THIS SALVAGE BADLY ENOUGH IS ALREADY DOING THE SAME.
OKAY, EVERYBODY, LISTEN UP!
TWENTY-SIX DAYS AGO, THE PENTAGON LOST TRACK OF A HIGHLY SOPHISTICATED SPY SATELLITE. HACKED INFO FROM THE AIR FORCE COMMAND CONFIRMS THIS SPACECRAFT WAS DESTROYED FIVE DAYS LATER WHEN IT BURNED UP UPON REENTRY TO THE EARTH'S ATMOSPHERE.
BUT EVERYTHING THAT WAS PUBLICALLY KNOWN ABOUT THE MEDICI 3 PROGRAM IS THAT IT WAS A RADIO TELESCOPE LAUNCHED TO SEE DEEP INTO THE COSMOS.
JUST A DIPLOMATIC MISSION TO ALDERAAN... AM I RIGHT?
YOU'VE BEEN PART OF MY SALVAGE TEAM FOR ALMOST A MONTH. YOU BROUGHT US THIS LEAD BASED ON SOME CONSPIRACY THEORY ABOUT THE MEDICI PROGRAM THAT CHECKS OUT...
AND YOU'RE GOING TO UNDERMINE ME NOW?
IT'S JUST THAT WHEN I'M ORDINARILY FACED WITH THE PROSPECT OF THINGS FROM OUTER SPACE... I NEED A CHECK.
A HEALTHY DOSE OF SKEPTICISM TO MAKE ME A BETTER TRUE BELIEVER.
AND HERE I JUST THOUGHT YOU WERE ATTRACTED TO REDHEADS, MR. BLAKE.
DUDE, YOU'VE GOT THE WORST CODENAME I'VE EVER HEARD!
ANTHONY BLAKE.

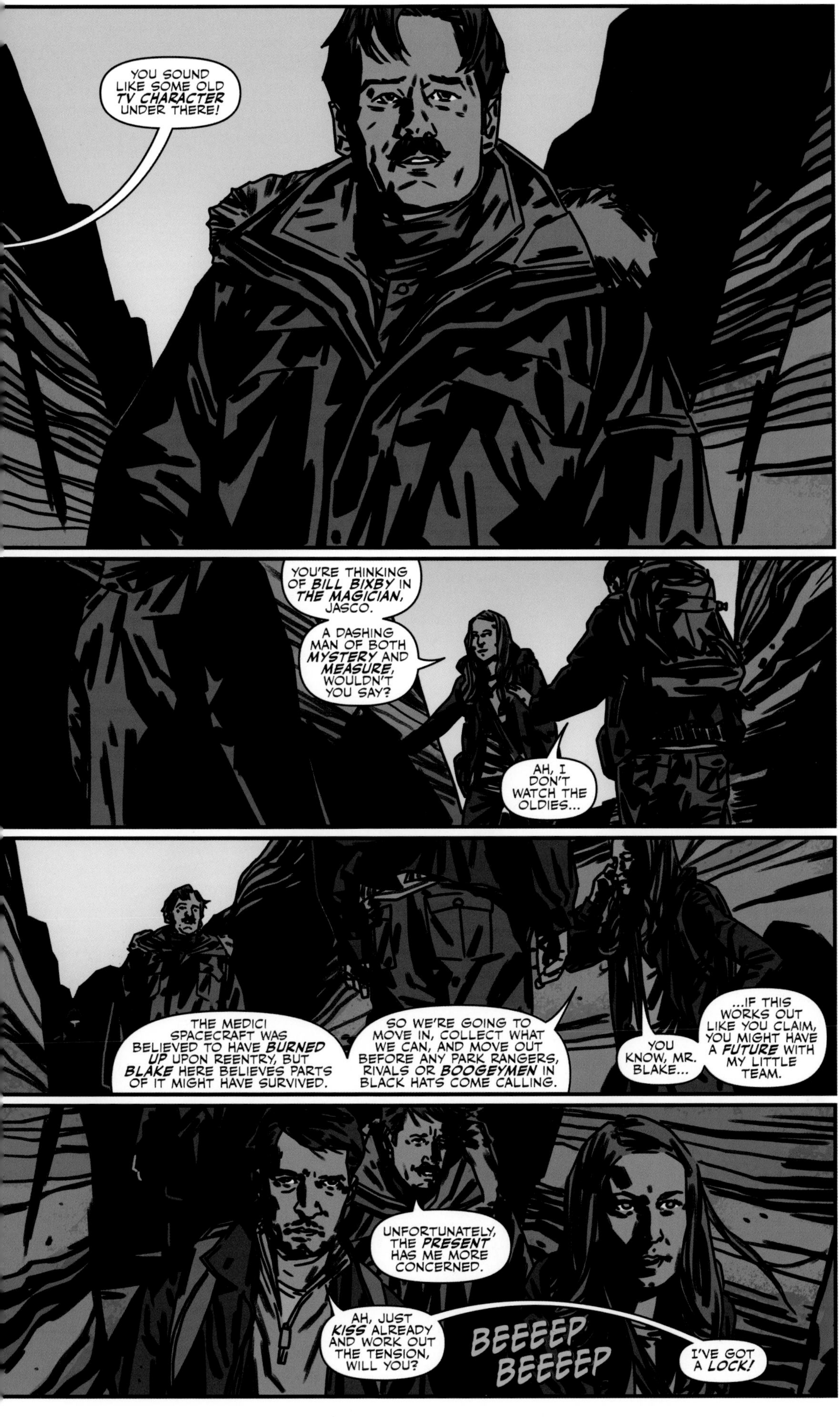
YOU SOUND LIKE SOME OLD TV CHARACTER UNDER THERE!
YOU'RE THINKING OF BILL BIXBY IN THE MAGICIAN, JASCO.
A DASHING MAN OF BOTH MYSTERY AND MEASURE, WOULDN'T YOU SAY?
AH, I DON'T WATCH THE OLDIES...
THE MEDICI SPACECRAFT WAS BELIEVED TO HAVE BURNED UP UPON REENTRY, BUT BLAKE HERE BELIEVES PARTS OF IT MIGHT HAVE SURVIVED.
SO WE'RE GOING TO MOVE IN, COLLECT WHAT WE CAN, AND MOVE OUT BEFORE ANY PARK RANGERS, RIVALS OR BOOGEYMEN IN BLACK HATS COME CALLING.
YOU KNOW, MR. BLAKE...
...IF THIS WORKS OUT LIKE YOU CLAIM, YOU MIGHT HAVE A FUTURE WITH MY LITTLE TEAM.
UNFORTUNATELY, THE PRESENT HAS ME MORE CONCERNED.
AH, JUST KISS ALREADY AND WORK OUT THE TENSION, WILL YOU?
BEEEEP BEEEEP
I'VE GOT A LOCK!

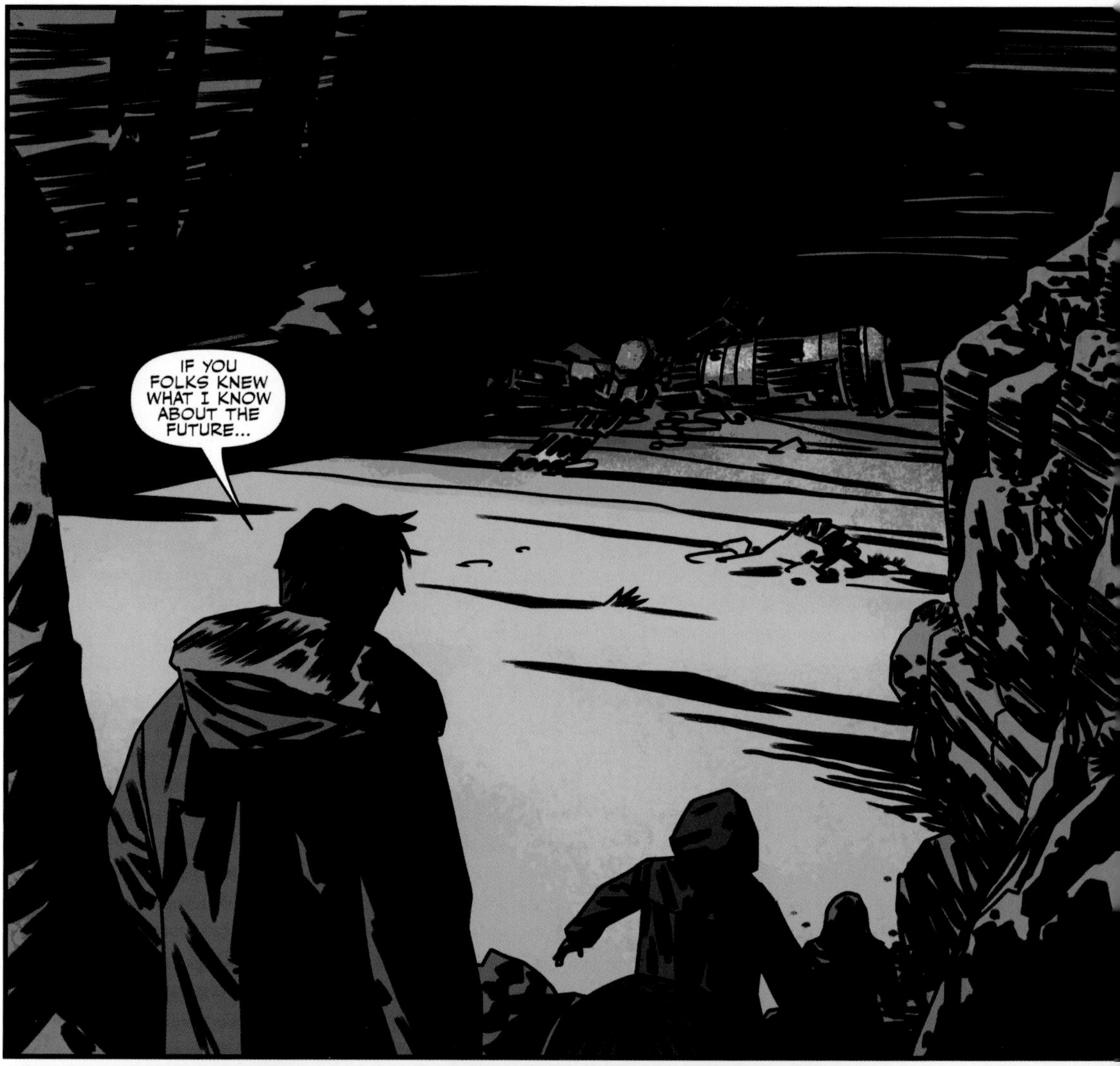
IF YOU FOLKS KNEW WHAT I KNOW ABOUT THE FUTURE...

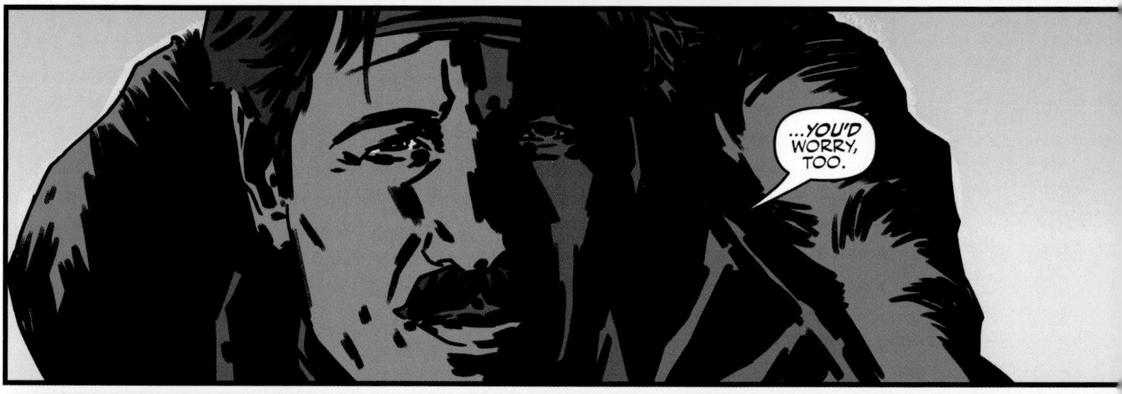
...YOU'D WORRY, TOO.

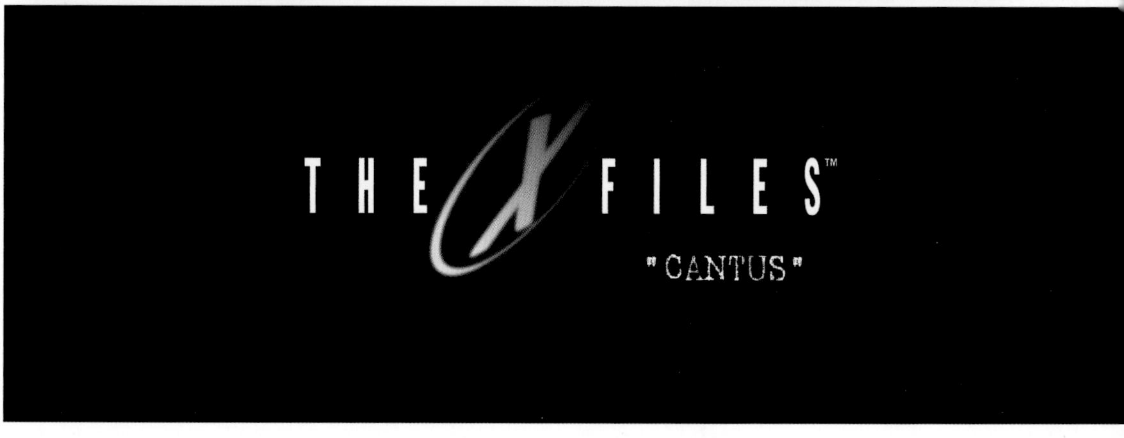
THE X FILES™
"CANTUS"

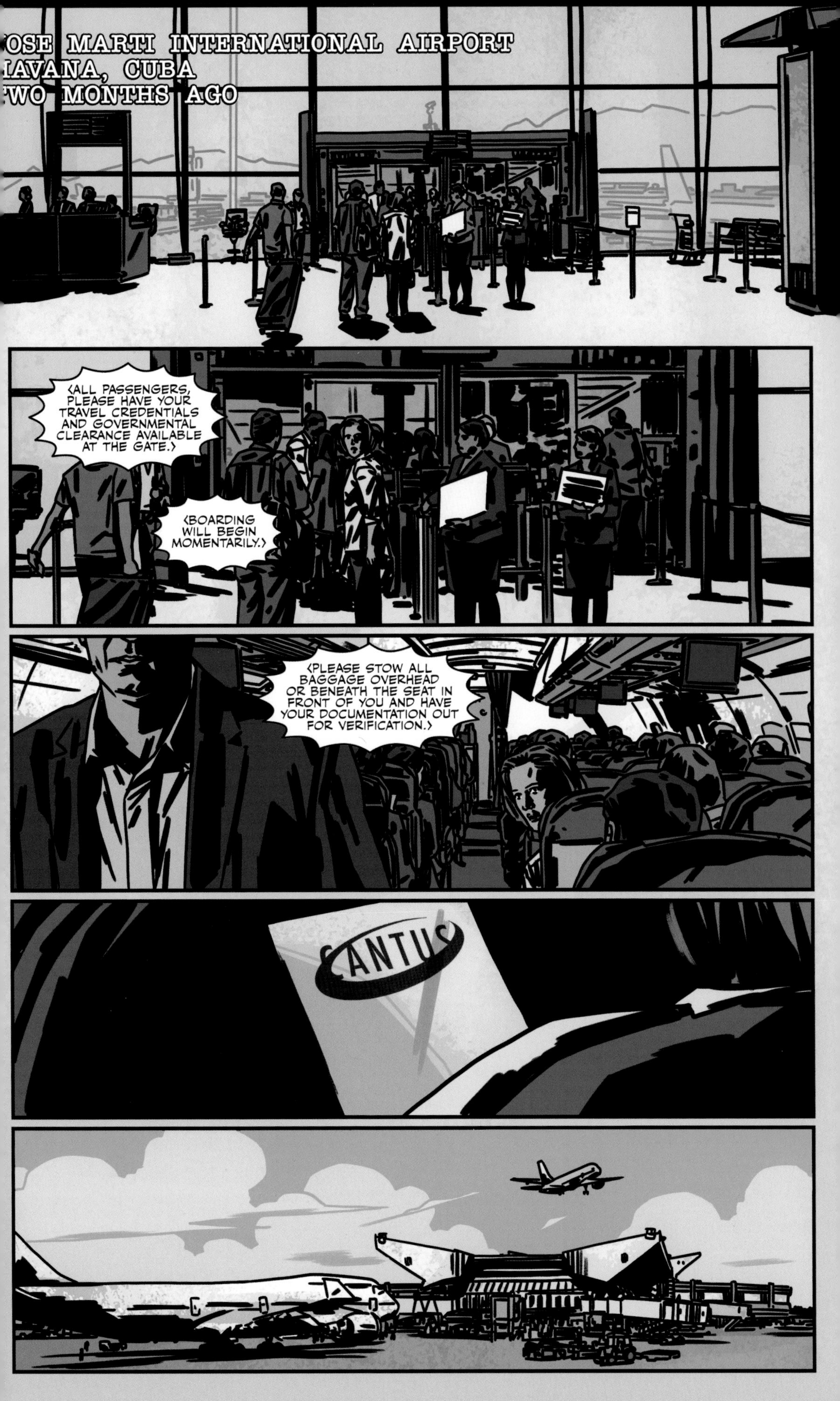
OSE MARTI INTERNATIONAL AIRPORT
IAVANA, CUBA
WO MONTHS AGO
‹ALL PASSENGERS, PLEASE HAVE YOUR TRAVEL CREDENTIALS AND GOVERNMENTAL CLEARANCE AVAILABLE AT THE GATE.›
‹BOARDING WILL BEGIN MOMENTARILY.›
‹PLEASE STOW ALL BAGGAGE OVERHEAD OR BENEATH THE SEAT IN FRONT OF YOU AND HAVE YOUR DOCUMENTATION OUT FOR VERIFICATION.›
CANTUS

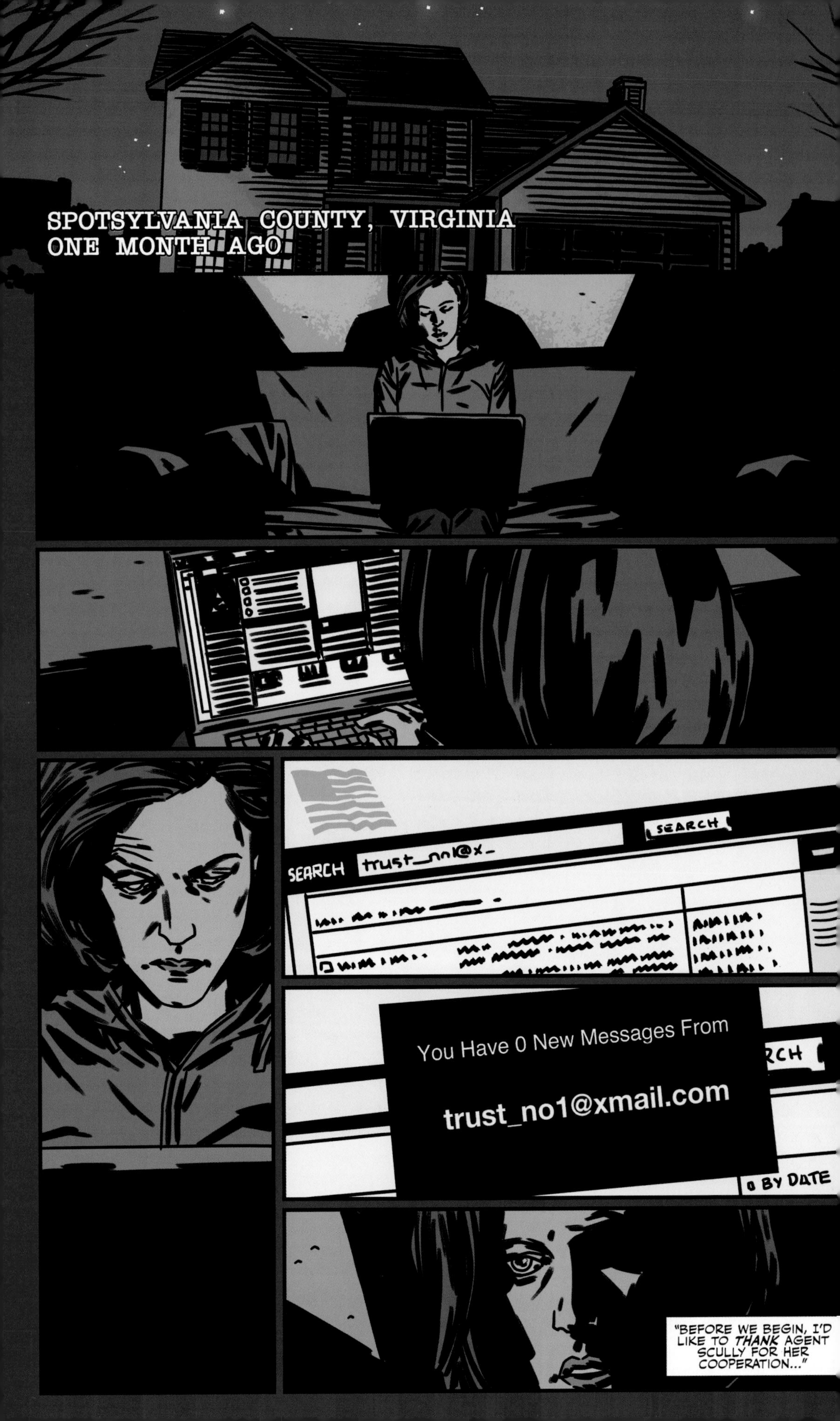
SPOTSYLVANIA COUNTY, VIRGINIA
ONE MONTH AGO
SEARCH
SEARCH trust_no1@x_
You Have 0 New Messages From
trust_no1@xmail.com
BY DATE
"BEFORE WE BEGIN, I'D LIKE TO THANK AGENT SCULLY FOR HER COOPERATION..."

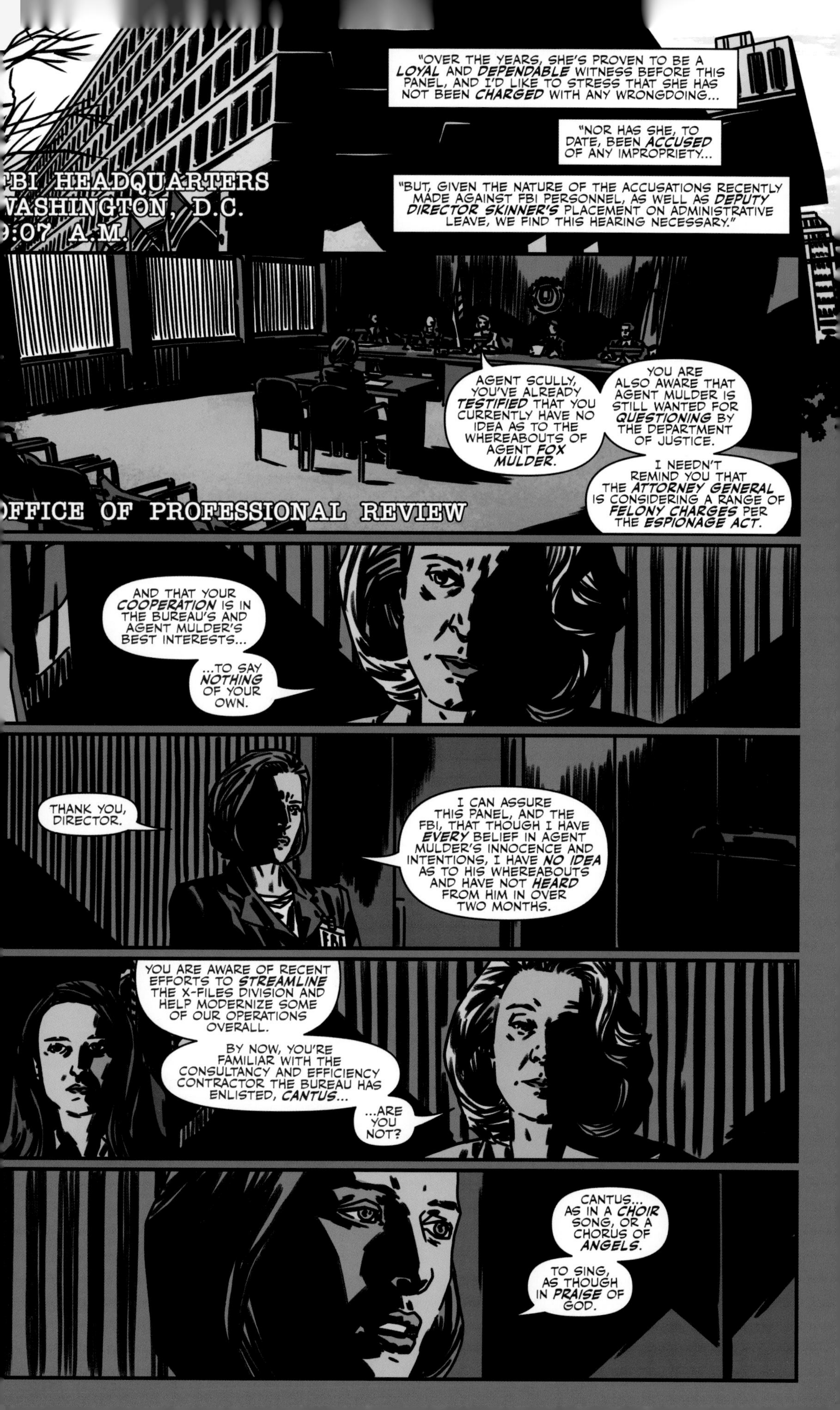
FBI HEADQUARTERS
WASHINGTON, D.C.
9:07 A.M.
"OVER THE YEARS, SHE'S PROVEN TO BE A LOYAL AND DEPENDABLE WITNESS BEFORE THIS PANEL, AND I'D LIKE TO STRESS THAT SHE HAS NOT BEEN CHARGED WITH ANY WRONGDOING...
"NOR HAS SHE, TO DATE, BEEN ACCUSED OF ANY IMPROPRIETY...
"BUT, GIVEN THE NATURE OF THE ACCUSATIONS RECENTLY MADE AGAINST FBI PERSONNEL, AS WELL AS DEPUTY DIRECTOR SKINNER'S PLACEMENT ON ADMINISTRATIVE LEAVE, WE FIND THIS HEARING NECESSARY."
OFFICE OF PROFESSIONAL REVIEW
AGENT SCULLY, YOU'VE ALREADY TESTIFIED THAT YOU CURRENTLY HAVE NO IDEA AS TO THE WHEREABOUTS OF AGENT FOX MULDER.
YOU ARE ALSO AWARE THAT AGENT MULDER IS STILL WANTED FOR QUESTIONING BY THE DEPARTMENT OF JUSTICE.
I NEEDN'T REMIND YOU THAT THE ATTORNEY GENERAL IS CONSIDERING A RANGE OF FELONY CHARGES PER THE ESPIONAGE ACT.
AND THAT YOUR COOPERATION IS IN THE BUREAU'S AND AGENT MULDER'S BEST INTERESTS...
...TO SAY NOTHING OF YOUR OWN.
THANK YOU, DIRECTOR.
I CAN ASSURE THIS PANEL, AND THE FBI, THAT THOUGH I HAVE EVERY BELIEF IN AGENT MULDER'S INNOCENCE AND INTENTIONS, I HAVE NO IDEA AS TO HIS WHEREABOUTS AND HAVE NOT HEARD FROM HIM IN OVER TWO MONTHS.
YOU ARE AWARE OF RECENT EFFORTS TO STREAMLINE THE X-FILES DIVISION AND HELP MODERNIZE SOME OF OUR OPERATIONS OVERALL.
BY NOW, YOU'RE FAMILIAR WITH THE CONSULTANCY AND EFFICIENCY CONTRACTOR THE BUREAU HAS ENLISTED, CANTUS...
...ARE YOU NOT?
CANTUS... AS IN A CHOIR SONG, OR A CHORUS OF ANGELS.
TO SING, AS THOUGH IN PRAISE OF GOD.

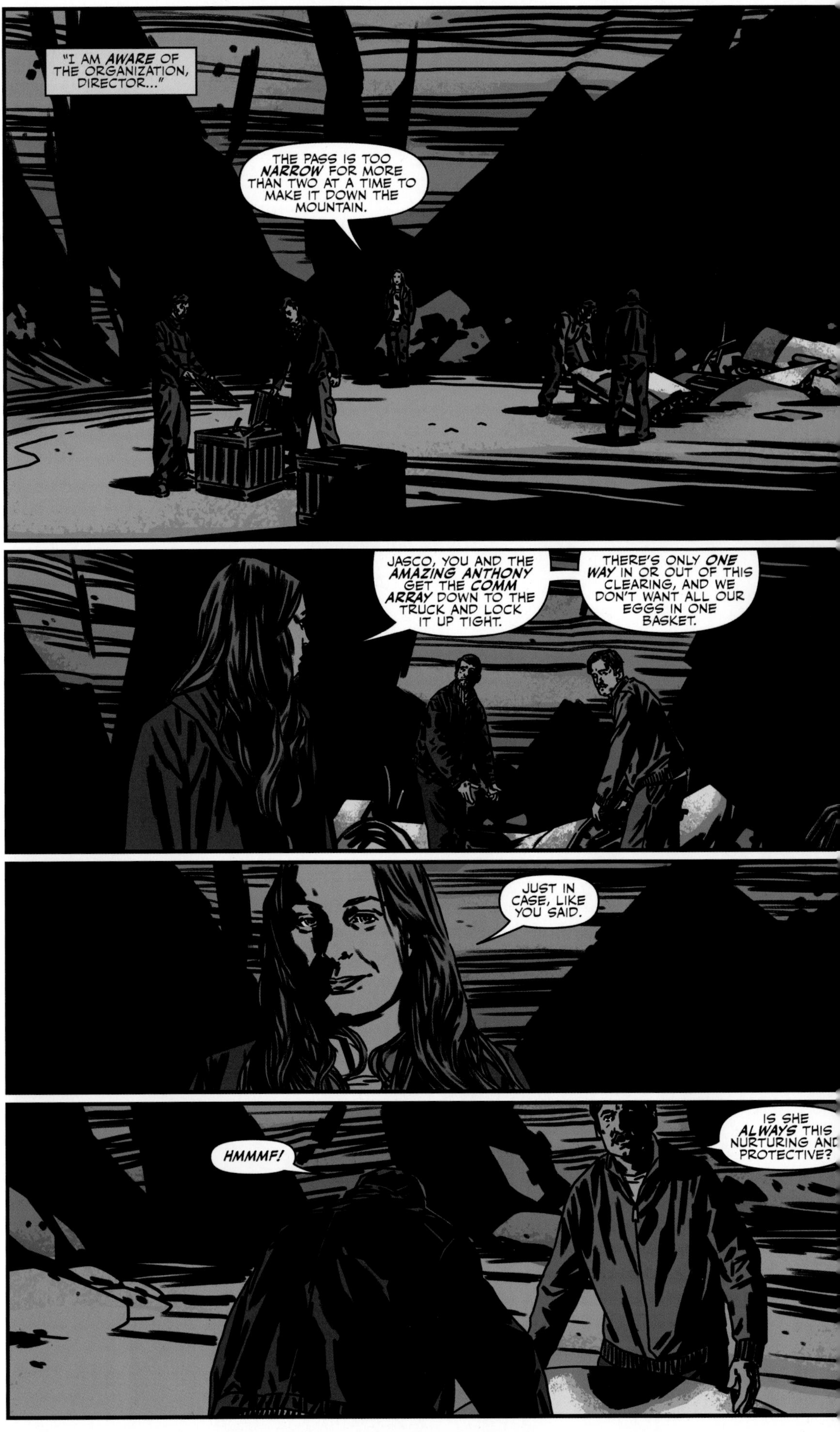
"I AM AWARE OF THE ORGANIZATION, DIRECTOR..."
THE PASS IS TOO NARROW FOR MORE THAN TWO AT A TIME TO MAKE IT DOWN THE MOUNTAIN.
JASCO, YOU AND THE AMAZING ANTHONY GET THE COMM ARRAY DOWN TO THE TRUCK AND LOCK IT UP TIGHT.
THERE'S ONLY ONE WAY IN OR OUT OF THIS CLEARING, AND WE DON'T WANT ALL OUR EGGS IN ONE BASKET.
JUST IN CASE, LIKE YOU SAID.
HMMMF!
IS SHE ALWAYS THIS NURTURING AND PROTECTIVE?

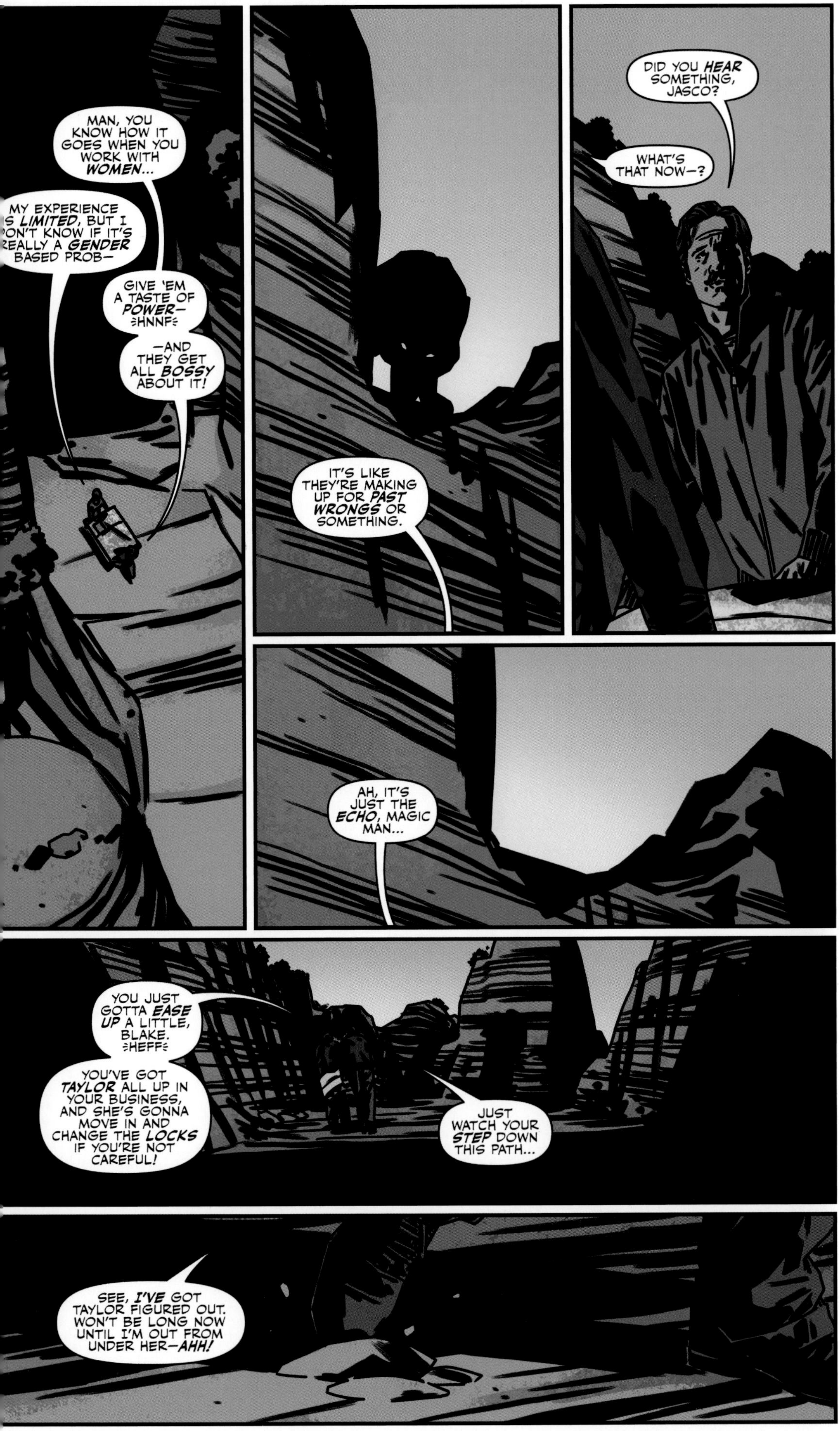
MAN, YOU KNOW HOW IT GOES WHEN YOU WORK WITH WOMEN...
MY EXPERIENCE IS LIMITED, BUT I DON'T KNOW IF IT'S REALLY A GENDER BASED PROB—
GIVE 'EM A TASTE OF POWER— HNNF
—AND THEY GET ALL BOSSY ABOUT IT!
IT'S LIKE THEY'RE MAKING UP FOR PAST WRONGS OR SOMETHING.
DID YOU HEAR SOMETHING, JASCO?
WHAT'S THAT NOW—?
AH, IT'S JUST THE ECHO, MAGIC MAN...
YOU JUST GOTTA EASE UP A LITTLE, BLAKE. HEFF
YOU'VE GOT TAYLOR ALL UP IN YOUR BUSINESS, AND SHE'S GONNA MOVE IN AND CHANGE THE LOCKS IF YOU'RE NOT CAREFUL!
JUST WATCH YOUR STEP DOWN THIS PATH...
SEE, I'VE GOT TAYLOR FIGURED OUT. WON'T BE LONG NOW UNTIL I'M OUT FROM UNDER HER—AHH!

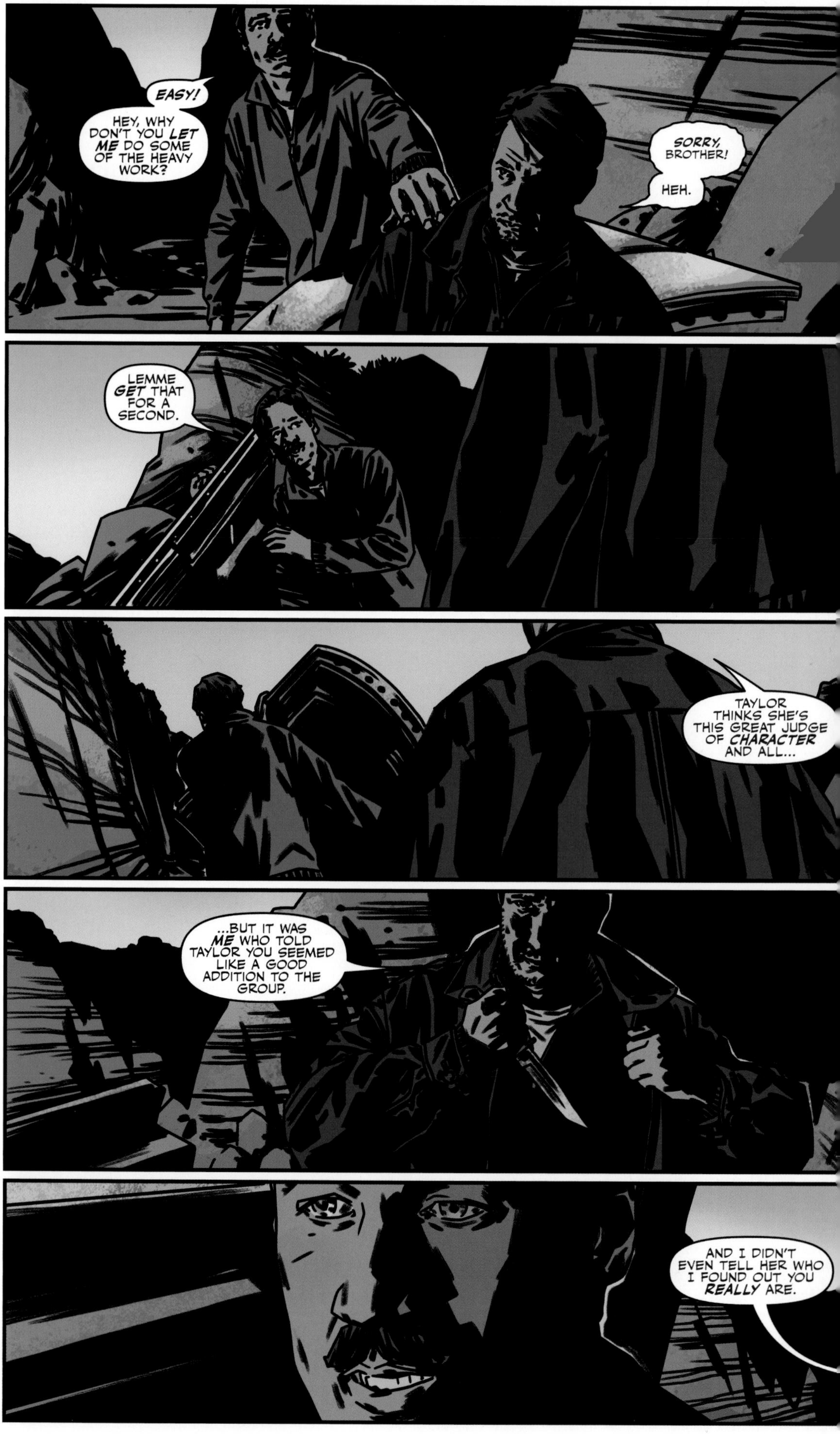
EASY!
HEY, WHY DON'T YOU LET ME DO SOME OF THE HEAVY WORK?
SORRY, BROTHER!
HEH.
LEMME GET THAT FOR A SECOND.
TAYLOR THINKS SHE'S THIS GREAT JUDGE OF CHARACTER AND ALL...
...BUT IT WAS ME WHO TOLD TAYLOR YOU SEEMED LIKE A GOOD ADDITION TO THE GROUP.
AND I DIDN'T EVEN TELL HER WHO I FOUND OUT YOU REALLY ARE.

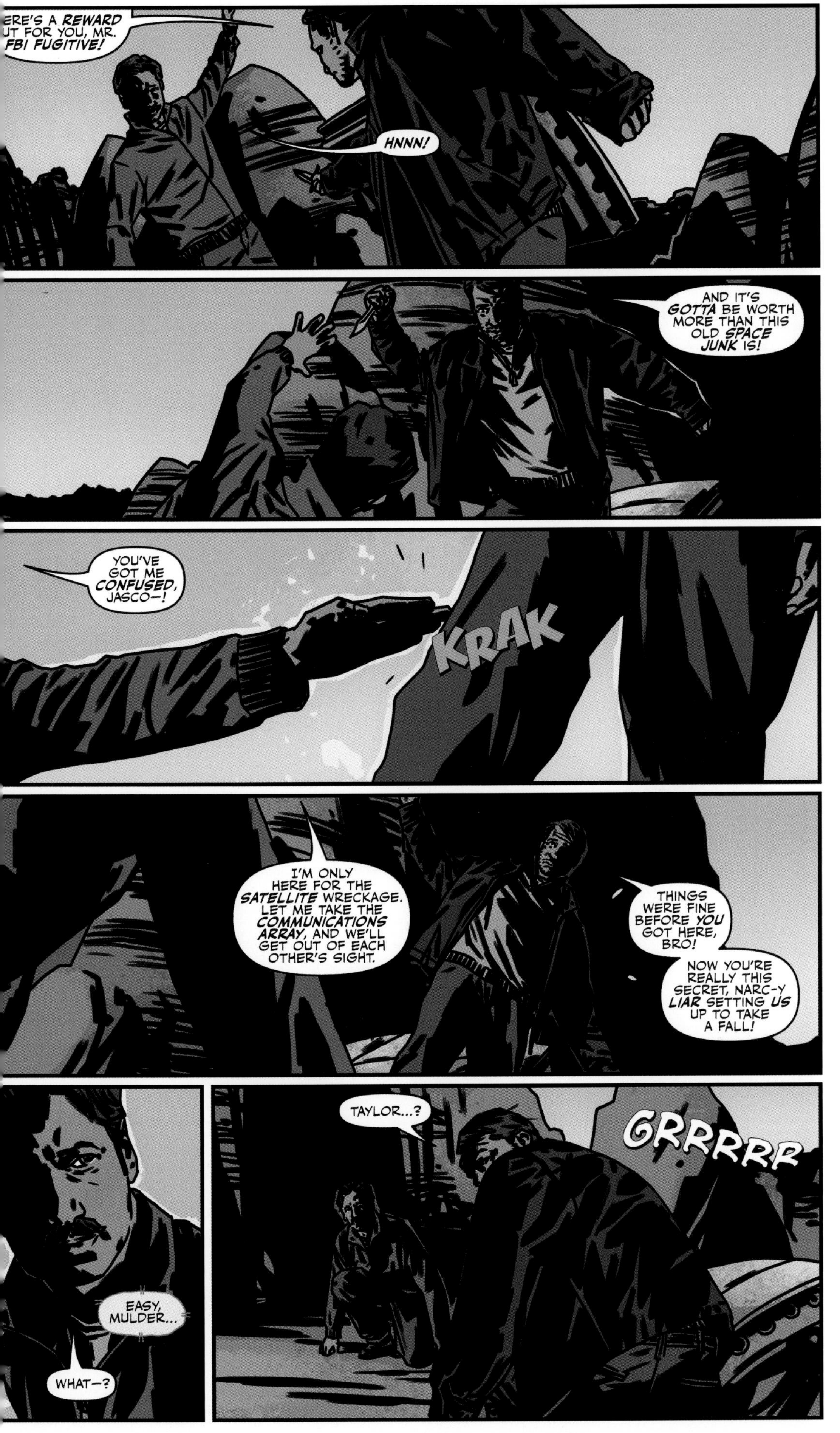

ERE'S A REWARD
UT FOR YOU, MR.
FBI FUGITIVE!
HNNN!
AND IT'S GOTTA BE WORTH MORE THAN THIS OLD SPACE JUNK IS!
YOU'VE GOT ME CONFUSED, JASCO—!
KRAK
I'M ONLY HERE FOR THE SATELLITE WRECKAGE. LET ME TAKE THE COMMUNICATIONS ARRAY, AND WE'LL GET OUT OF EACH OTHER'S SIGHT.
THINGS WERE FINE BEFORE YOU GOT HERE, BRO!
NOW YOU'RE REALLY THIS SECRET, NARC-Y LIAR SETTING US UP TO TAKE A FALL!
EASY, MULDER...
WHAT—?
TAYLOR...?
GRRRRRR

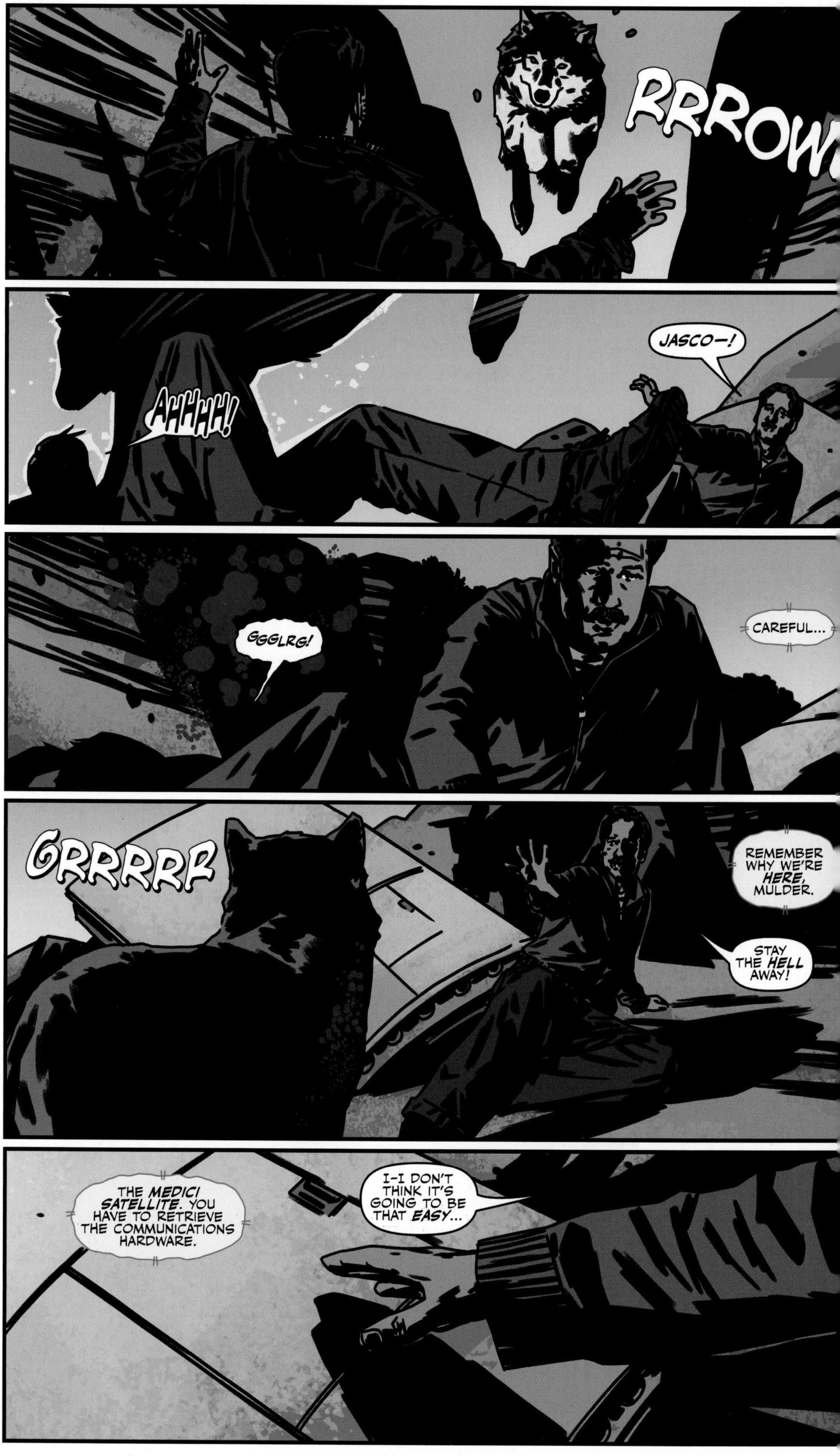
RRROW
JASCO—!
AHHHH!
GGGLRG!
CAREFUL...
GRRRRR
REMEMBER WHY WE'RE HERE, MULDER.
STAY THE HELL AWAY!
THE MEDICI SATELLITE. YOU HAVE TO RETRIEVE THE COMMUNICATIONS HARDWARE.
I-I DON'T THINK IT'S GOING TO BE THAT EASY...

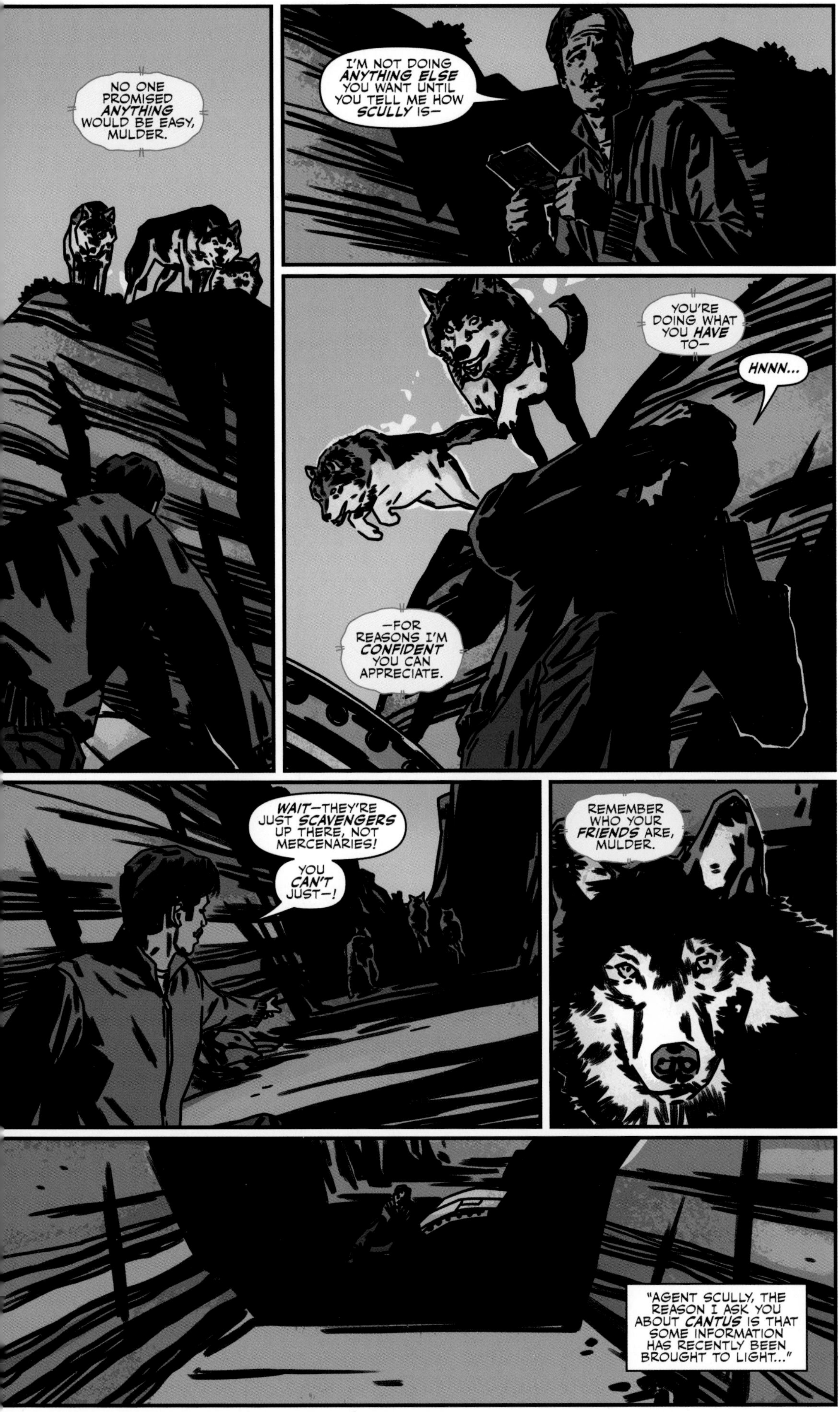
NO ONE PROMISED ANYTHING WOULD BE EASY, MULDER.
I'M NOT DOING ANYTHING ELSE YOU WANT UNTIL YOU TELL ME HOW SCULLY IS—
YOU'RE DOING WHAT YOU HAVE TO—
HNNN...
—FOR REASONS I'M CONFIDENT YOU CAN APPRECIATE.
WAIT—THEY'RE JUST SCAVENGERS UP THERE, NOT MERCENARIES!
YOU CAN'T JUST—!
REMEMBER WHO YOUR FRIENDS ARE, MULDER.
"AGENT SCULLY, THE REASON I ASK YOU ABOUT CANTUS IS THAT SOME INFORMATION HAS RECENTLY BEEN BROUGHT TO LIGHT..."

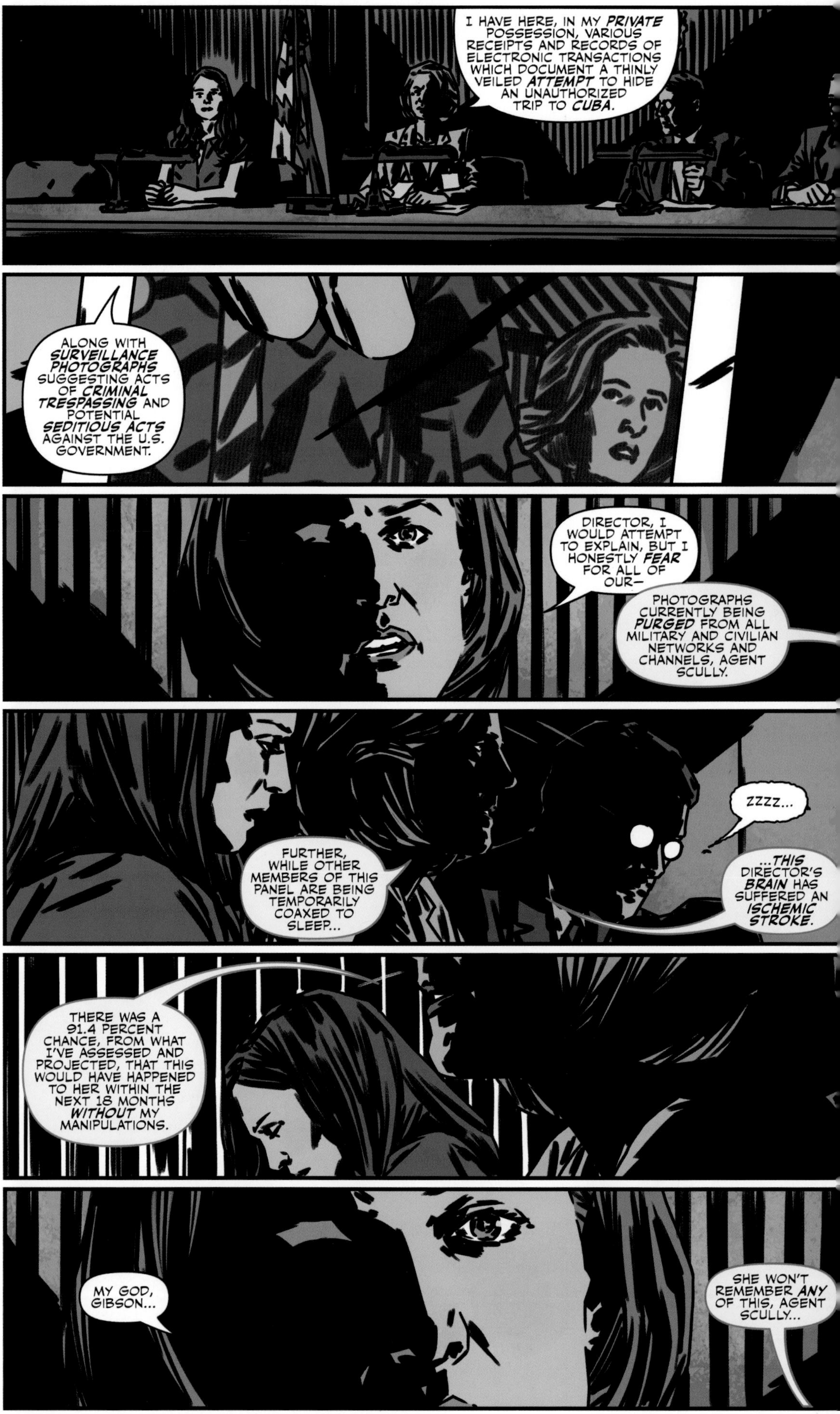

I HAVE HERE, IN MY PRIVATE POSSESSION, VARIOUS RECEIPTS AND RECORDS OF ELECTRONIC TRANSACTIONS WHICH DOCUMENT A THINLY VEILED ATTEMPT TO HIDE AN UNAUTHORIZED TRIP TO CUBA.
ALONG WITH SURVEILLANCE PHOTOGRAPHS SUGGESTING ACTS OF CRIMINAL TRESPASSING AND POTENTIAL SEDITIOUS ACTS AGAINST THE U.S. GOVERNMENT.
DIRECTOR, I WOULD ATTEMPT TO EXPLAIN, BUT I HONESTLY FEAR FOR ALL OF OUR—
PHOTOGRAPHS CURRENTLY BEING PURGED FROM ALL MILITARY AND CIVILIAN NETWORKS AND CHANNELS, AGENT SCULLY.
FURTHER, WHILE OTHER MEMBERS OF THIS PANEL ARE BEING TEMPORARILY COAXED TO SLEEP...
ZZZZ...
...THIS DIRECTOR'S BRAIN HAS SUFFERED AN ISCHEMIC STROKE.
THERE WAS A 91.4 PERCENT CHANCE, FROM WHAT I'VE ASSESSED AND PROJECTED, THAT THIS WOULD HAVE HAPPENED TO HER WITHIN THE NEXT 18 MONTHS WITHOUT MY MANIPULATIONS.
MY GOD, GIBSON...
SHE WON'T REMEMBER ANY OF THIS, AGENT SCULLY...

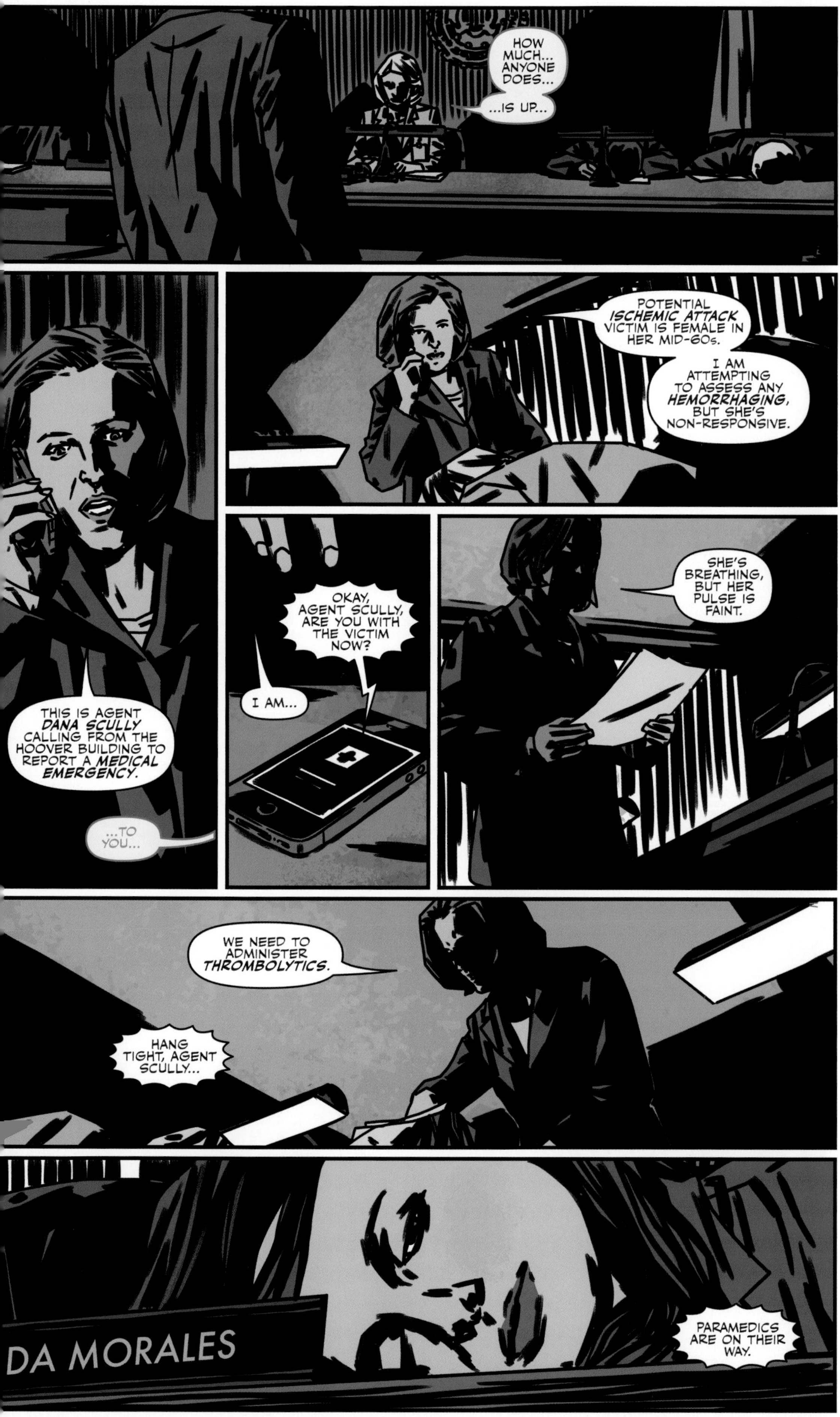
HOW MUCH... ANYONE DOES...
...IS UP...
THIS IS AGENT DANA SCULLY CALLING FROM THE HOOVER BUILDING TO REPORT A MEDICAL EMERGENCY.
...TO YOU...
POTENTIAL ISCHEMIC ATTACK VICTIM IS FEMALE IN HER MID-60s.
I AM ATTEMPTING TO ASSESS ANY HEMORRHAGING, BUT SHE'S NON-RESPONSIVE.
OKAY, AGENT SCULLY, ARE YOU WITH THE VICTIM NOW?
I AM...
SHE'S BREATHING, BUT HER PULSE IS FAINT.
WE NEED TO ADMINISTER THROMBOLYTICS.
HANG TIGHT, AGENT SCULLY...
DA MORALES
PARAMEDICS ARE ON THEIR WAY.

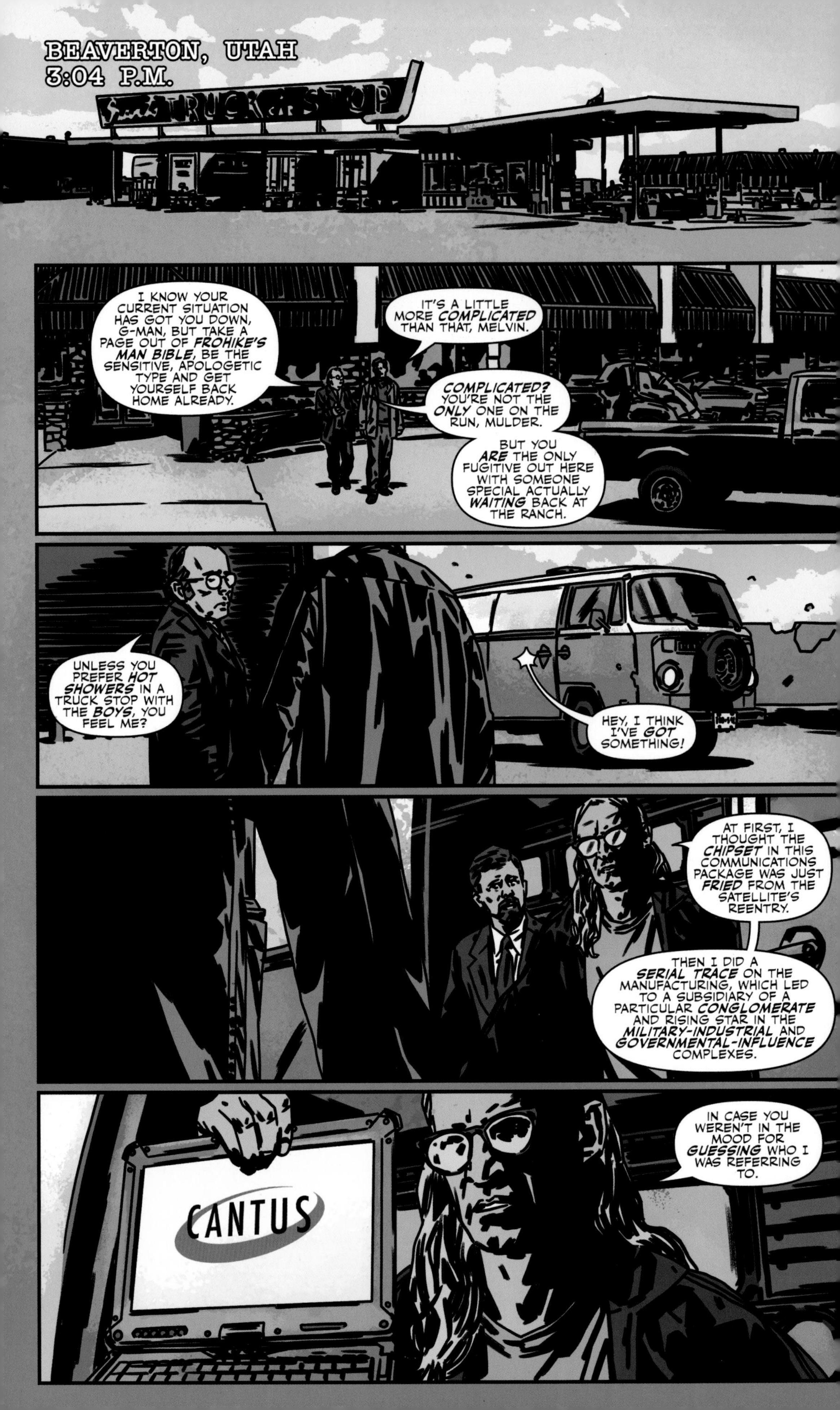

BEAVERTON, UTAH
3:04 P.M.
I KNOW YOUR CURRENT SITUATION HAS GOT YOU DOWN, G-MAN, BUT TAKE A PAGE OUT OF FROHIKE'S MAN BIBLE, BE THE SENSITIVE, APOLOGETIC TYPE AND GET YOURSELF BACK HOME ALREADY.
IT'S A LITTLE MORE COMPLICATED THAN THAT, MELVIN.
COMPLICATED? YOU'RE NOT THE ONLY ONE ON THE RUN, MULDER.
BUT YOU ARE THE ONLY FUGITIVE OUT HERE WITH SOMEONE SPECIAL ACTUALLY WAITING BACK AT THE RANCH.
UNLESS YOU PREFER HOT SHOWERS IN A TRUCK STOP WITH THE BOYS, YOU FEEL ME?
HEY, I THINK I'VE GOT SOMETHING!
AT FIRST, I THOUGHT THE CHIPSET IN THIS COMMUNICATIONS PACKAGE WAS JUST FRIED FROM THE SATELLITE'S REENTRY.
THEN I DID A SERIAL TRACE ON THE MANUFACTURING, WHICH LED TO A SUBSIDIARY OF A PARTICULAR CONGLOMERATE AND RISING STAR IN THE MILITARY-INDUSTRIAL AND GOVERNMENTAL-INFLUENCE COMPLEXES.
CANTUS
IN CASE YOU WEREN'T IN THE MOOD FOR GUESSING WHO I WAS REFERRING TO.

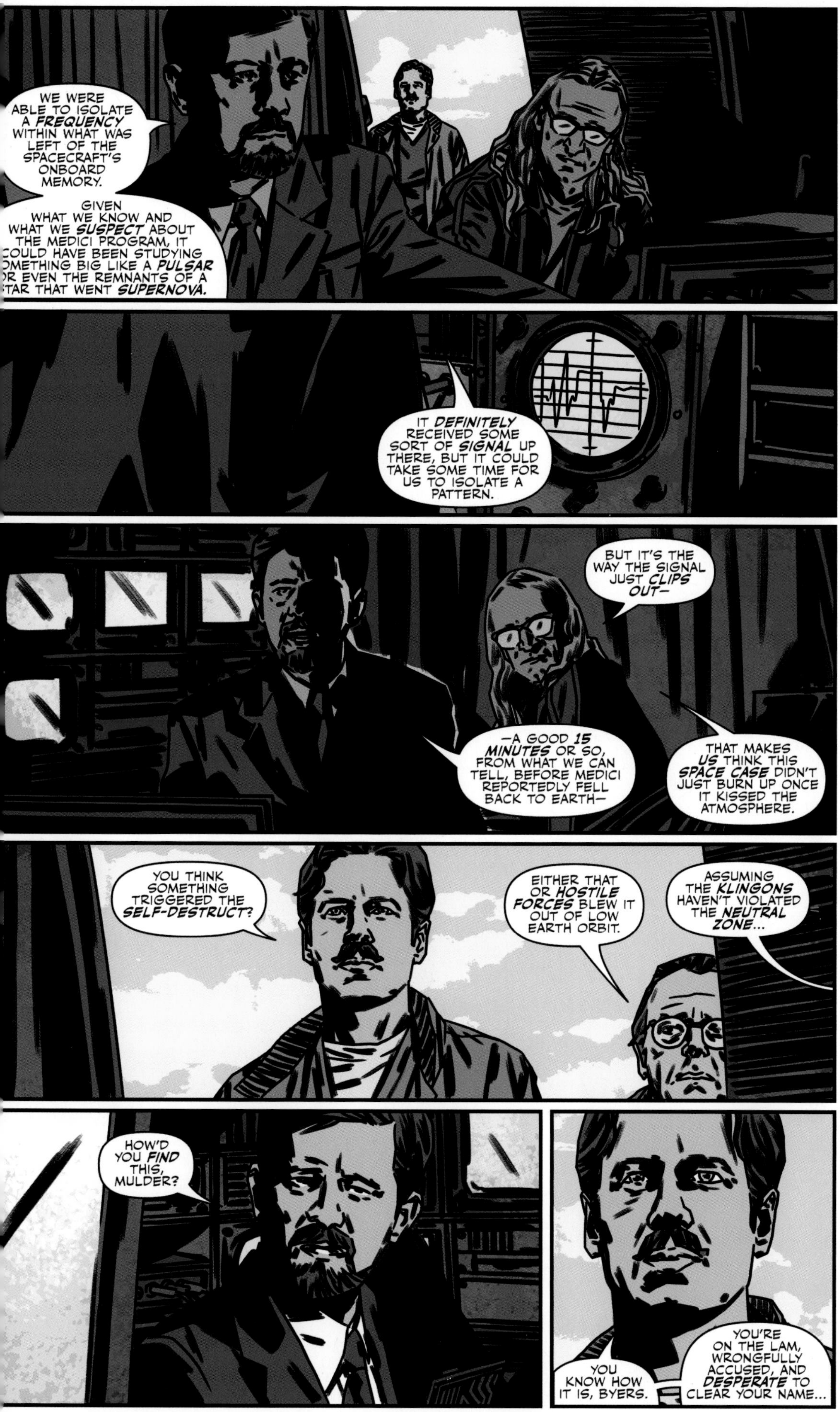
WE WERE ABLE TO ISOLATE A FREQUENCY WITHIN WHAT WAS LEFT OF THE SPACECRAFT'S ONBOARD MEMORY.
GIVEN WHAT WE KNOW AND WHAT WE SUSPECT ABOUT THE MEDICI PROGRAM, IT COULD HAVE BEEN STUDYING SOMETHING BIG LIKE A PULSAR OR EVEN THE REMNANTS OF A STAR THAT WENT SUPERNOVA.
IT DEFINITELY RECEIVED SOME SORT OF SIGNAL UP THERE, BUT IT COULD TAKE SOME TIME FOR US TO ISOLATE A PATTERN.
BUT IT'S THE WAY THE SIGNAL JUST CLIPS OUT—
—A GOOD 15 MINUTES OR SO, FROM WHAT WE CAN TELL, BEFORE MEDICI REPORTEDLY FELL BACK TO EARTH—
THAT MAKES US THINK THIS SPACE CASE DIDN'T JUST BURN UP ONCE IT KISSED THE ATMOSPHERE.
YOU THINK SOMETHING TRIGGERED THE SELF-DESTRUCT?
EITHER THAT OR HOSTILE FORCES BLEW IT OUT OF LOW EARTH ORBIT.
ASSUMING THE KLINGONS HAVEN'T VIOLATED THE NEUTRAL ZONE...
HOW'D YOU FIND THIS, MULDER?
YOU'RE ON THE LAM, WRONGFULLY ACCUSED, AND DESPERATE TO CLEAR YOUR NAME...
YOU KNOW HOW IT IS, BYERS.

"...IT OPENS YOU UP TO *ALL KINDS* OF UNFORESEEN POSSIBILITIES."

I WAS WONDERING WHEN YOU'D BE BACK.

I NEED *MULDER'S HELP* NOW.

YOU *KNOW* WHERE HE IS...

NOT WELL *ENOUGH!*

YOU'RE A *TRAITOR.* YOU'RE A *KILLER.*

YOU'RE OUT OF YOUR *MIND,* GIBSON!

MULDER IS *PROTECTING* YOU, AGENT SCULLY.

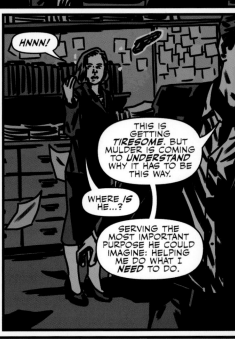

HNNN!

THIS IS GETTING *TIRESOME.* BUT MULDER IS COMING TO *UNDERSTAND* WHY IT HAS TO BE THIS WAY.

WHERE *IS* HE...?

SERVING THE MOST IMPORTANT PURPOSE HE COULD IMAGINE: HELPING ME DO WHAT I *NEED* TO DO.

WHAT ABOUT ME, GIBSON?

WHAT AM *I* SUPPOSED TO DO NOW?

HELP *HIM,* OF COURSE.

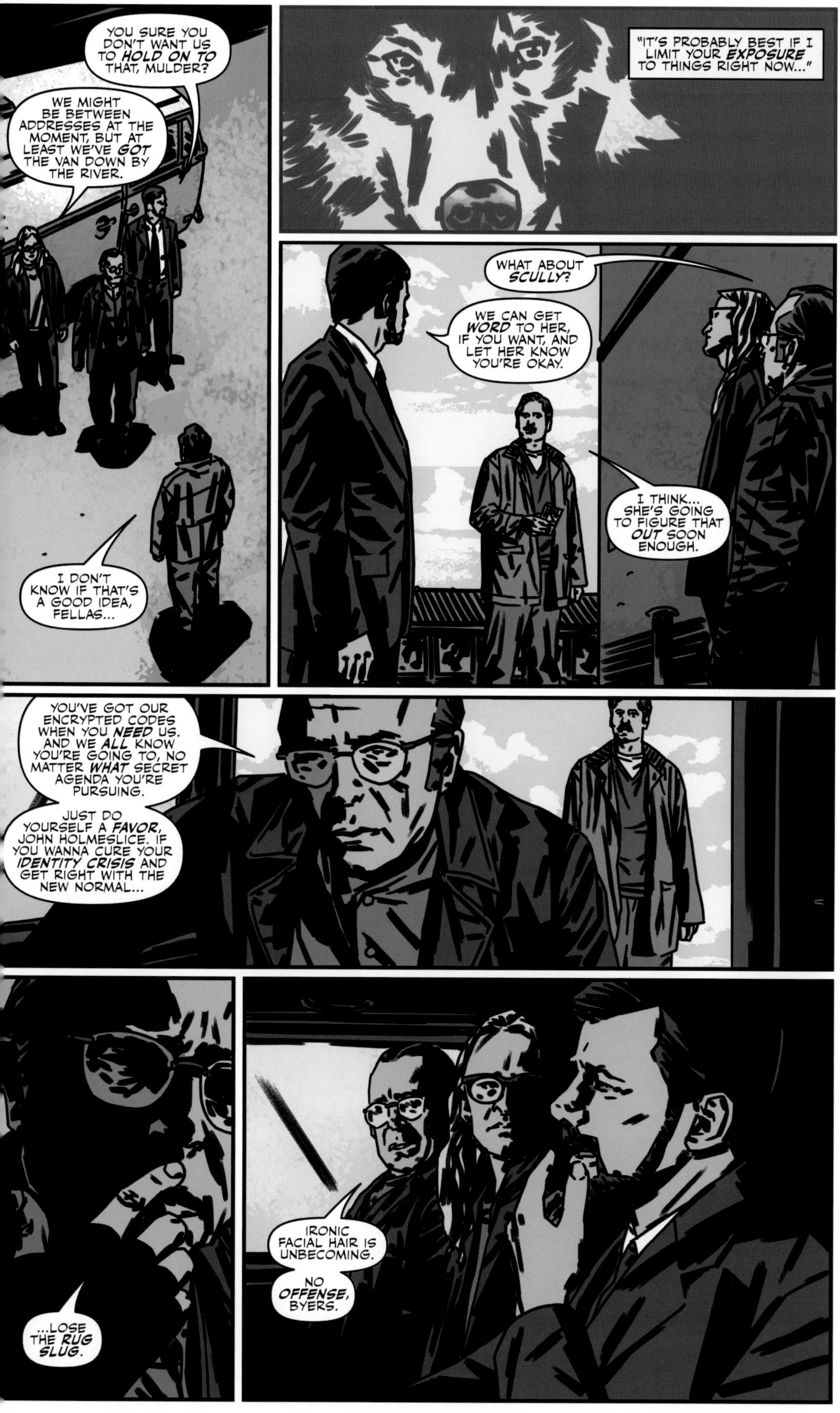
YOU SURE YOU DON'T WANT US TO HOLD ON TO THAT, MULDER?
WE MIGHT BE BETWEEN ADDRESSES AT THE MOMENT, BUT AT LEAST WE'VE GOT THE VAN DOWN BY THE RIVER.
I DON'T KNOW IF THAT'S A GOOD IDEA, FELLAS...
"IT'S PROBABLY BEST IF I LIMIT YOUR EXPOSURE TO THINGS RIGHT NOW..."
WHAT ABOUT SCULLY?
WE CAN GET WORD TO HER, IF YOU WANT, AND LET HER KNOW YOU'RE OKAY.
I THINK... SHE'S GOING TO FIGURE THAT OUT SOON ENOUGH.
YOU'VE GOT OUR ENCRYPTED CODES WHEN YOU NEED US. AND WE ALL KNOW YOU'RE GOING TO, NO MATTER WHAT SECRET AGENDA YOU'RE PURSUING.
JUST DO YOURSELF A FAVOR, JOHN HOLMESLICE. IF YOU WANNA CURE YOUR IDENTITY CRISIS AND GET RIGHT WITH THE NEW NORMAL...
...LOSE THE RUG SLUG.
IRONIC FACIAL HAIR IS UNBECOMING.
NO OFFENSE, BYERS.

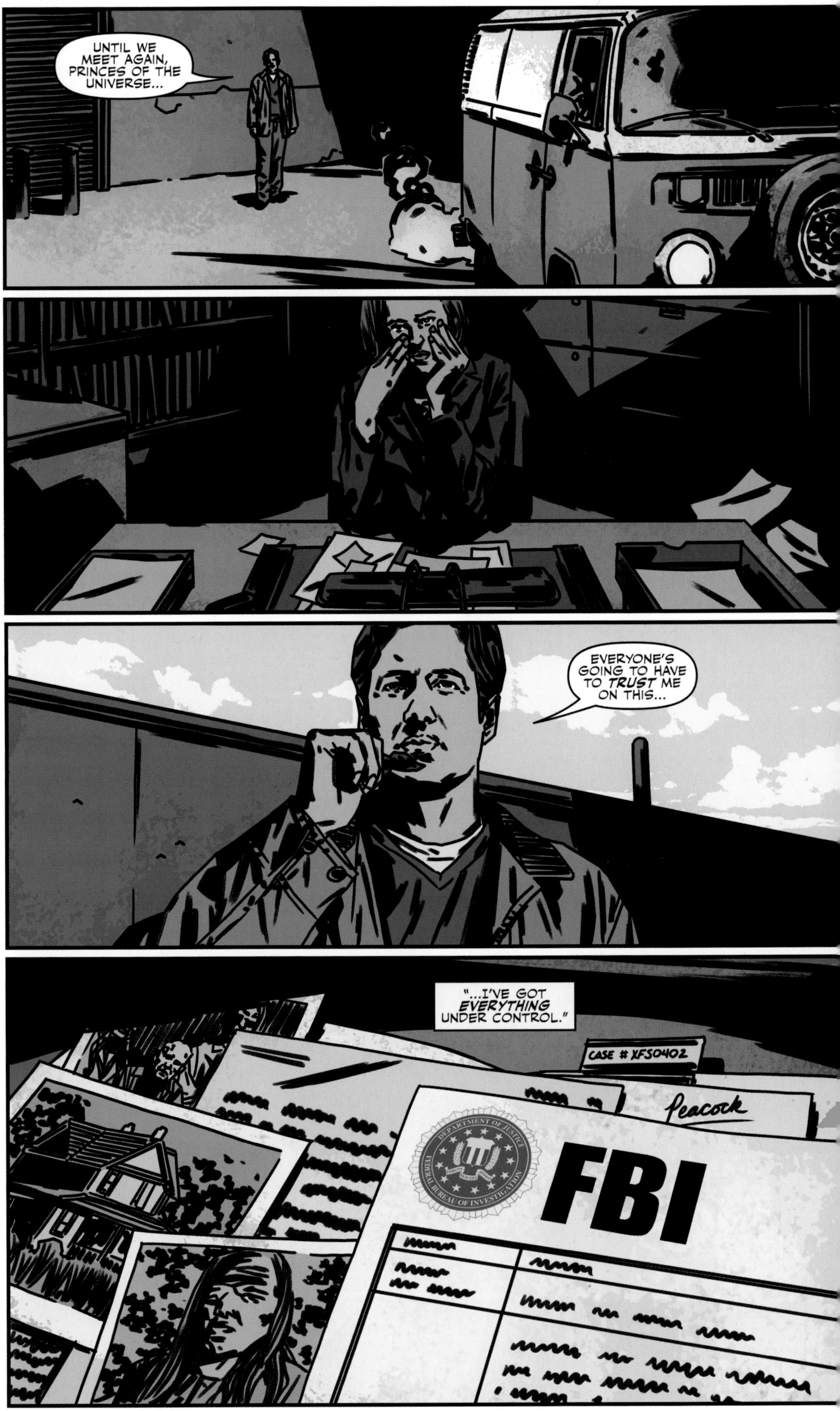
UNTIL WE MEET AGAIN, PRINCES OF THE UNIVERSE...
EVERYONE'S GOING TO HAVE TO *TRUST* ME ON THIS...
"...I'VE GOT *EVERYTHING* UNDER CONTROL."
CASE # XFS0402
Peacock
FBI
DEPARTMENT OF JUSTICE
FEDERAL BUREAU OF INVESTIGATION

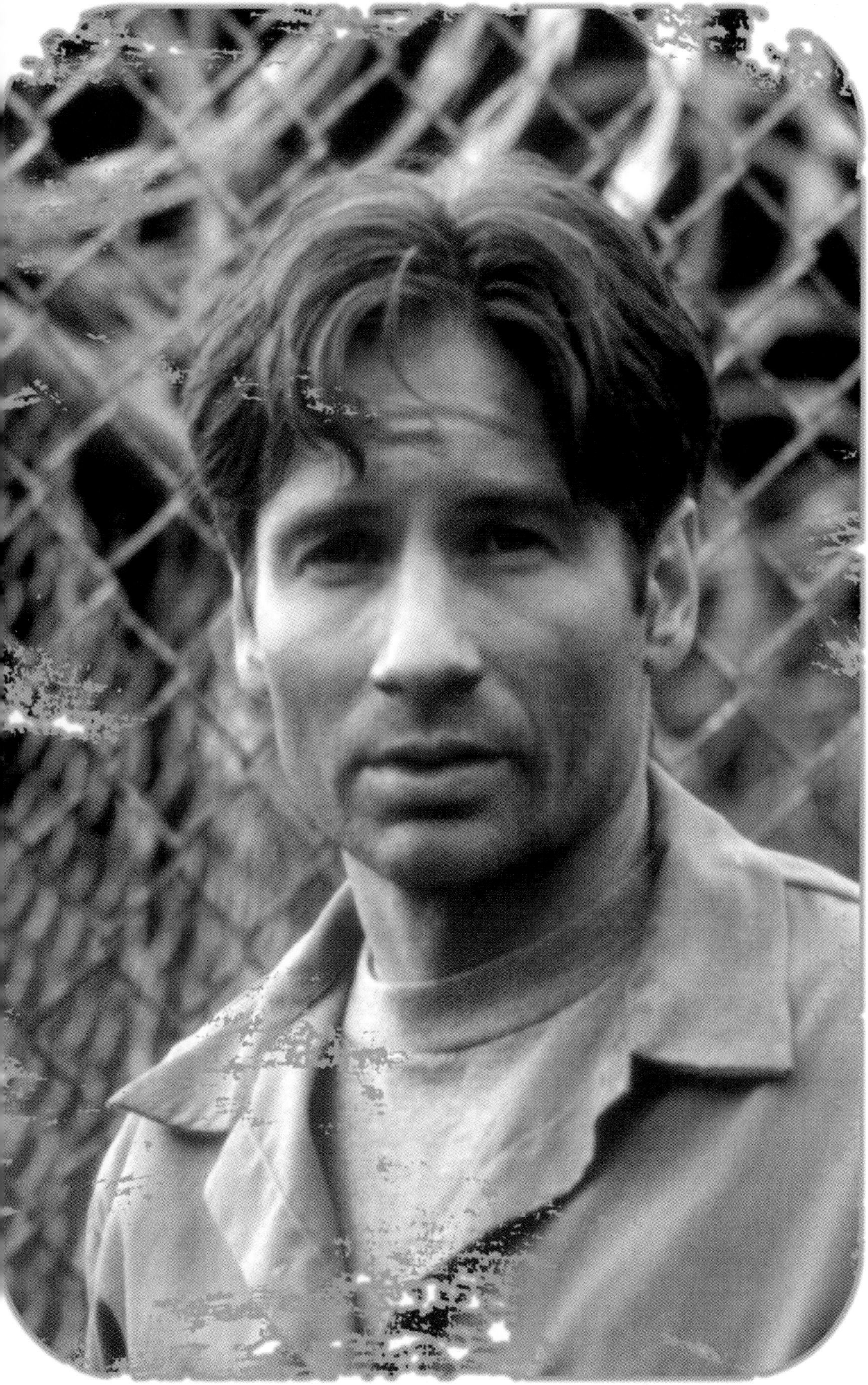

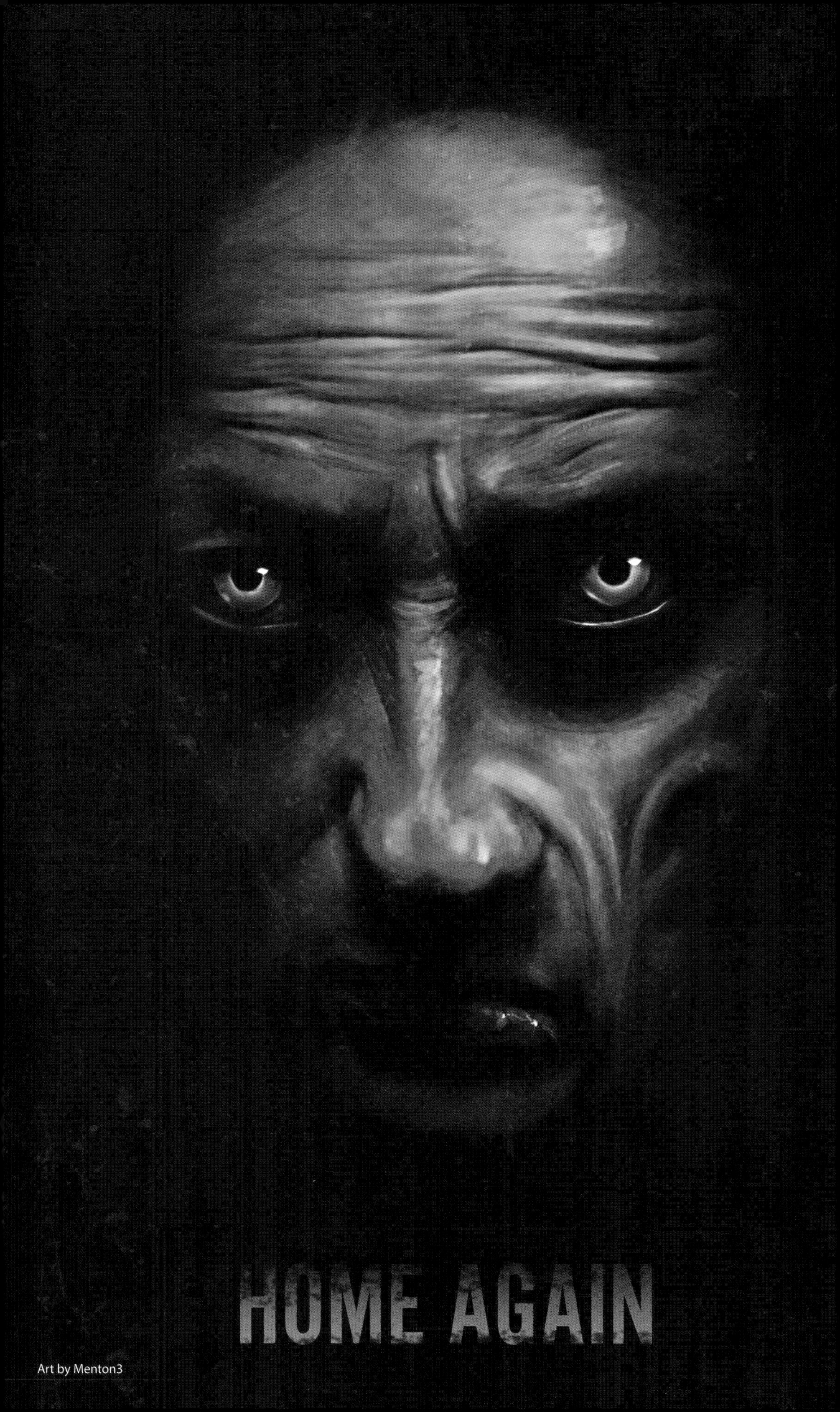
HOME AGAIN

Art by Menton3

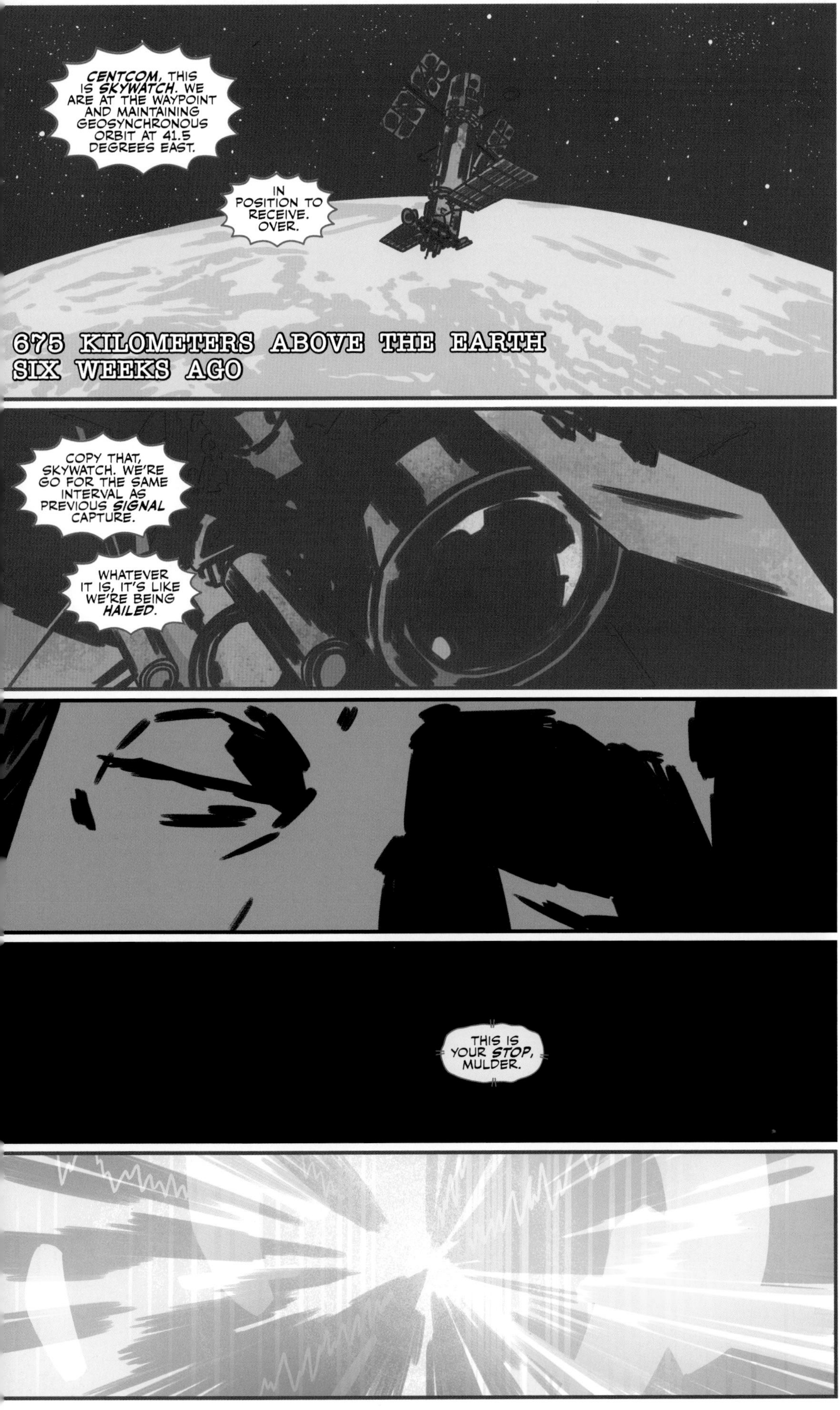
CENTCOM, THIS IS SKYWATCH. WE ARE AT THE WAYPOINT AND MAINTAINING GEOSYNCHRONOUS ORBIT AT 41.5 DEGREES EAST.
IN POSITION TO RECEIVE. OVER.
675 KILOMETERS ABOVE THE EARTH
SIX WEEKS AGO
COPY THAT, SKYWATCH. WE'RE GO FOR THE SAME INTERVAL AS PREVIOUS SIGNAL CAPTURE.
WHATEVER IT IS, IT'S LIKE WE'RE BEING HAILED.
THIS IS YOUR STOP, MULDER.

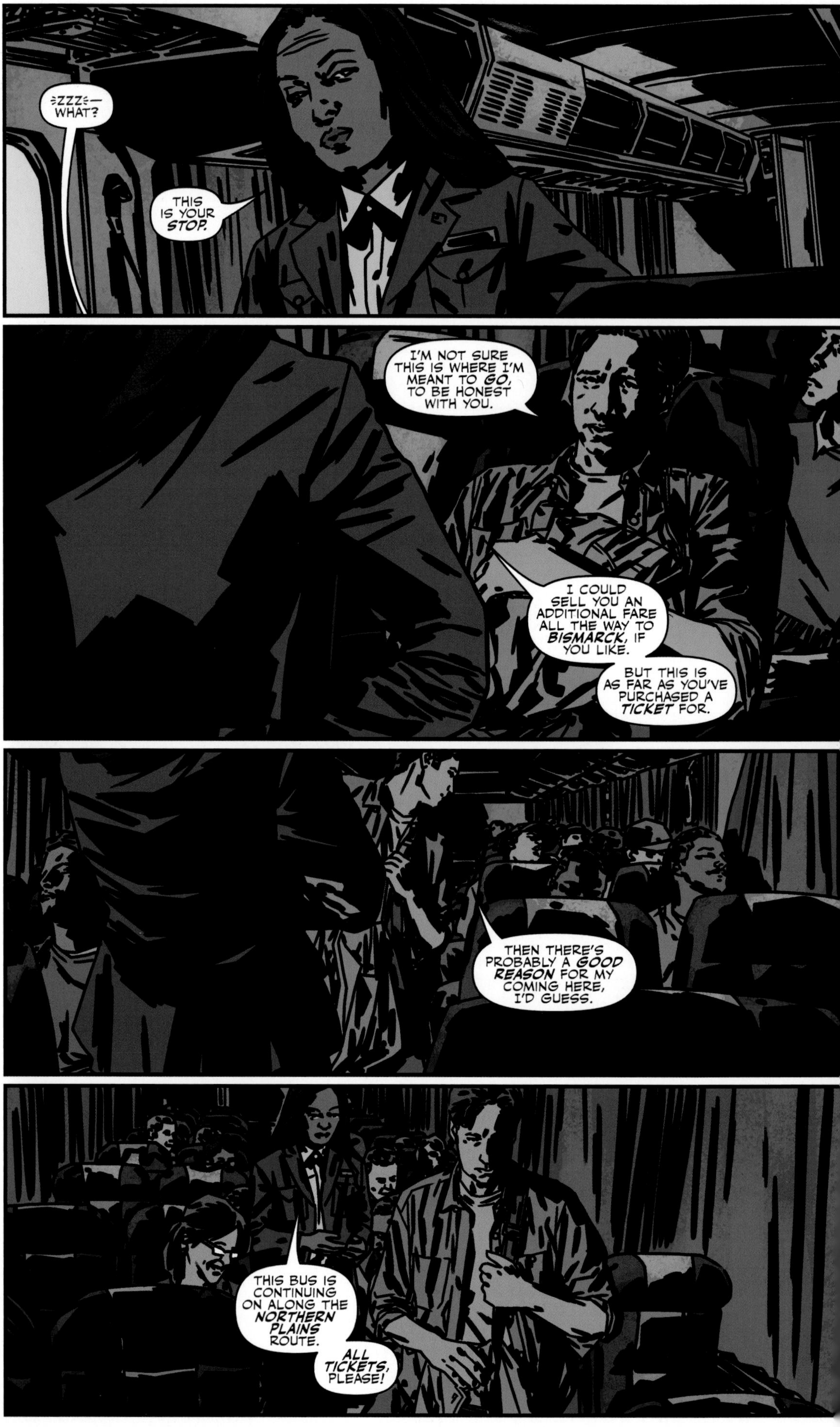

ZZZ— WHAT?
THIS IS YOUR STOP.
I'M NOT SURE THIS IS WHERE I'M MEANT TO GO, TO BE HONEST WITH YOU.
I COULD SELL YOU AN ADDITIONAL FARE ALL THE WAY TO BISMARCK, IF YOU LIKE.
BUT THIS IS AS FAR AS YOU'VE PURCHASED A TICKET FOR.
THEN THERE'S PROBABLY A GOOD REASON FOR MY COMING HERE, I'D GUESS.
THIS BUS IS CONTINUING ON ALONG THE NORTHERN PLAINS ROUTE.
ALL TICKETS, PLEASE!

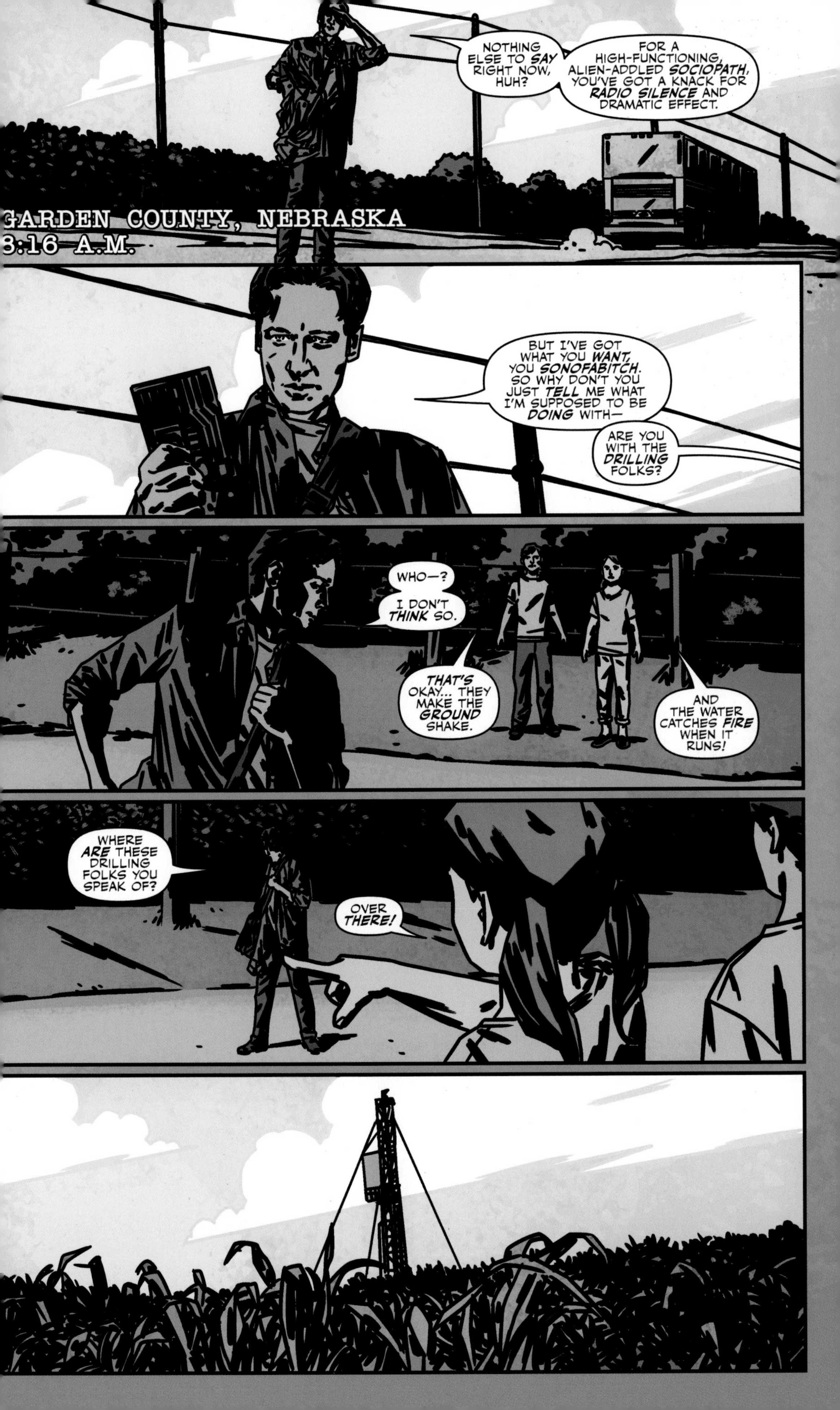
NOTHING ELSE TO SAY RIGHT NOW, HUH?
FOR A HIGH-FUNCTIONING, ALIEN-ADDLED SOCIOPATH, YOU'VE GOT A KNACK FOR RADIO SILENCE AND DRAMATIC EFFECT.
GARDEN COUNTY, NEBRASKA
3:16 A.M.
BUT I'VE GOT WHAT YOU WANT, YOU SONOFABITCH. SO WHY DON'T YOU JUST TELL ME WHAT I'M SUPPOSED TO BE DOING WITH—
ARE YOU WITH THE DRILLING FOLKS?
WHO—?
I DON'T THINK SO.
THAT'S OKAY... THEY MAKE THE GROUND SHAKE.
AND THE WATER CATCHES FIRE WHEN IT RUNS!
WHERE ARE THESE DRILLING FOLKS YOU SPEAK OF?
OVER THERE!

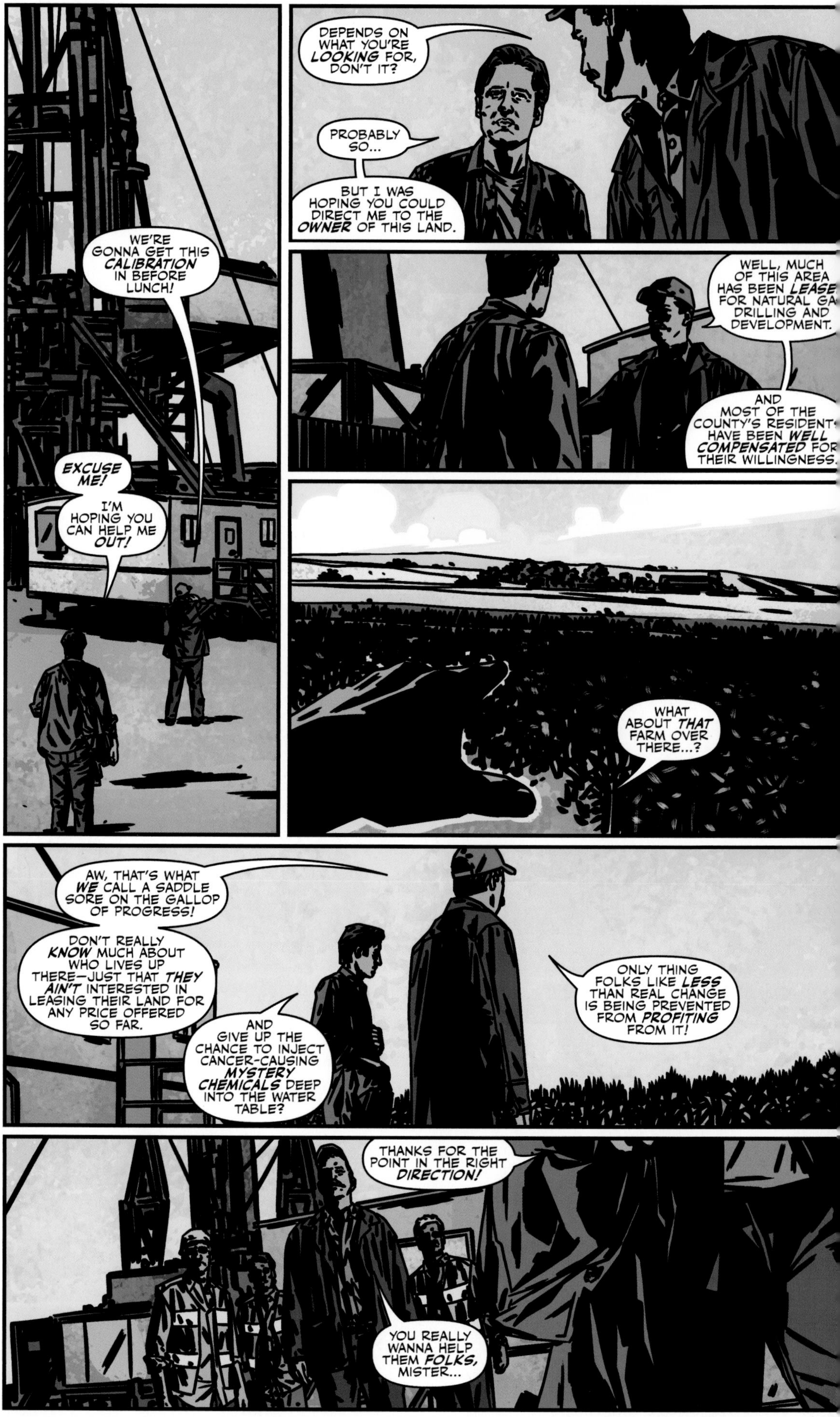
WE'RE GONNA GET THIS CALIBRATION IN BEFORE LUNCH!
EXCUSE ME!
I'M HOPING YOU CAN HELP ME OUT!
DEPENDS ON WHAT YOU'RE LOOKING FOR, DON'T IT?
PROBABLY SO...
BUT I WAS HOPING YOU COULD DIRECT ME TO THE OWNER OF THIS LAND.
WELL, MUCH OF THIS AREA HAS BEEN LEASE FOR NATURAL GA DRILLING AND DEVELOPMENT.
AND MOST OF THE COUNTY'S RESIDENT HAVE BEEN WELL COMPENSATED FOR THEIR WILLINGNESS.
WHAT ABOUT THAT FARM OVER THERE...?
AW, THAT'S WHAT WE CALL A SADDLE SORE ON THE GALLOP OF PROGRESS!
DON'T REALLY KNOW MUCH ABOUT WHO LIVES UP THERE—JUST THAT THEY AIN'T INTERESTED IN LEASING THEIR LAND FOR ANY PRICE OFFERED SO FAR.
AND GIVE UP THE CHANCE TO INJECT CANCER-CAUSING MYSTERY CHEMICALS DEEP INTO THE WATER TABLE?
ONLY THING FOLKS LIKE LESS THAN REAL CHANGE IS BEING PREVENTED FROM PROFITING FROM IT!
THANKS FOR THE POINT IN THE RIGHT DIRECTION!
YOU REALLY WANNA HELP THEM FOLKS, MISTER...

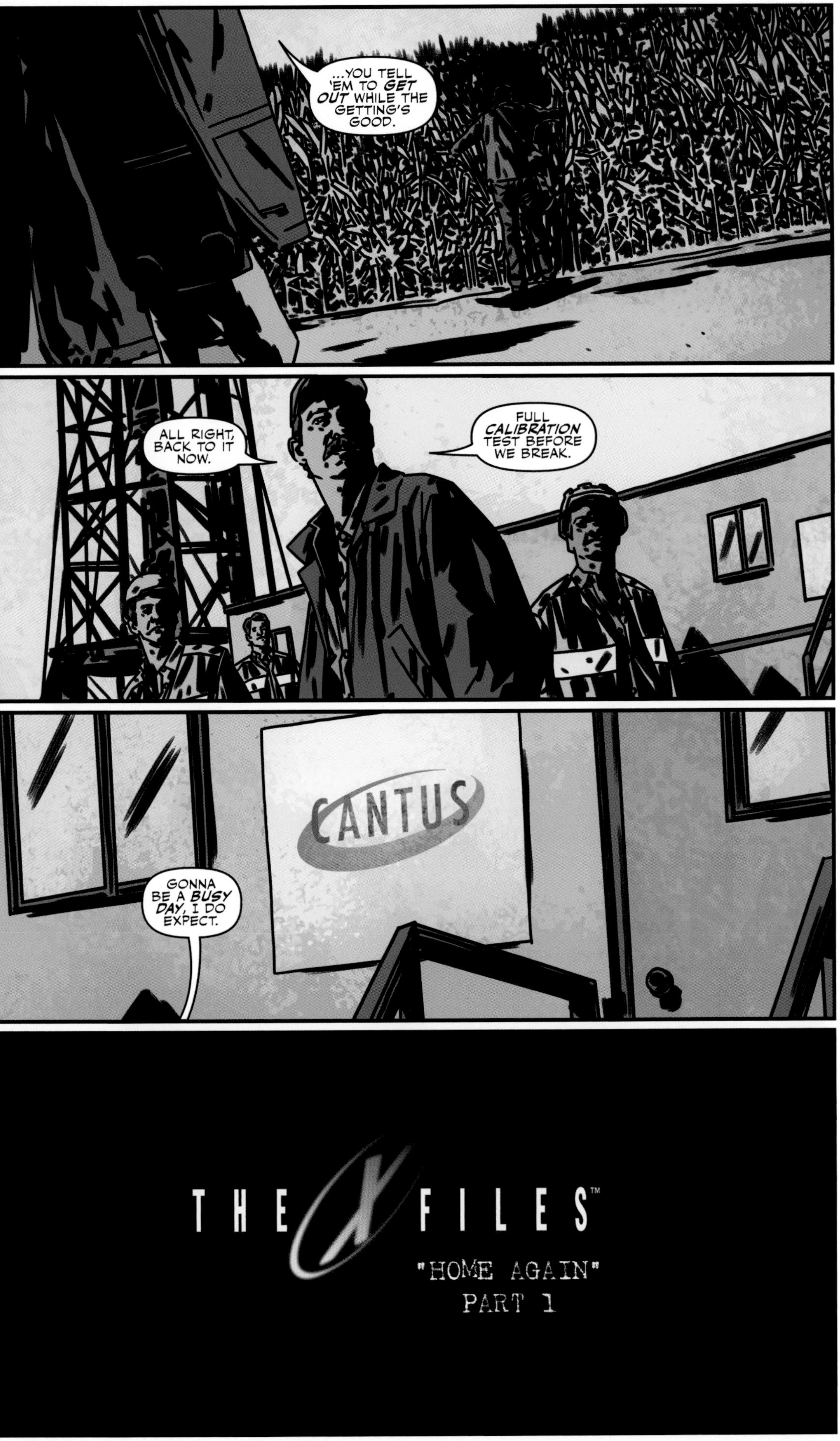
...YOU TELL 'EM TO *GET OUT* WHILE THE GETTING'S GOOD.
ALL RIGHT, BACK TO IT NOW.
FULL *CALIBRATION* TEST BEFORE WE BREAK.
CANTUS
GONNA BE A *BUSY DAY*, I DO EXPECT.
THE X FILES™
"HOME AGAIN"
PART 1

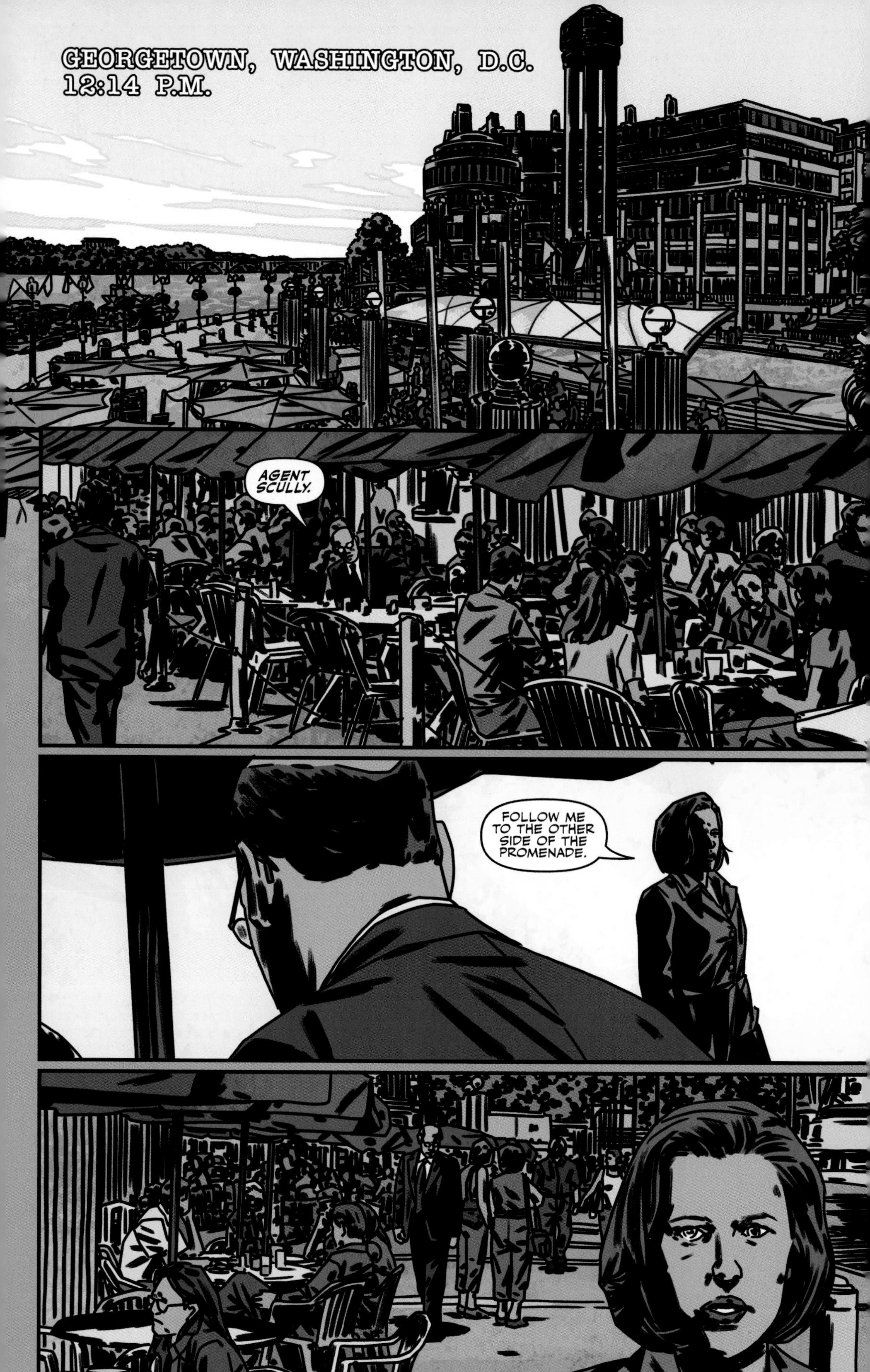
GEORGETOWN, WASHINGTON, D.C.
12:14 P.M.
AGENT SCULLY.
FOLLOW ME TO THE OTHER SIDE OF THE PROMENADE.

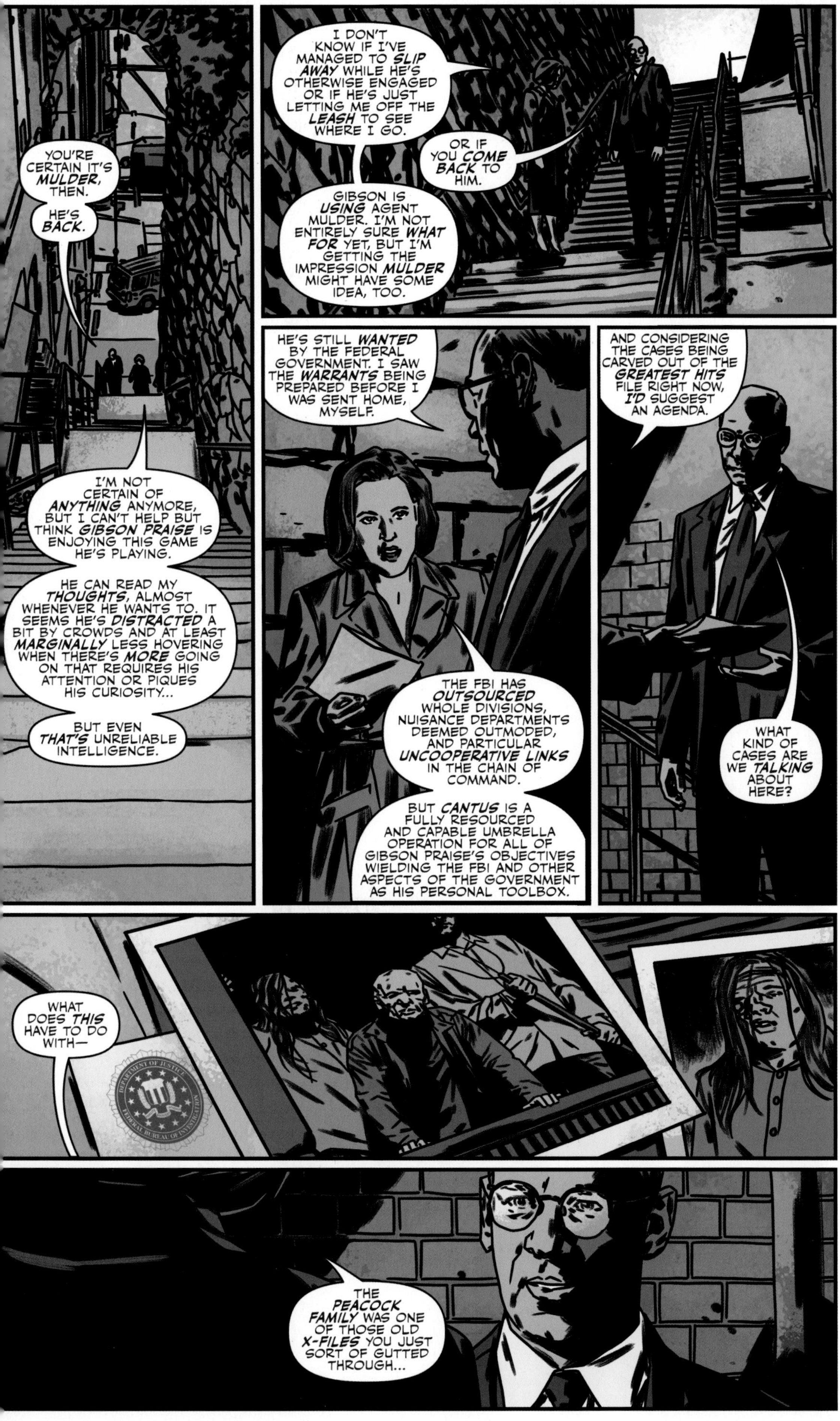
YOU'RE CERTAIN IT'S MULDER, THEN.
HE'S BACK.
I'M NOT CERTAIN OF ANYTHING ANYMORE, BUT I CAN'T HELP BUT THINK GIBSON PRAISE IS ENJOYING THIS GAME HE'S PLAYING.
HE CAN READ MY THOUGHTS, ALMOST WHENEVER HE WANTS TO. IT SEEMS HE'S DISTRACTED A BIT BY CROWDS AND AT LEAST MARGINALLY LESS HOVERING WHEN THERE'S MORE GOING ON THAT REQUIRES HIS ATTENTION OR PIQUES HIS CURIOSITY...
BUT EVEN THAT'S UNRELIABLE INTELLIGENCE.
I DON'T KNOW IF I'VE MANAGED TO SLIP AWAY WHILE HE'S OTHERWISE ENGAGED OR IF HE'S JUST LETTING ME OFF THE LEASH TO SEE WHERE I GO.
OR IF YOU COME BACK TO HIM.
GIBSON IS USING AGENT MULDER. I'M NOT ENTIRELY SURE WHAT FOR YET, BUT I'M GETTING THE IMPRESSION MULDER MIGHT HAVE SOME IDEA, TOO.
HE'S STILL WANTED BY THE FEDERAL GOVERNMENT. I SAW THE WARRANTS BEING PREPARED BEFORE I WAS SENT HOME, MYSELF.
THE FBI HAS OUTSOURCED WHOLE DIVISIONS, NUISANCE DEPARTMENTS DEEMED OUTMODED, AND PARTICULAR UNCOOPERATIVE LINKS IN THE CHAIN OF COMMAND.
BUT CANTUS IS A FULLY RESOURCED AND CAPABLE UMBRELLA OPERATION FOR ALL OF GIBSON PRAISE'S OBJECTIVES WIELDING THE FBI AND OTHER ASPECTS OF THE GOVERNMENT AS HIS PERSONAL TOOLBOX.
AND CONSIDERING THE CASES BEING CARVED OUT OF THE GREATEST HITS FILE RIGHT NOW, I'D SUGGEST AN AGENDA.
WHAT KIND OF CASES ARE WE TALKING ABOUT HERE?
WHAT DOES THIS HAVE TO DO WITH—
DEPARTMENT OF JUSTICE
FEDERAL BUREAU OF INVESTIGATION
THE PEACOCK FAMILY WAS ONE OF THOSE OLD X-FILES YOU JUST SORT OF GUTTED THROUGH...

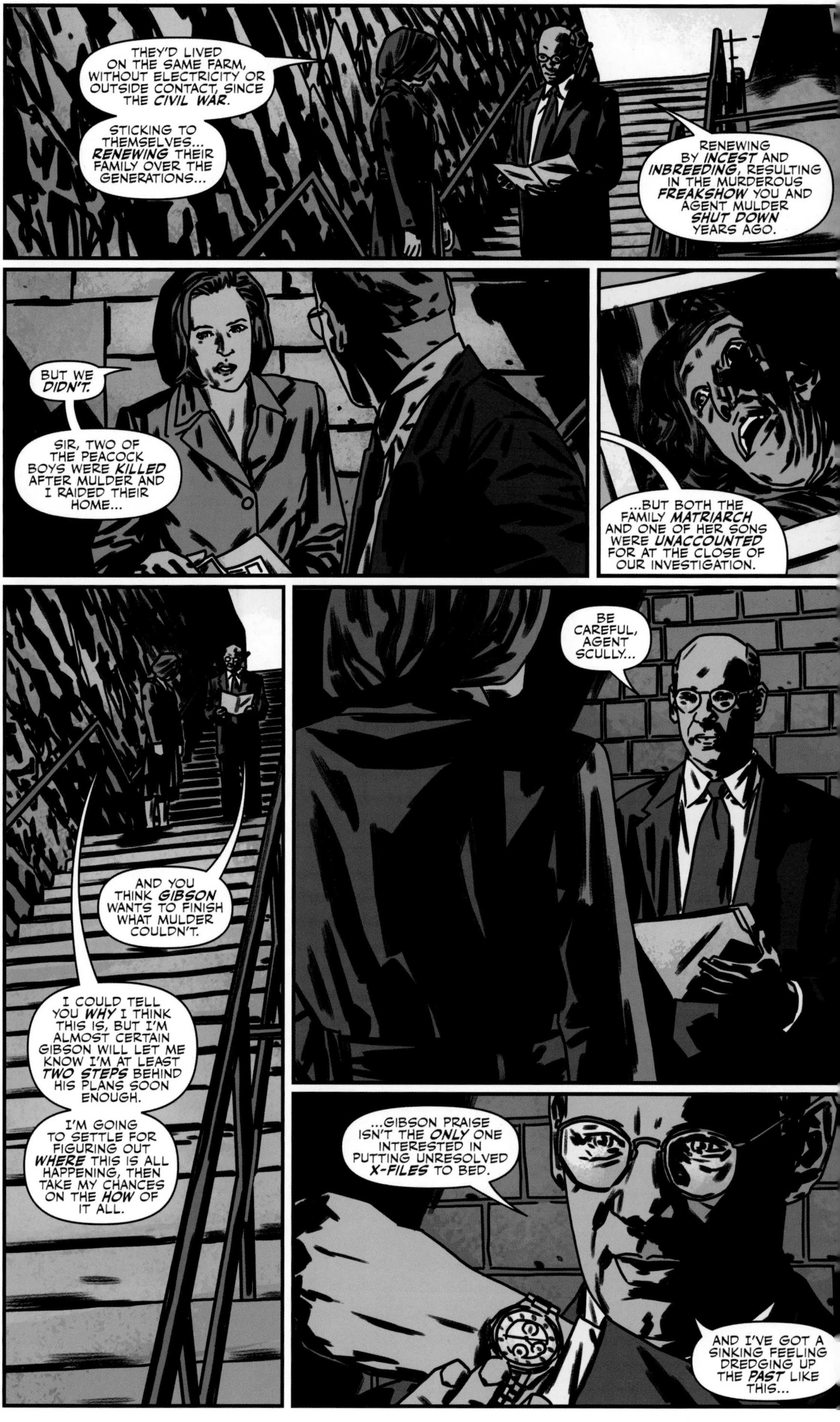
THEY'D LIVED ON THE SAME FARM, WITHOUT ELECTRICITY OR OUTSIDE CONTACT, SINCE THE CIVIL WAR.
STICKING TO THEMSELVES... RENEWING THEIR FAMILY OVER THE GENERATIONS...
RENEWING BY INCEST AND INBREEDING, RESULTING IN THE MURDEROUS FREAKSHOW YOU AND AGENT MULDER SHUT DOWN YEARS AGO.
BUT WE DIDN'T.
SIR, TWO OF THE PEACOCK BOYS WERE KILLED AFTER MULDER AND I RAIDED THEIR HOME...
...BUT BOTH THE FAMILY MATRIARCH AND ONE OF HER SONS WERE UNACCOUNTED FOR AT THE CLOSE OF OUR INVESTIGATION.
AND YOU THINK GIBSON WANTS TO FINISH WHAT MULDER COULDN'T.
I COULD TELL YOU WHY I THINK THIS IS, BUT I'M ALMOST CERTAIN GIBSON WILL LET ME KNOW I'M AT LEAST TWO STEPS BEHIND HIS PLANS SOON ENOUGH.
I'M GOING TO SETTLE FOR FIGURING OUT WHERE THIS IS ALL HAPPENING, THEN TAKE MY CHANCES ON THE HOW OF IT ALL.
BE CAREFUL, AGENT SCULLY...
...GIBSON PRAISE ISN'T THE ONLY ONE INTERESTED IN PUTTING UNRESOLVED X-FILES TO BED.
AND I'VE GOT A SINKING FEELING DREDGING UP THE PAST LIKE THIS...

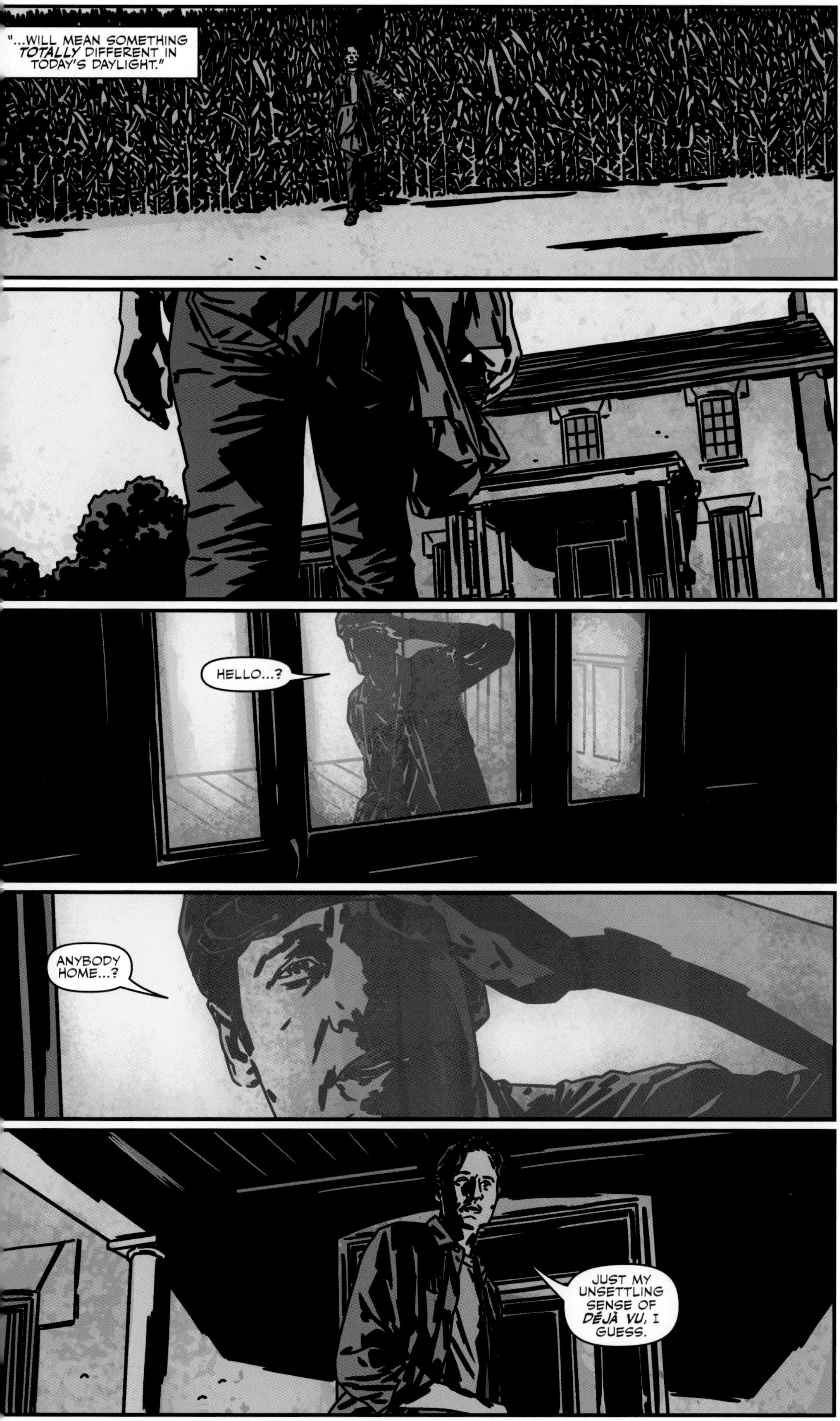
"...WILL MEAN SOMETHING *TOTALLY* DIFFERENT IN TODAY'S DAYLIGHT."
HELLO...?
ANYBODY HOME...?
JUST MY UNSETTLING SENSE OF *DÉJÀ VU*, I GUESS.

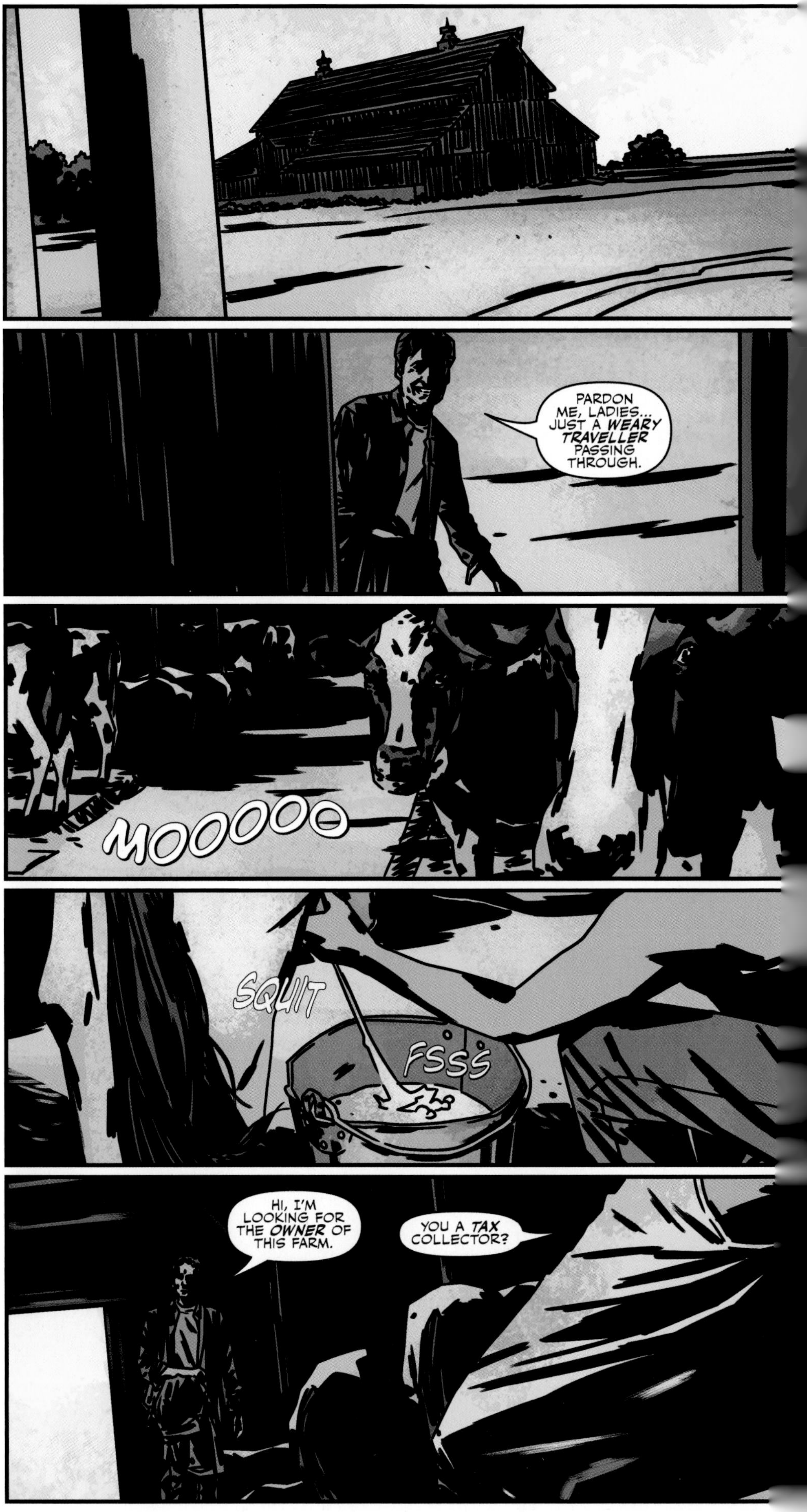

PARDON ME, LADIES... JUST A WEARY TRAVELLER PASSING THROUGH.
MOOOOO
SQUIT
FSSS
HI, I'M LOOKING FOR THE OWNER OF THIS FARM.
YOU A TAX COLLECTOR?

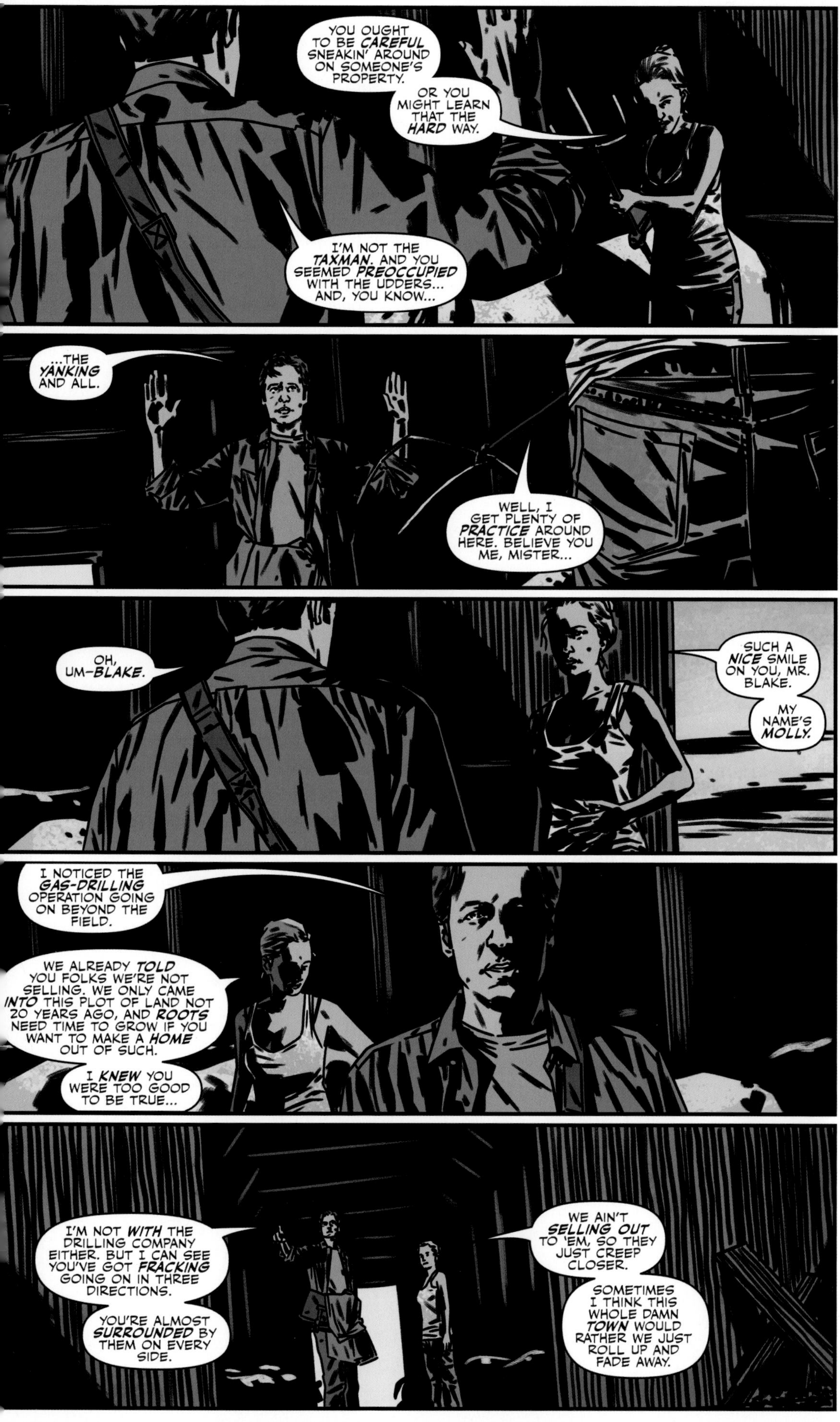
YOU OUGHT TO BE CAREFUL SNEAKIN' AROUND ON SOMEONE'S PROPERTY.
OR YOU MIGHT LEARN THAT THE HARD WAY.
I'M NOT THE TAXMAN. AND YOU SEEMED PREOCCUPIED WITH THE UDDERS... AND, YOU KNOW...
...THE YANKING AND ALL.
WELL, I GET PLENTY OF PRACTICE AROUND HERE. BELIEVE YOU ME, MISTER...
OH, UM--BLAKE.
SUCH A NICE SMILE ON YOU, MR. BLAKE.
MY NAME'S MOLLY.
I NOTICED THE GAS-DRILLING OPERATION GOING ON BEYOND THE FIELD.
WE ALREADY TOLD YOU FOLKS WE'RE NOT SELLING. WE ONLY CAME INTO THIS PLOT OF LAND NOT 20 YEARS AGO, AND ROOTS NEED TIME TO GROW IF YOU WANT TO MAKE A HOME OUT OF SUCH.
I KNEW YOU WERE TOO GOOD TO BE TRUE...
I'M NOT WITH THE DRILLING COMPANY EITHER. BUT I CAN SEE YOU'VE GOT FRACKING GOING ON IN THREE DIRECTIONS.
YOU'RE ALMOST SURROUNDED BY THEM ON EVERY SIDE.
WE AIN'T SELLING OUT TO 'EM, SO THEY JUST CREEP CLOSER.
SOMETIMES I THINK THIS WHOLE DAMN TOWN WOULD RATHER WE JUST ROLL UP AND FADE AWAY.

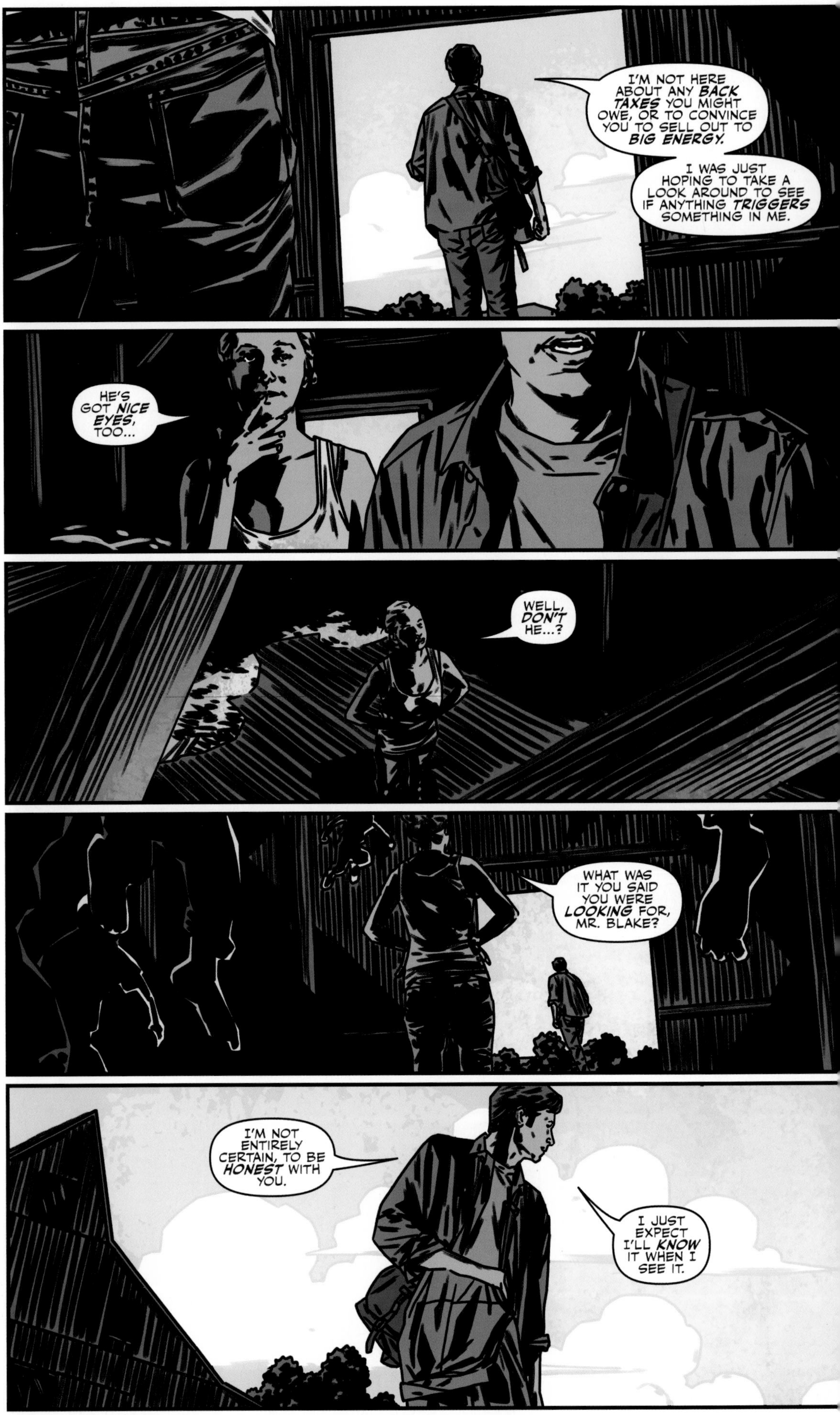

I'M NOT HERE ABOUT ANY BACK TAXES YOU MIGHT OWE, OR TO CONVINCE YOU TO SELL OUT TO BIG ENERGY.
I WAS JUST HOPING TO TAKE A LOOK AROUND TO SEE IF ANYTHING TRIGGERS SOMETHING IN ME.
HE'S GOT NICE EYES, TOO...
WELL, DON'T HE...?
WHAT WAS IT YOU SAID YOU WERE LOOKING FOR, MR. BLAKE?
I'M NOT ENTIRELY CERTAIN, TO BE HONEST WITH YOU.
I JUST EXPECT I'LL KNOW IT WHEN I SEE IT.

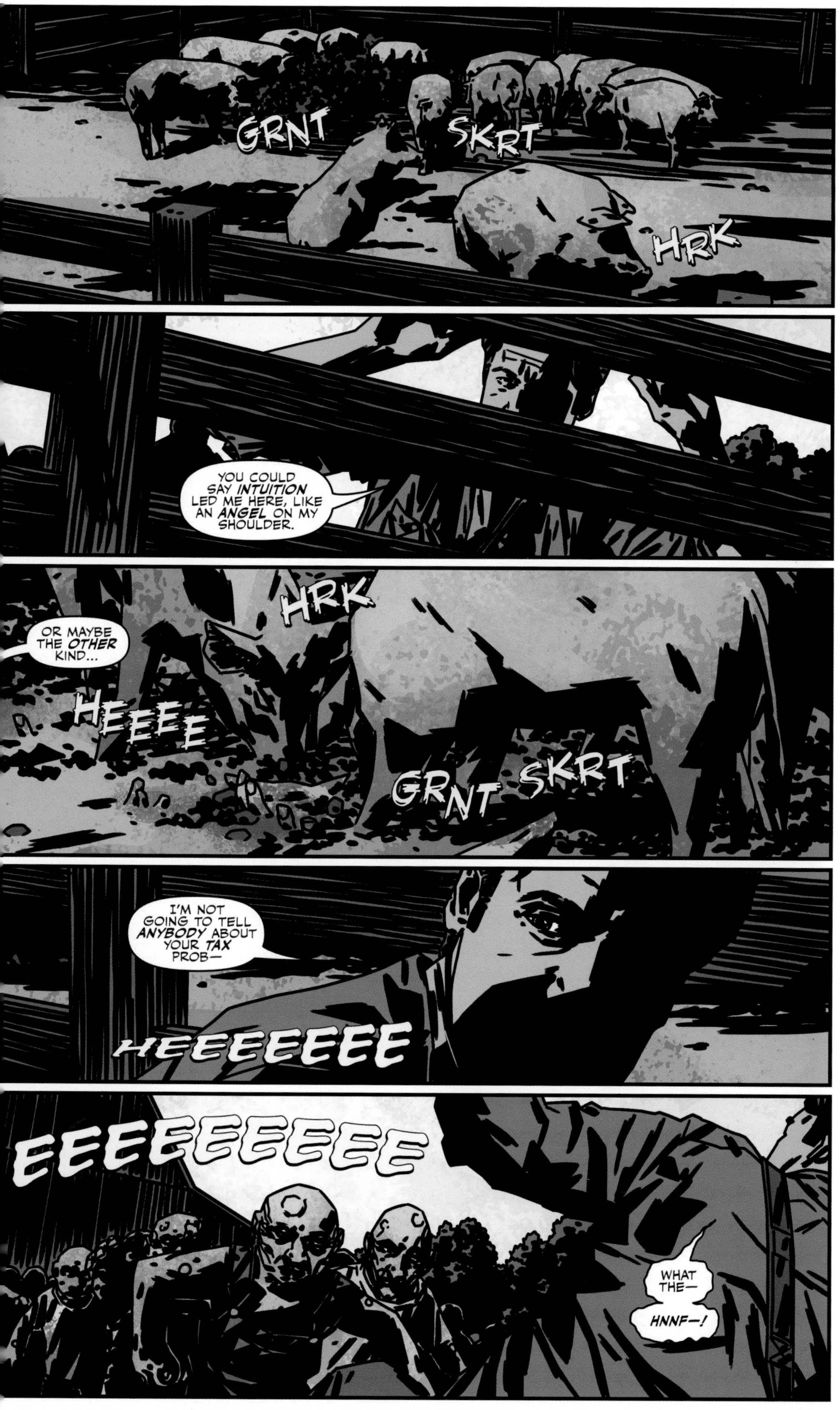
GRNT
SKRT
HRK
YOU COULD SAY INTUITION LED ME HERE, LIKE AN ANGEL ON MY SHOULDER.
HRK
OR MAYBE THE OTHER KIND...
HEEEEE
GRNT SKRT
I'M NOT GOING TO TELL ANYBODY ABOUT YOUR TAX PROB—
HEEEEEEEE
EEEEEEEEEE
WHAT THE—
HNNF—!

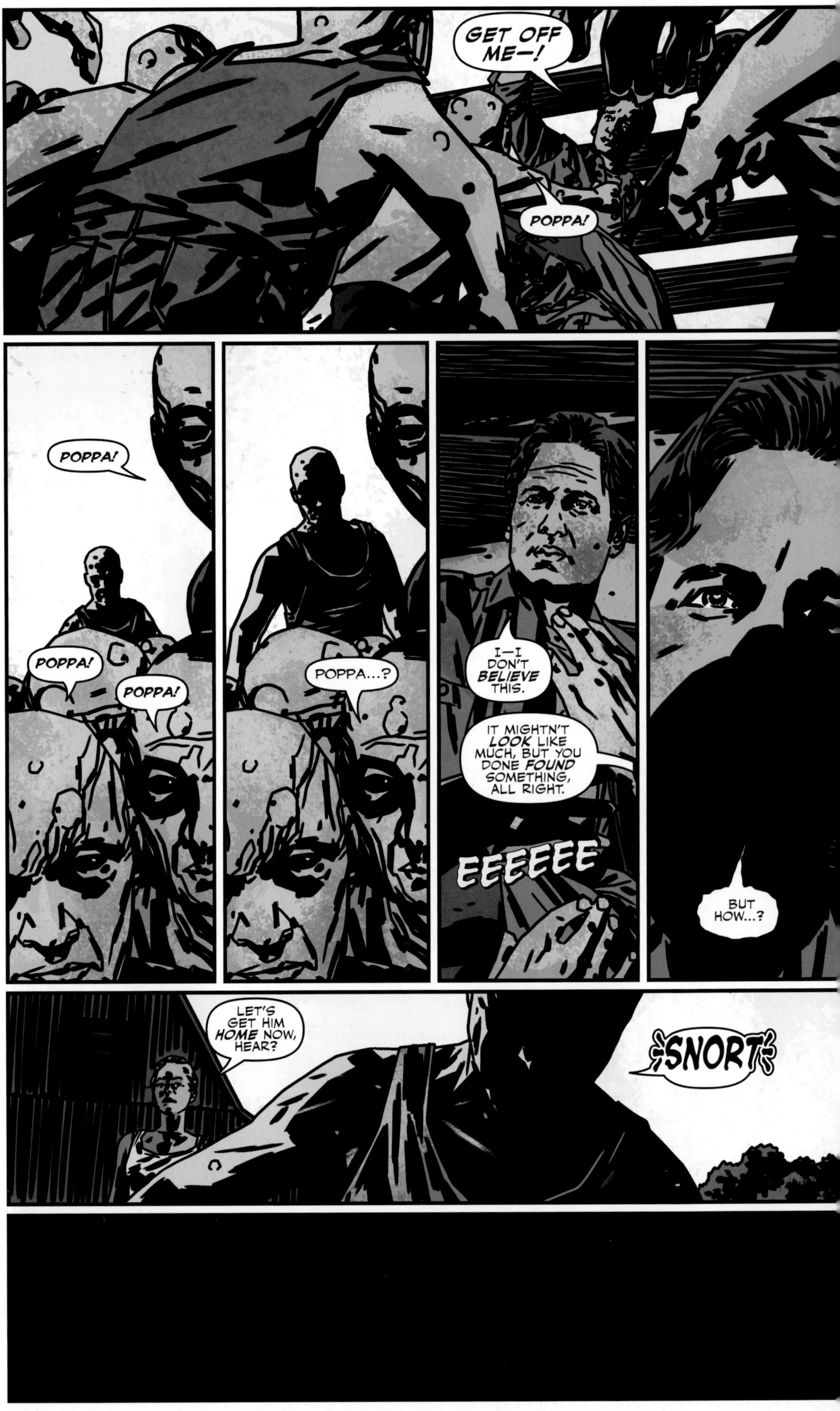
GET OFF ME—!
POPPA!
POPPA!
POPPA!
POPPA!
POPPA...?
I—I DON'T BELIEVE THIS.
IT MIGHTN'T LOOK LIKE MUCH, BUT YOU DONE FOUND SOMETHING, ALL RIGHT.
EEEEEE
BUT HOW...?
LET'S GET HIM HOME NOW, HEAR?
SNORT

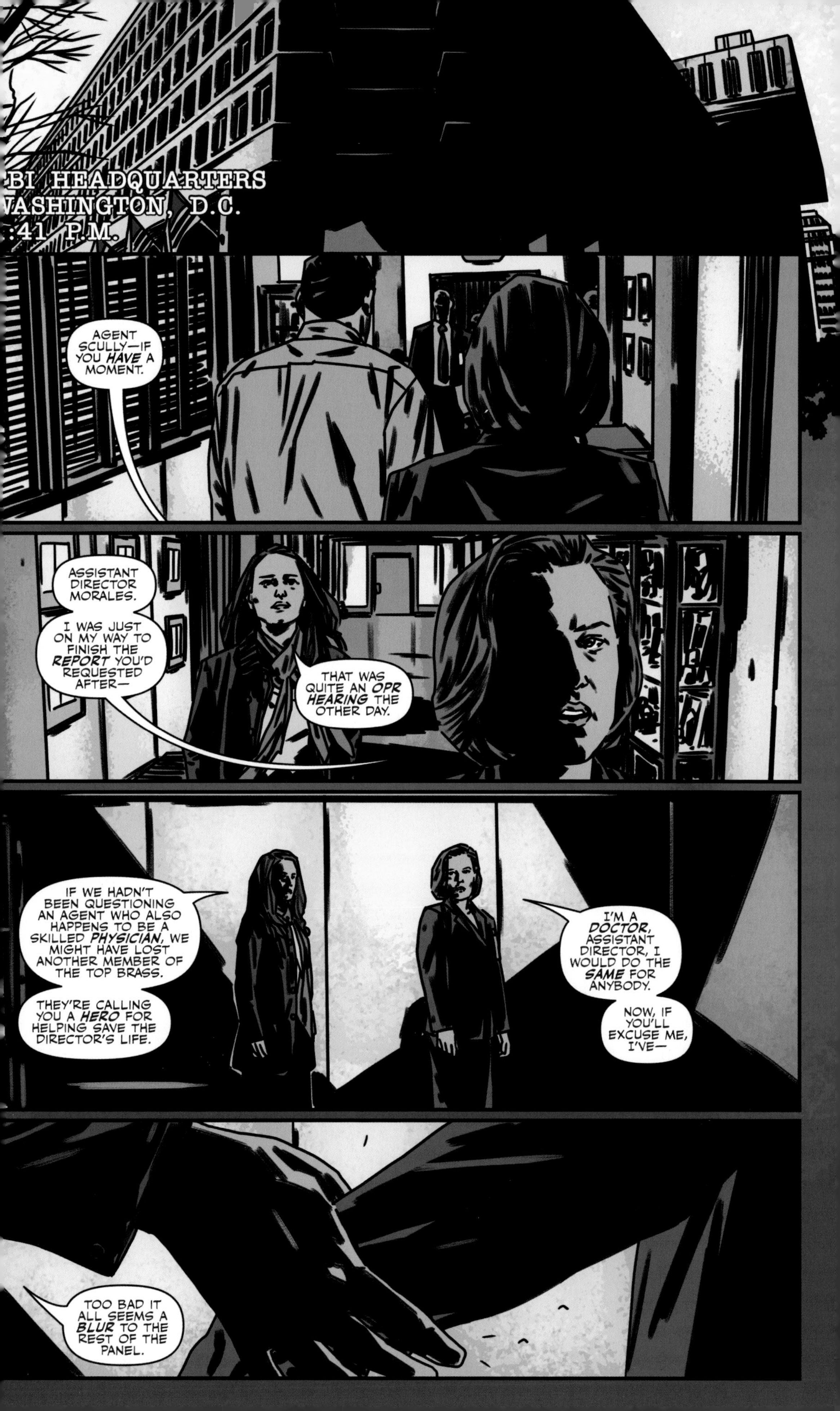

BI HEADQUARTERS
VASHINGTON, D.C.
:41 P.M.
AGENT SCULLY—IF YOU *HAVE* A MOMENT.
ASSISTANT DIRECTOR MORALES.
I WAS JUST ON MY WAY TO FINISH THE *REPORT* YOU'D REQUESTED AFTER—
THAT WAS QUITE AN *OPR HEARING* THE OTHER DAY.
IF WE HADN'T BEEN QUESTIONING AN AGENT WHO ALSO HAPPENS TO BE A SKILLED *PHYSICIAN*, WE MIGHT HAVE LOST ANOTHER MEMBER OF THE TOP BRASS.
THEY'RE CALLING YOU A *HERO* FOR HELPING SAVE THE DIRECTOR'S LIFE.
I'M A *DOCTOR*, ASSISTANT DIRECTOR, I WOULD DO THE *SAME* FOR ANYBODY.
NOW, IF YOU'LL EXCUSE ME, I'VE—
TOO BAD IT ALL SEEMS A *BLUR* TO THE REST OF THE PANEL.

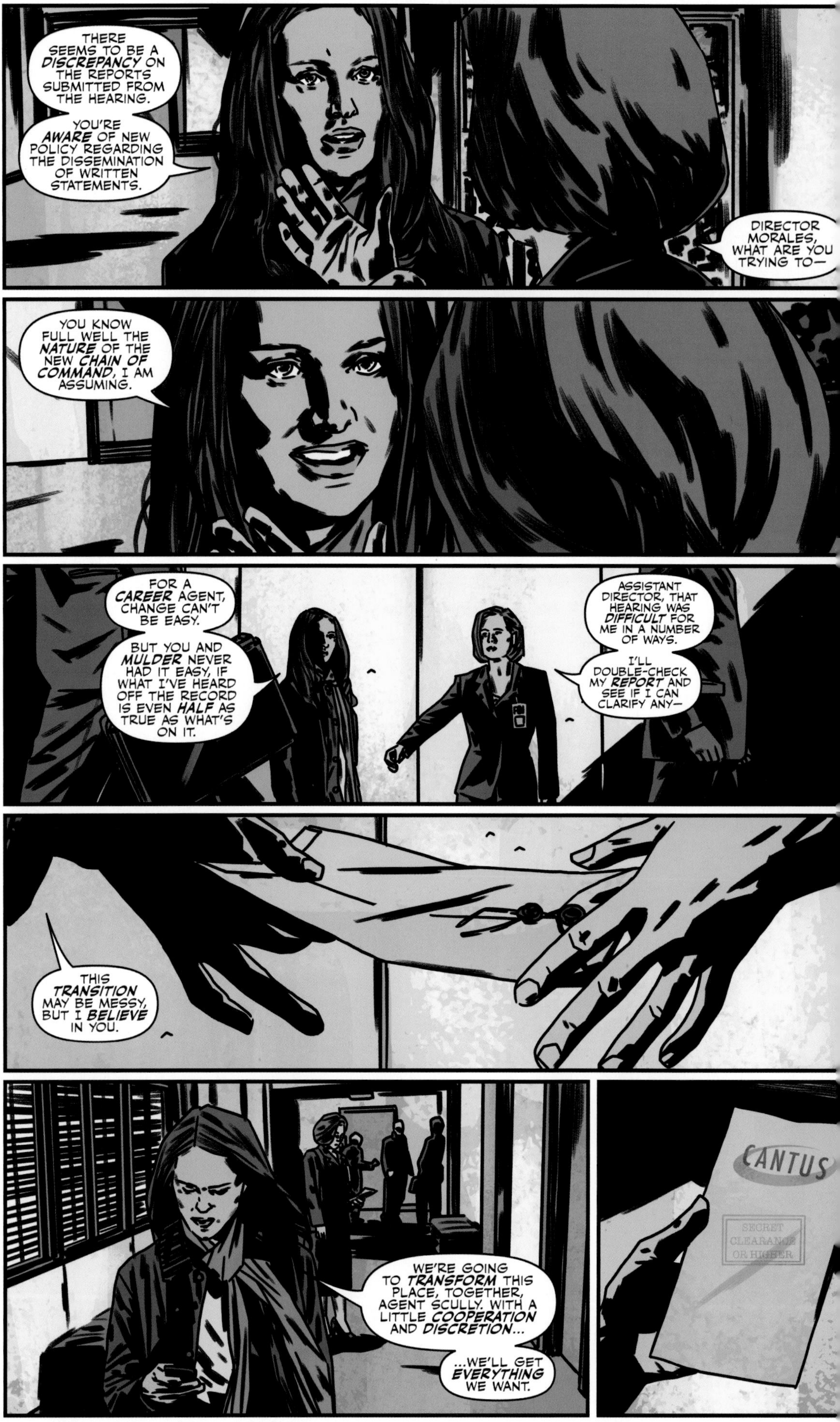
THERE SEEMS TO BE A *DISCREPANCY* ON THE REPORTS SUBMITTED FROM THE HEARING.
YOU'RE *AWARE* OF NEW POLICY REGARDING THE DISSEMINATION OF WRITTEN STATEMENTS.
DIRECTOR MORALES, WHAT ARE YOU TRYING TO—
YOU KNOW FULL WELL THE *NATURE* OF THE NEW *CHAIN OF COMMAND*, I AM ASSUMING.
FOR A *CAREER* AGENT, CHANGE CAN'T BE EASY.
BUT YOU AND *MULDER* NEVER HAD IT EASY, IF WHAT I'VE HEARD OFF THE RECORD IS EVEN *HALF* AS TRUE AS WHAT'S ON IT.
ASSISTANT DIRECTOR, THAT HEARING WAS *DIFFICULT* FOR ME IN A NUMBER OF WAYS.
I'LL DOUBLE-CHECK MY *REPORT* AND SEE IF I CAN CLARIFY ANY—
THIS *TRANSITION* MAY BE MESSY, BUT I *BELIEVE* IN YOU.
WE'RE GOING TO *TRANSFORM* THIS PLACE, TOGETHER, AGENT SCULLY. WITH A LITTLE *COOPERATION* AND *DISCRETION*...
...WE'LL GET *EVERYTHING* WE WANT.
CANTUS
SECRET CLEARANCE OR HIGHER

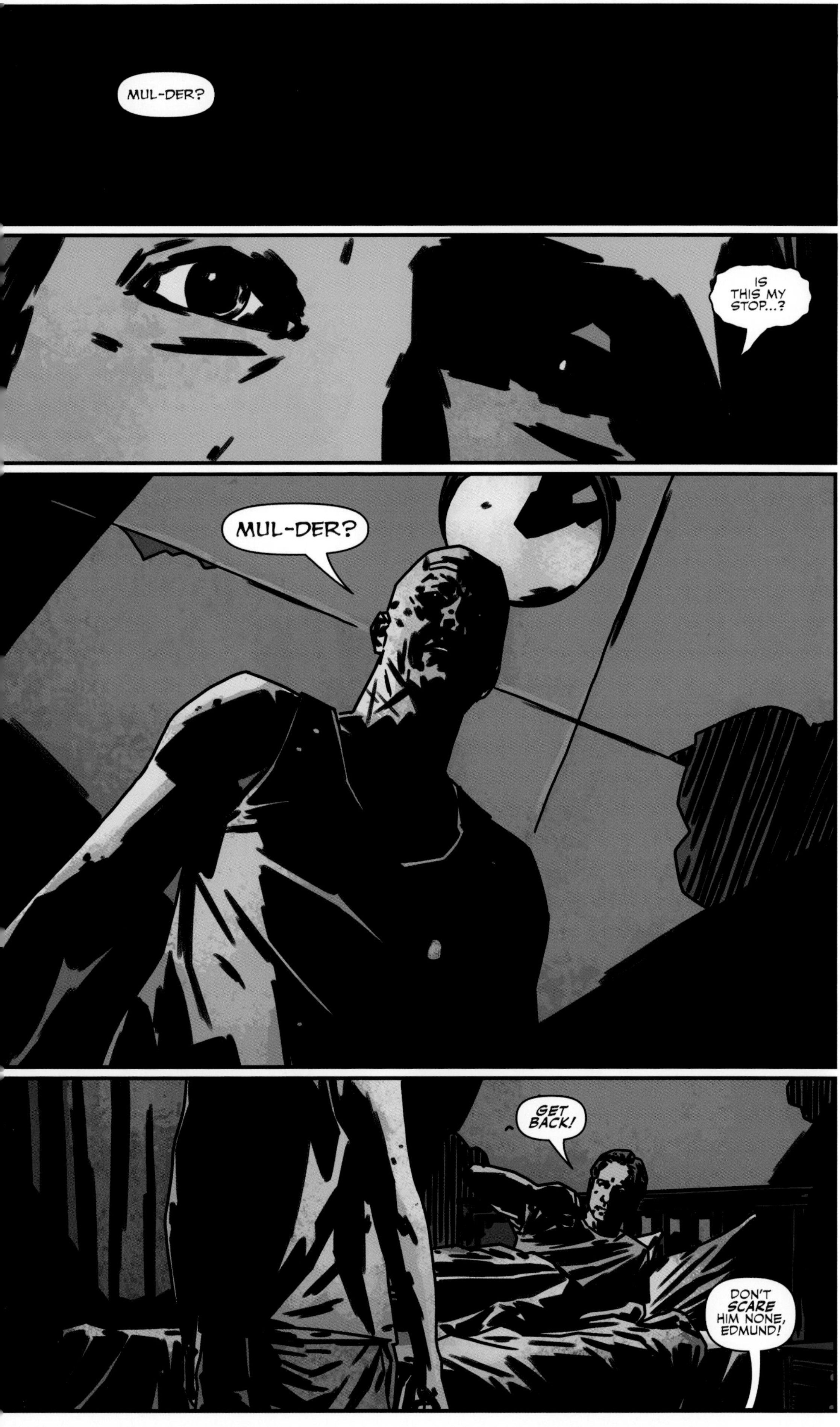
MUL-DER?
IS THIS MY STOP...?
MUL-DER?
GET BACK!
DON'T SCARE HIM NONE, EDMUND!

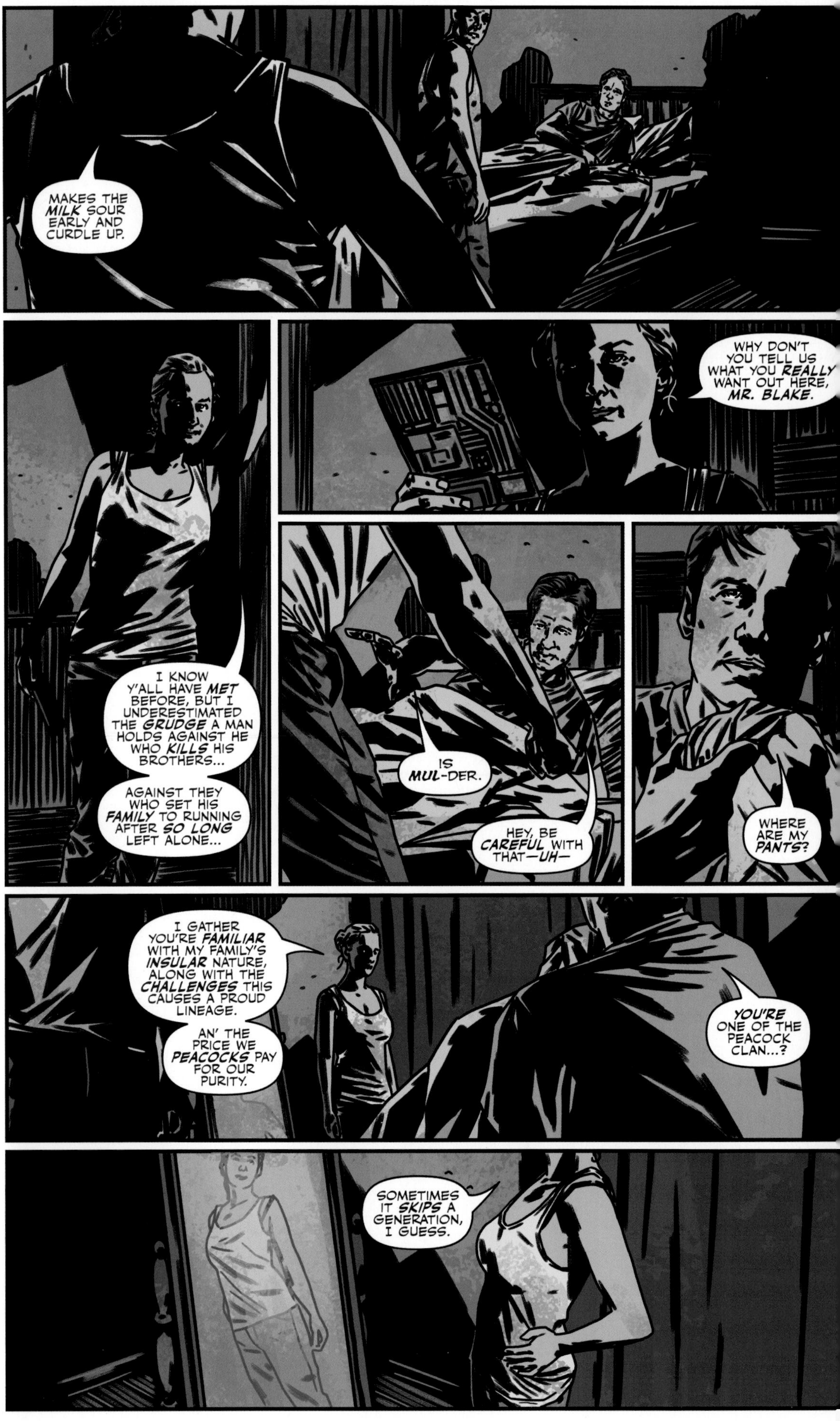

MAKES THE MILK SOUR EARLY AND CURDLE UP.
I KNOW Y'ALL HAVE MET BEFORE, BUT I UNDERESTIMATED THE GRUDGE A MAN HOLDS AGAINST HE WHO KILLS HIS BROTHERS...
AGAINST THEY WHO SET HIS FAMILY TO RUNNING AFTER SO LONG LEFT ALONE...
WHY DON'T YOU TELL US WHAT YOU REALLY WANT OUT HERE, MR. BLAKE.
IS MUL-DER.
HEY, BE CAREFUL WITH THAT—UH—
WHERE ARE MY PANTS?
I GATHER YOU'RE FAMILIAR WITH MY FAMILY'S INSULAR NATURE, ALONG WITH THE CHALLENGES THIS CAUSES A PROUD LINEAGE.
AN' THE PRICE WE PEACOCKS PAY FOR OUR PURITY.
YOU'RE ONE OF THE PEACOCK CLAN...?
SOMETIMES IT SKIPS A GENERATION, I GUESS.

POPPA...?

THE **PEACOCKS** IS IN NEED OF **NEW BLOOD**. SOMEONE WE **KNOW** IS A STRONG, FORMIDABLE MAN.

DOWN! GET OFF—!

POPPA!

POPPA!

EDMUND CREIGHTON PEACOCK HAS SIRED **HUNDREDS** OF MY DEAR BROTHERS AND SISTERS OVER THESE MANY YEARS... BUT HIS **POTENCY**, IT APPEARS, HAS REACHED ITS END.

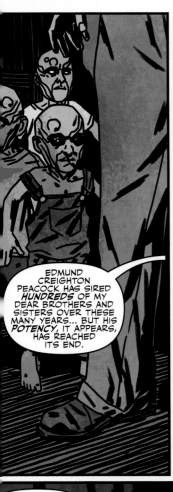

YOU'RE **NOT** SUGGESTING—

ONE OF THE BEST THINGS ABOUT **MILKING COWS** ALL DAY... YOU DEVELOP A PARTICULAR **FEEL** FOR IT.

I'M GONNA TAKE A **PASS** ON BEING YOUR BABY DADDY, HATE TO BREAK IT TO YOU.

WHAT— US?

GROSS!

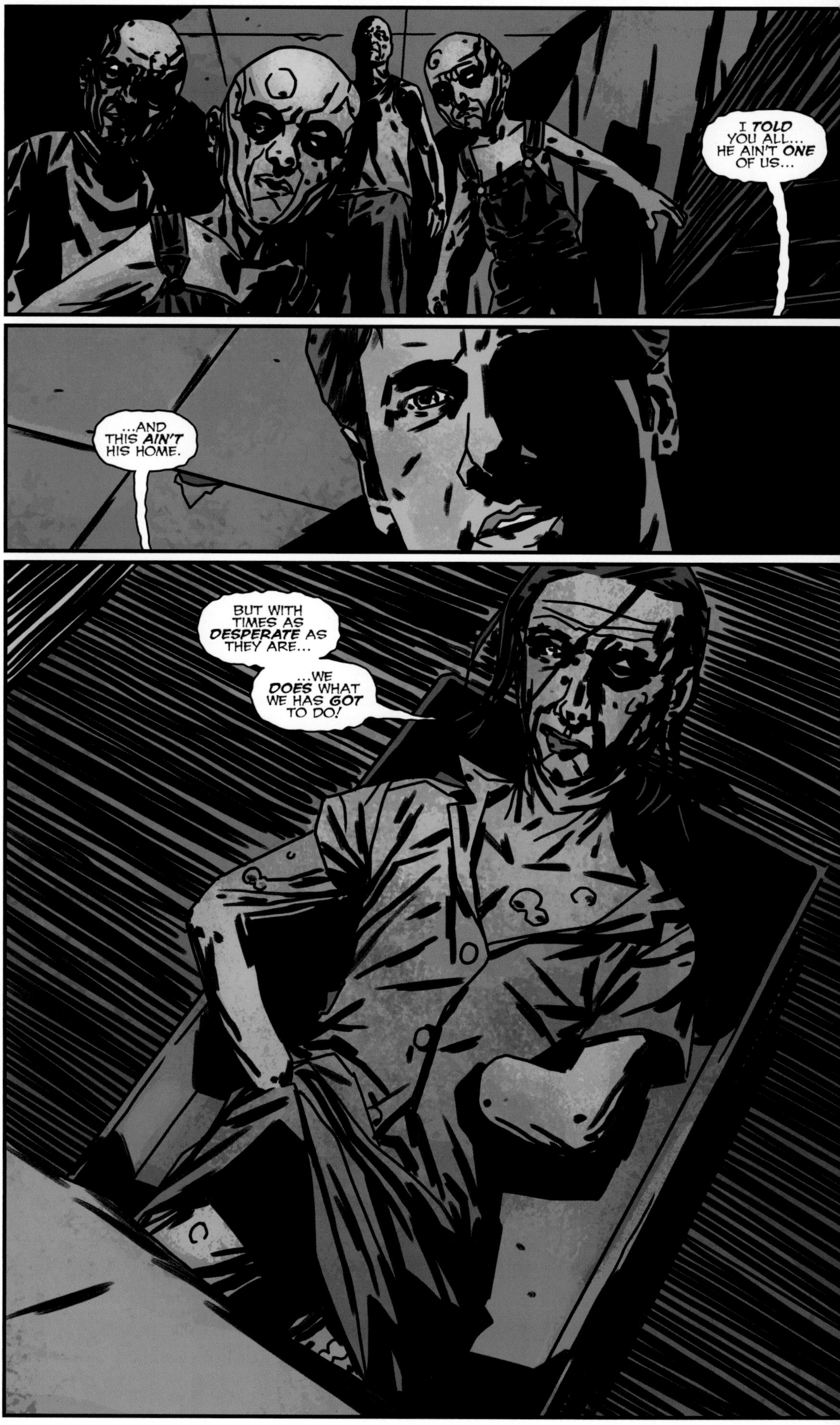
I *TOLD* YOU ALL... HE AIN'T *ONE* OF US...
...AND THIS *AIN'T* HIS HOME.
BUT WITH TIMES AS *DESPERATE* AS THEY ARE...
...WE *DOES* WHAT WE HAS *GOT* TO DO!

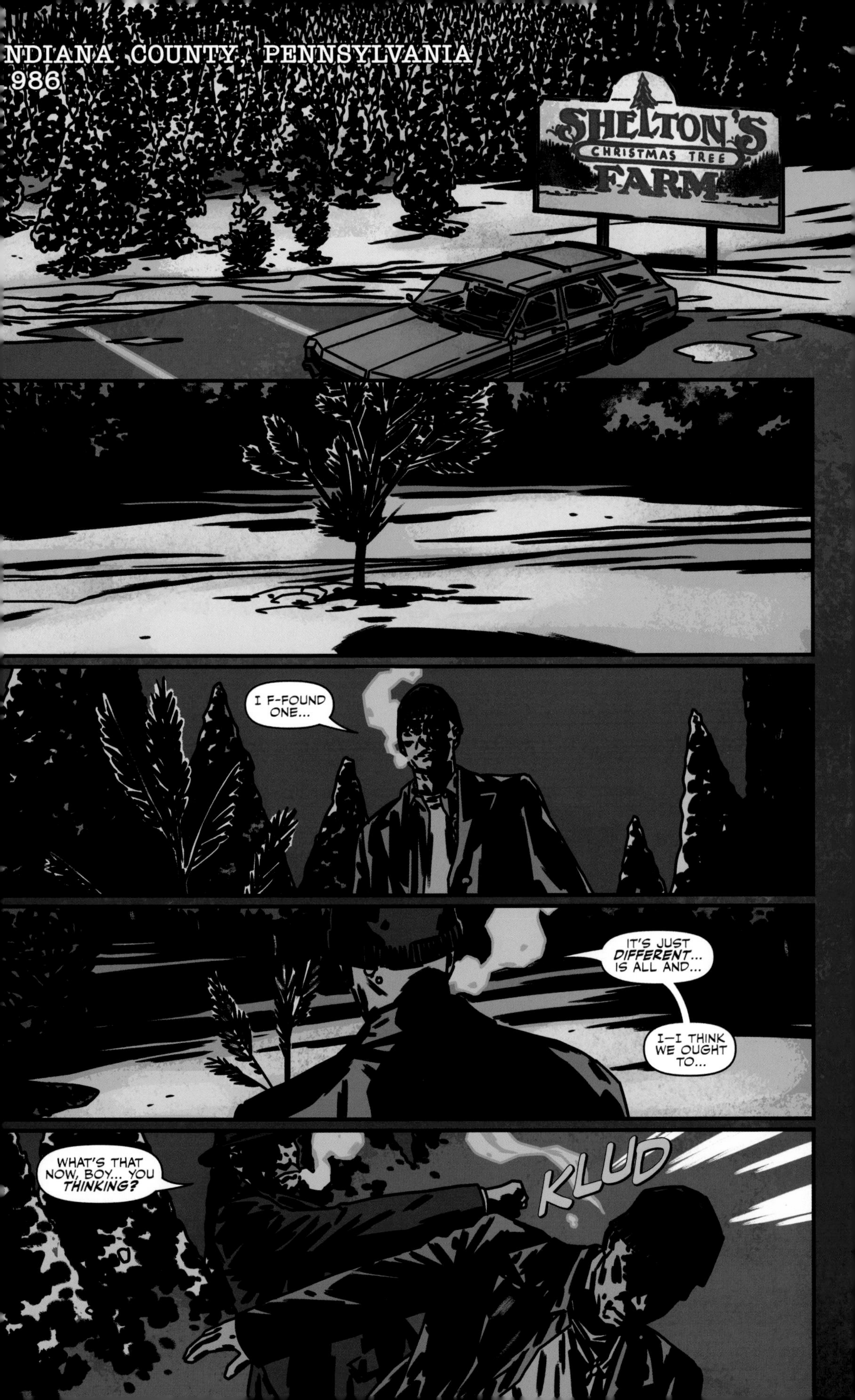
NDIANA COUNTY, PENNSYLVANIA
986
SHELTON'S CHRISTMAS TREE FARM
I F-FOUND ONE...
IT'S JUST *DIFFERENT*... IS ALL AND...
I—I THINK WE OUGHT TO...
WHAT'S THAT NOW, BOY... YOU *THINKING?*
KLUD

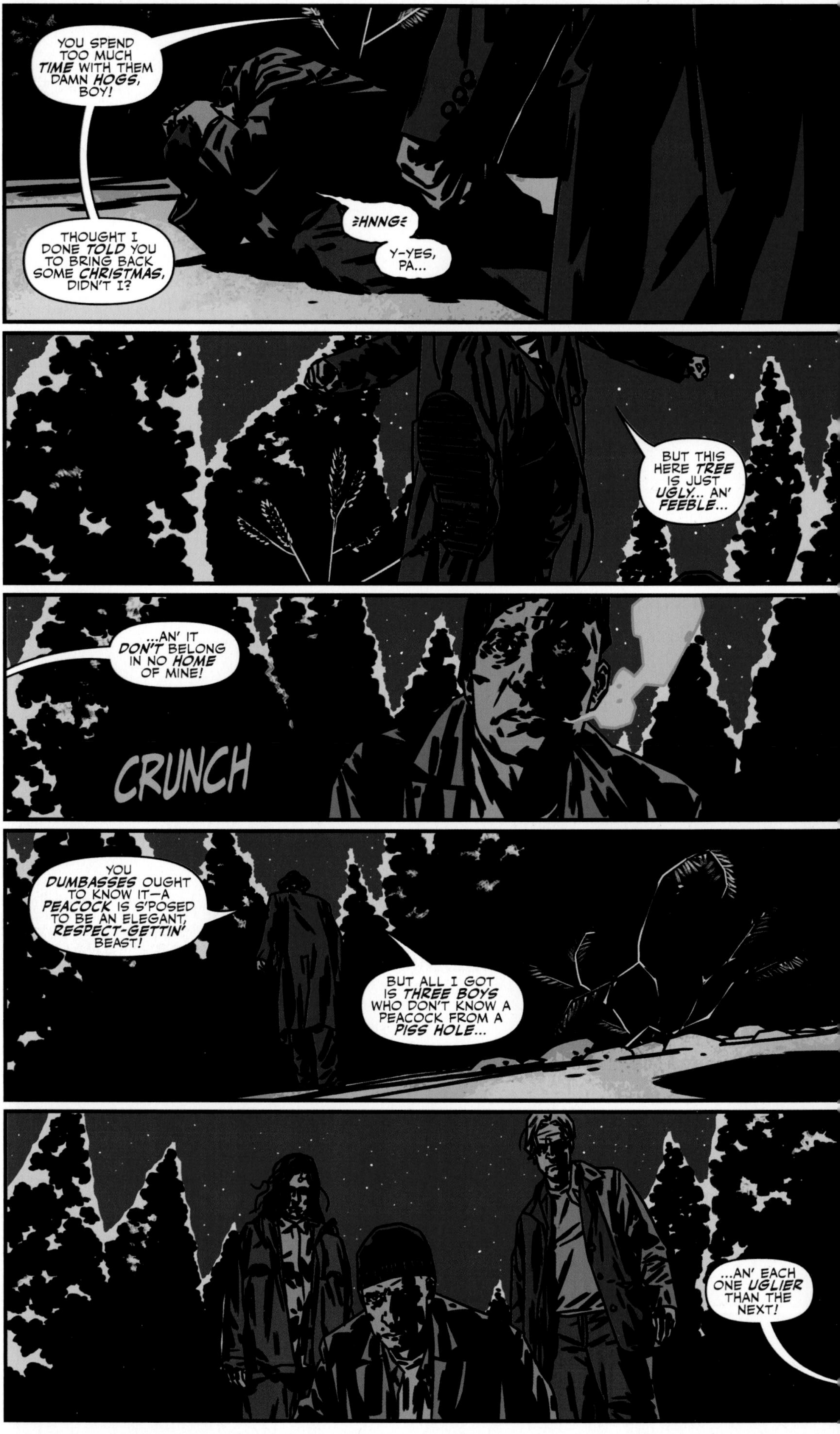
YOU SPEND TOO MUCH TIME WITH THEM DAMN HOGS, BOY!
THOUGHT I DONE TOLD YOU TO BRING BACK SOME CHRISTMAS, DIDN'T I?
HNNG
Y-YES, PA...
BUT THIS HERE TREE IS JUST UGLY... AN' FEEBLE...
...AN' IT DON'T BELONG IN NO HOME OF MINE!
CRUNCH
YOU DUMBASSES OUGHT TO KNOW IT—A PEACOCK IS S'POSED TO BE AN ELEGANT, RESPECT-GETTIN' BEAST!
BUT ALL I GOT IS THREE BOYS WHO DON'T KNOW A PEACOCK FROM A PISS HOLE...
...AN' EACH ONE UGLIER THAN THE NEXT!

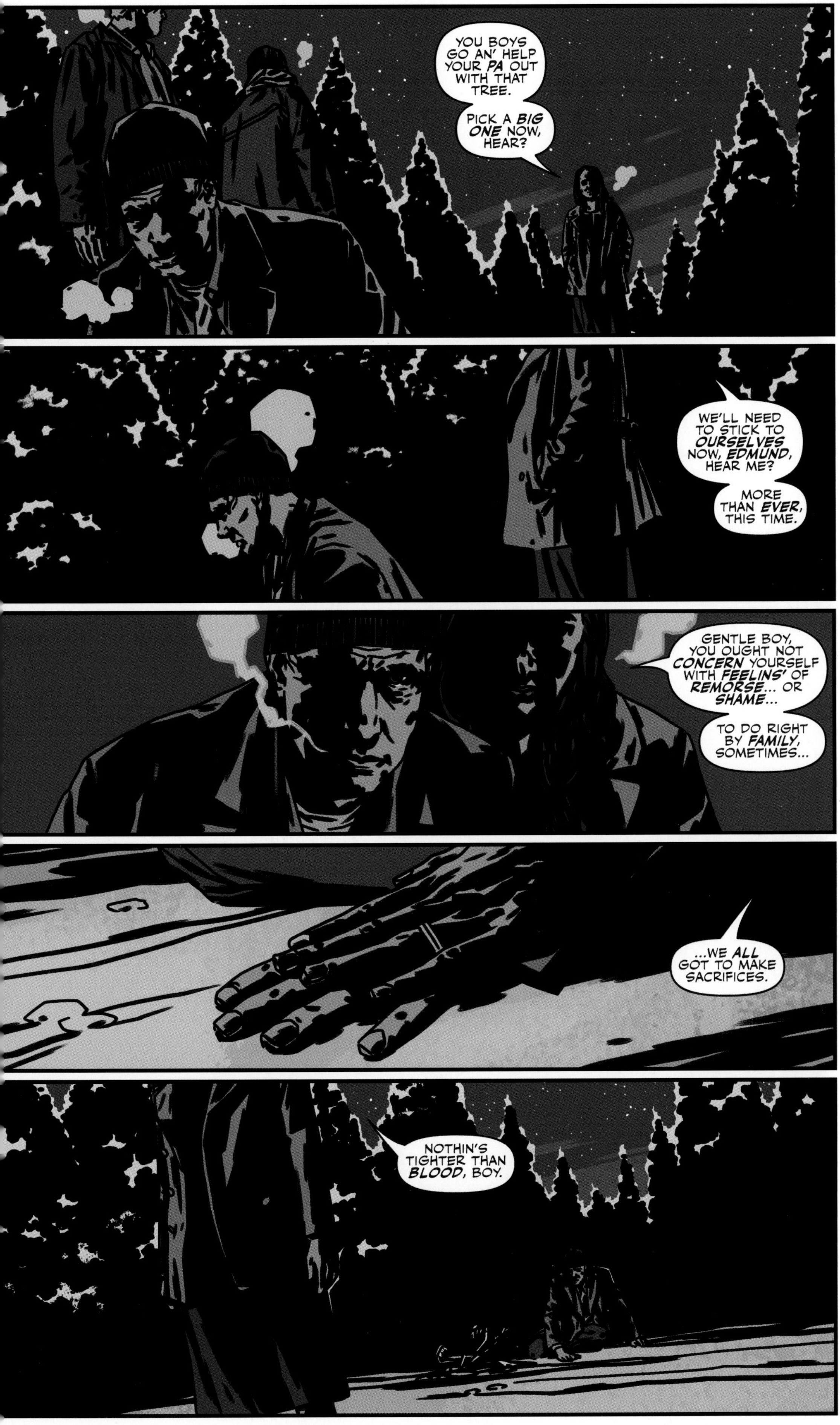

YOU BOYS GO AN' HELP YOUR PA OUT WITH THAT TREE.
PICK A BIG ONE NOW, HEAR?
WE'LL NEED TO STICK TO OURSELVES NOW, EDMUND, HEAR ME?
MORE THAN EVER, THIS TIME.
GENTLE BOY, YOU OUGHT NOT CONCERN YOURSELF WITH FEELINS' OF REMORSE... OR SHAME...
TO DO RIGHT BY FAMILY, SOMETIMES...
...WE ALL GOT TO MAKE SACRIFICES.
NOTHIN'S TIGHTER THAN BLOOD, BOY.

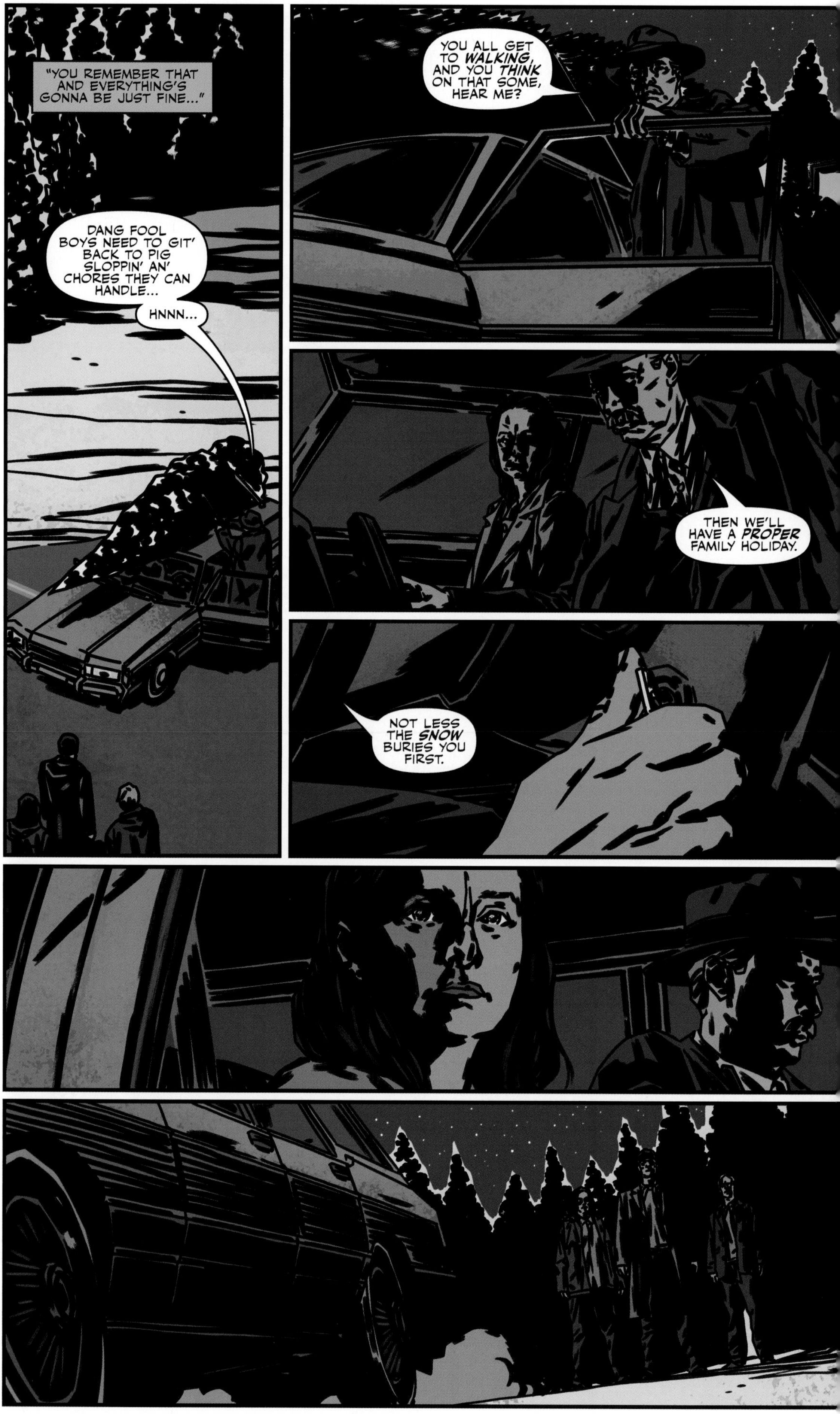

"YOU REMEMBER THAT AND EVERYTHING'S GONNA BE JUST FINE..."
DANG FOOL BOYS NEED TO GIT' BACK TO PIG SLOPPIN' AN' CHORES THEY CAN HANDLE...
HNNN...
YOU ALL GET TO WALKING, AND YOU THINK ON THAT SOME, HEAR ME?
THEN WE'LL HAVE A PROPER FAMILY HOLIDAY.
NOT LESS THE SNOW BURIES YOU FIRST.

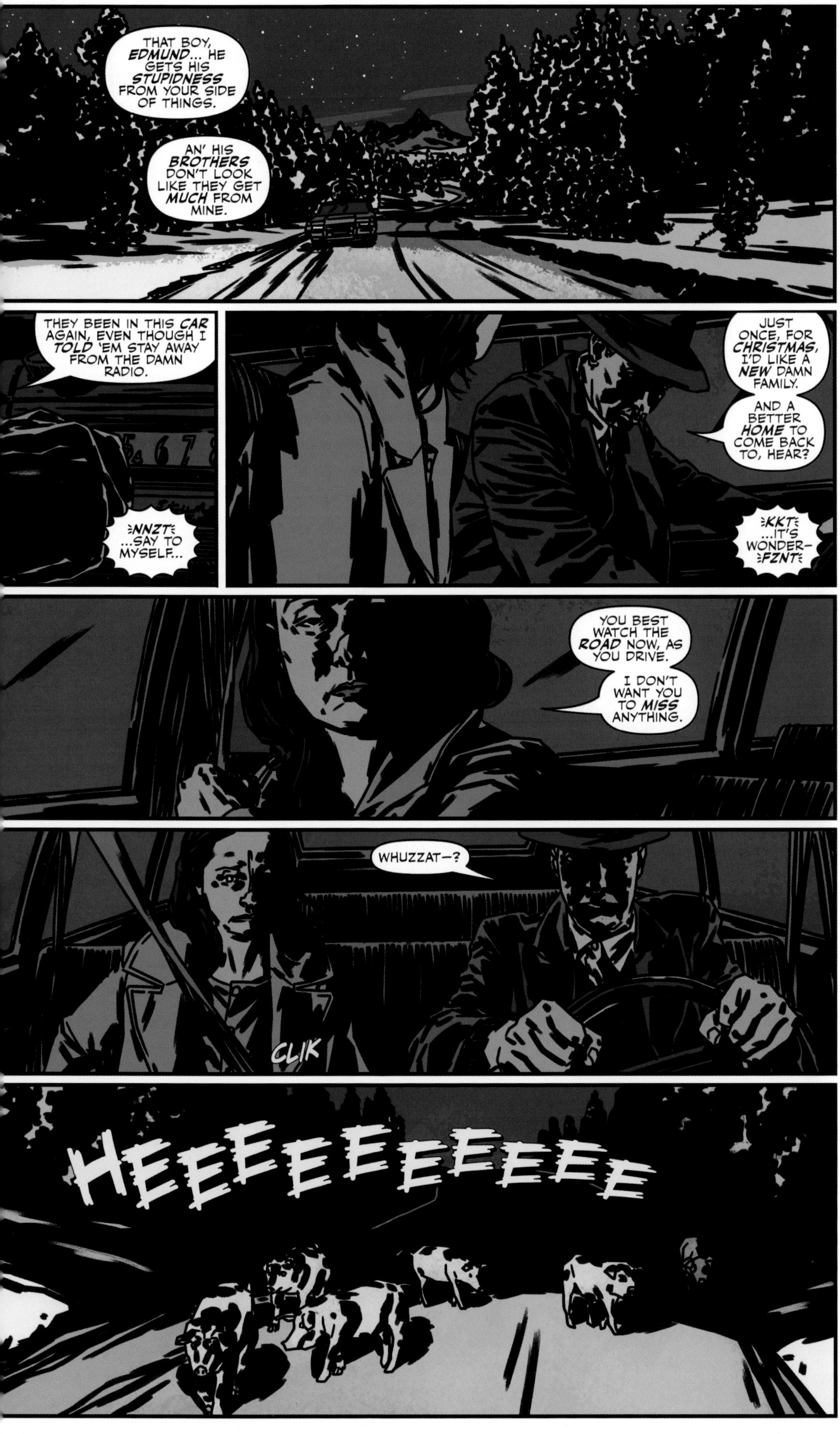

THAT BOY, EDMUND... HE GETS HIS STUPIDNESS FROM YOUR SIDE OF THINGS.
AN' HIS BROTHERS DON'T LOOK LIKE THEY GET MUCH FROM MINE.
THEY BEEN IN THIS CAR AGAIN, EVEN THOUGH I TOLD 'EM STAY AWAY FROM THE DAMN RADIO.
NNZT ...SAY TO MYSELF...
JUST ONCE, FOR CHRISTMAS, I'D LIKE A NEW DAMN FAMILY.
AND A BETTER HOME TO COME BACK TO, HEAR?
KKT ...IT'S WONDER- FZNT
YOU BEST WATCH THE ROAD NOW, AS YOU DRIVE.
I DON'T WANT YOU TO MISS ANYTHING.
WHUZZAT—?
CLIK
HEEEEEEEEEEE

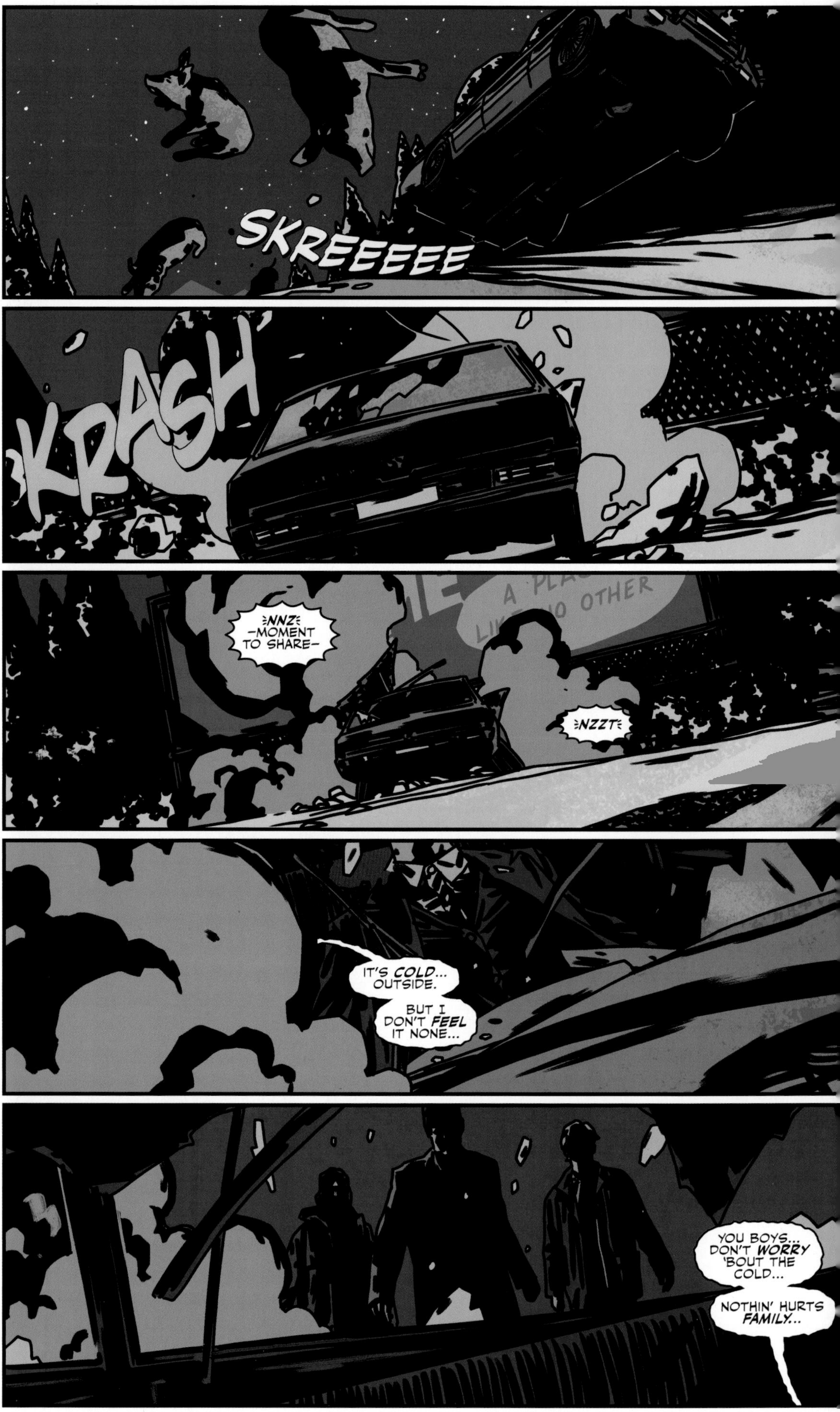

SKREEEEEE
KRASH
A PLA
LIKE NO OTHER
NNZ -MOMENT TO SHARE-
NZZT
IT'S COLD... OUTSIDE.
BUT I DON'T FEEL IT NONE...
YOU BOYS... DON'T WORRY 'BOUT THE COLD...
NOTHIN' HURTS FAMILY...

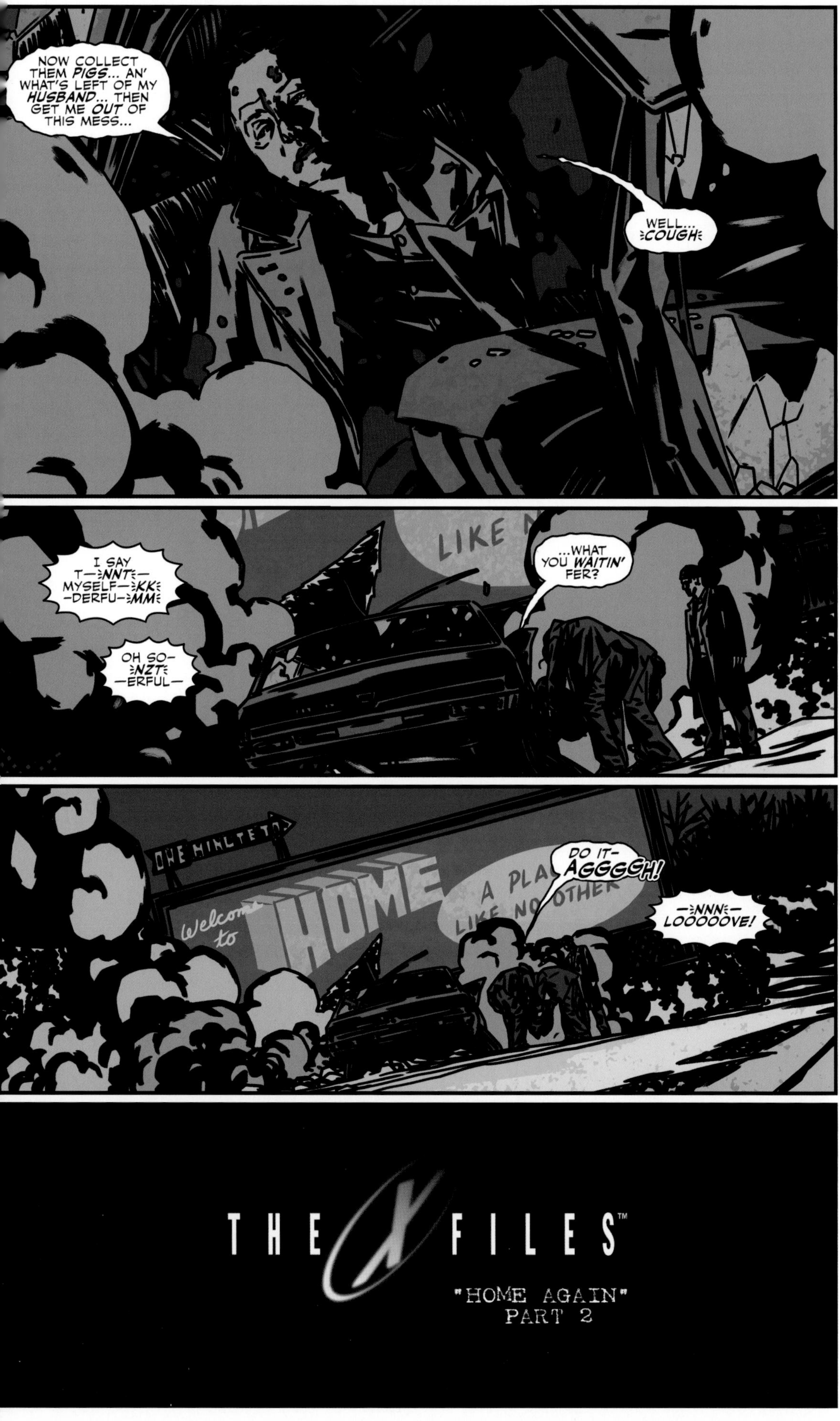
NOW COLLECT THEM PIGS... AN' WHAT'S LEFT OF MY HUSBAND... THEN GET ME OUT OF THIS MESS...
WELL... COUGH
LIKE N
I SAY T—NNT— MYSELF—KK —DERFU—MM
OH SO— NZT —ERFUL—
...WHAT YOU WAITIN' FER?
Welcome to
HOME
DO IT— AGGGGH!
—NNN— LOOOOOVE!
THE X FILES™
"HOME AGAIN"
PART 2

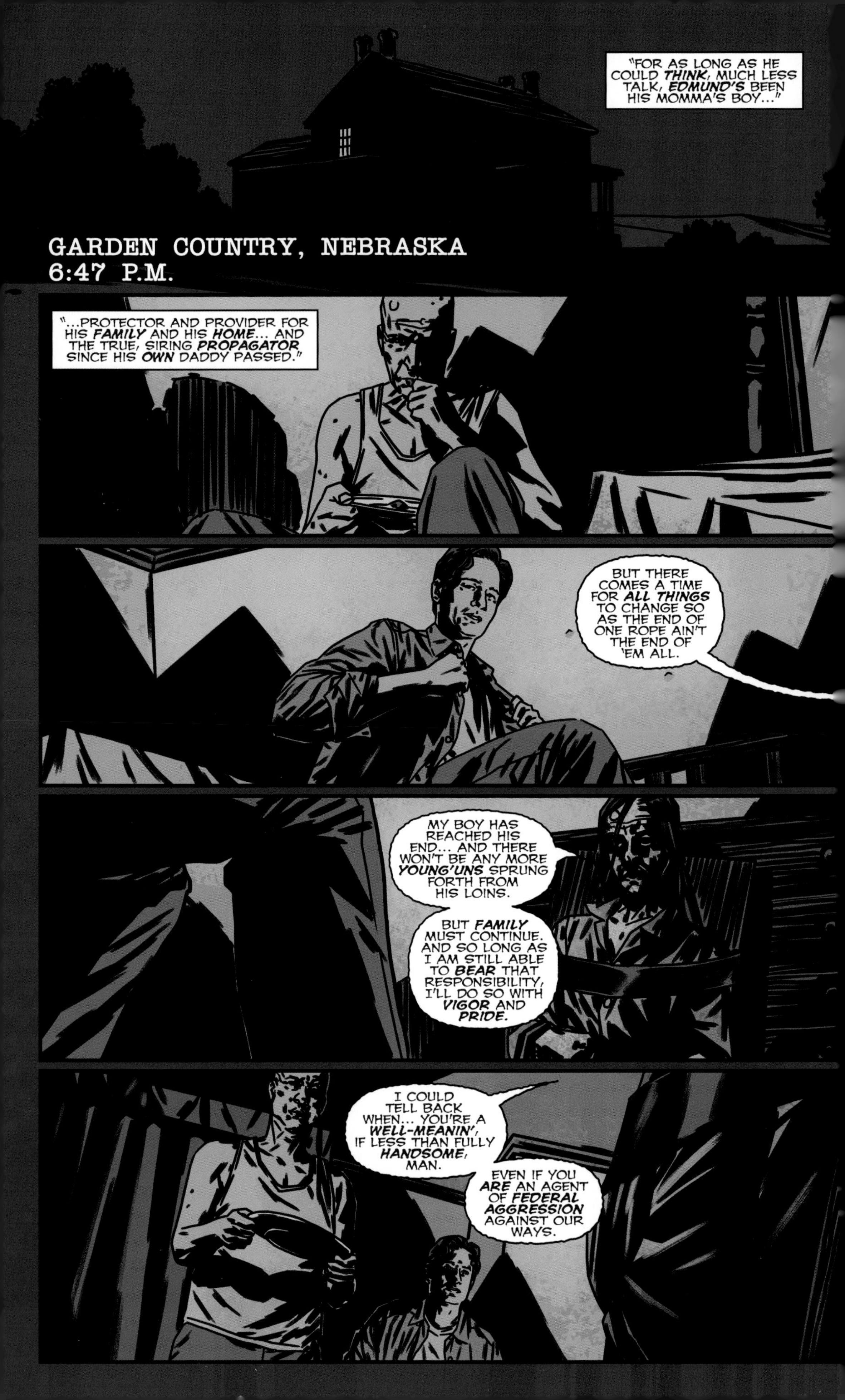
"FOR AS LONG AS HE COULD THINK, MUCH LESS TALK, EDMUND'S BEEN HIS MOMMA'S BOY..."
GARDEN COUNTRY, NEBRASKA
6:47 P.M.
"...PROTECTOR AND PROVIDER FOR HIS FAMILY AND HIS HOME... AND THE TRUE, SIRING PROPAGATOR SINCE HIS OWN DADDY PASSED."
BUT THERE COMES A TIME FOR ALL THINGS TO CHANGE SO AS THE END OF ONE ROPE AIN'T THE END OF 'EM ALL.
MY BOY HAS REACHED HIS END... AND THERE WON'T BE ANY MORE YOUNG'UNS SPRUNG FORTH FROM HIS LOINS.
BUT FAMILY MUST CONTINUE. AND SO LONG AS I AM STILL ABLE TO BEAR THAT RESPONSIBILITY, I'LL DO SO WITH VIGOR AND PRIDE.
I COULD TELL BACK WHEN... YOU'RE A WELL-MEANIN', IF LESS THAN FULLY HANDSOME, MAN.
EVEN IF YOU ARE AN AGENT OF FEDERAL AGGRESSION AGAINST OUR WAYS.

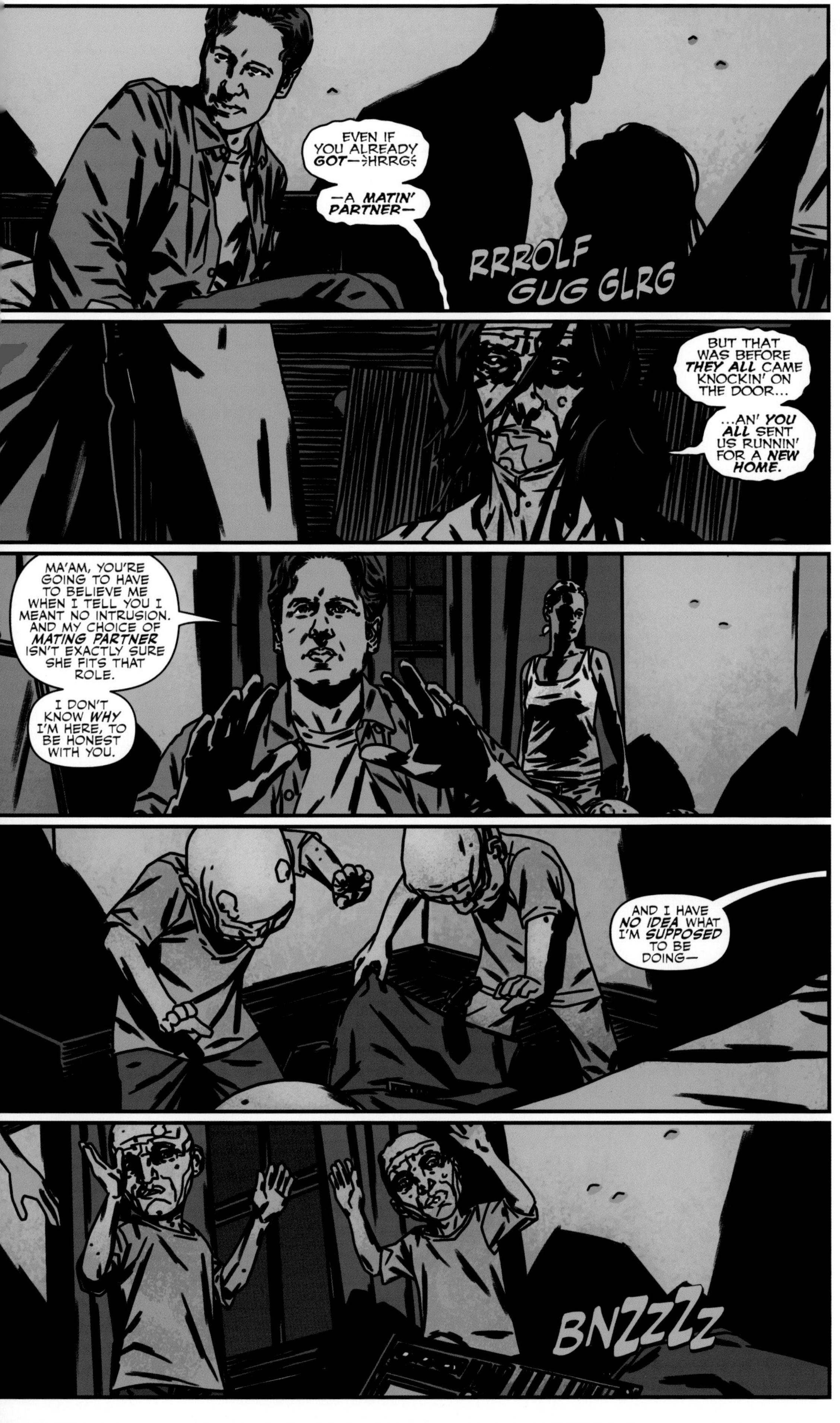
EVEN IF YOU ALREADY GOT—HRRG—
—A MATIN' PARTNER—
RRROLF GUG GLRG
BUT THAT WAS BEFORE THEY ALL CAME KNOCKIN' ON THE DOOR...
...AN' YOU ALL SENT US RUNNIN' FOR A NEW HOME.
MA'AM, YOU'RE GOING TO HAVE TO BELIEVE ME WHEN I TELL YOU I MEANT NO INTRUSION. AND MY CHOICE OF MATING PARTNER ISN'T EXACTLY SURE SHE FITS THAT ROLE.
I DON'T KNOW WHY I'M HERE, TO BE HONEST WITH YOU.
AND I HAVE NO IDEA WHAT I'M SUPPOSED TO BE DOING—
BNZZZZ

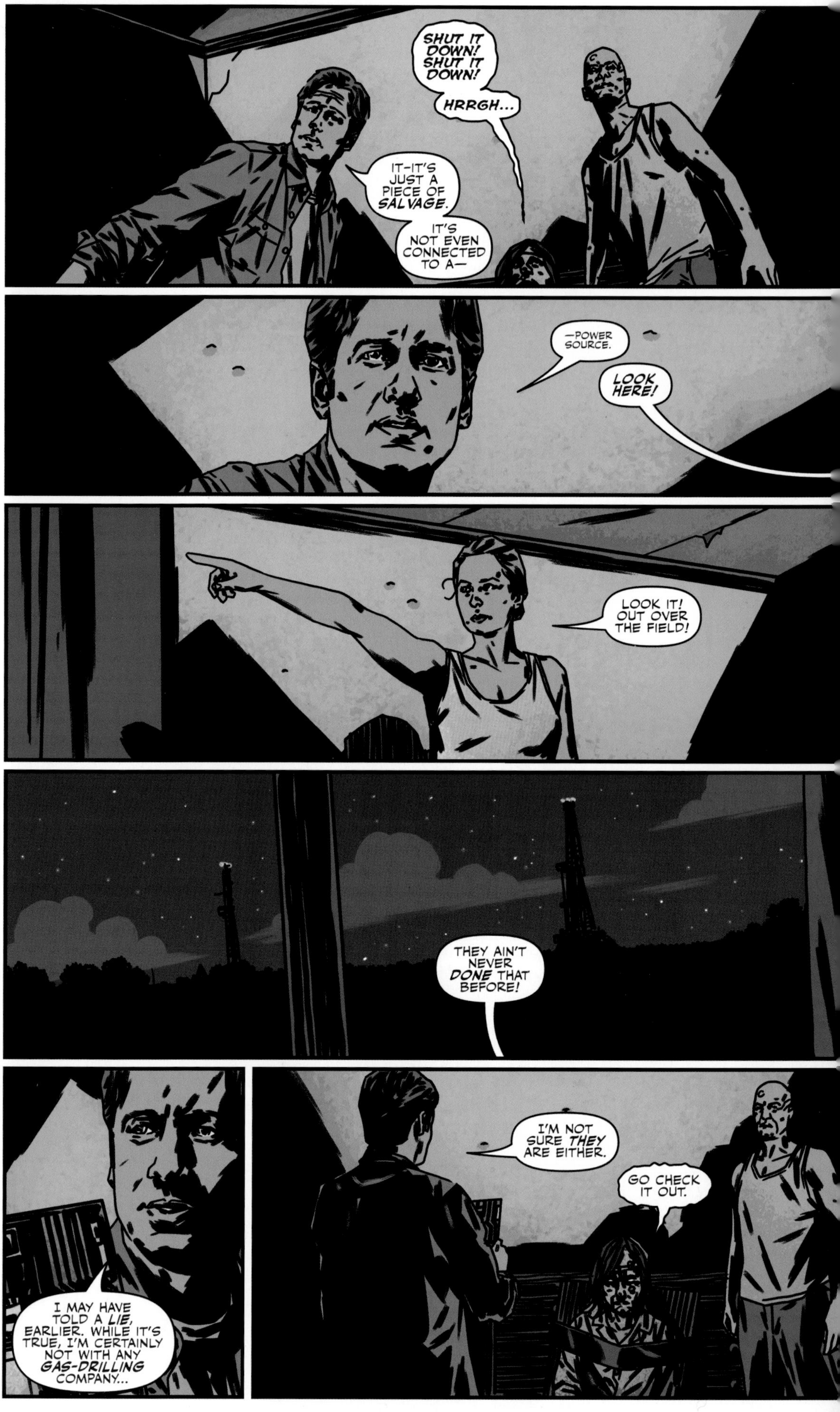
SHUT IT DOWN! SHUT IT DOWN!
HRRGH...
IT-IT'S JUST A PIECE OF SALVAGE.
IT'S NOT EVEN CONNECTED TO A—
—POWER SOURCE.
LOOK HERE!
LOOK IT! OUT OVER THE FIELD!
THEY AIN'T NEVER DONE THAT BEFORE!
I MAY HAVE TOLD A LIE, EARLIER. WHILE IT'S TRUE, I'M CERTAINLY NOT WITH ANY GAS-DRILLING COMPANY...
I'M NOT SURE THEY ARE EITHER.
GO CHECK IT OUT.

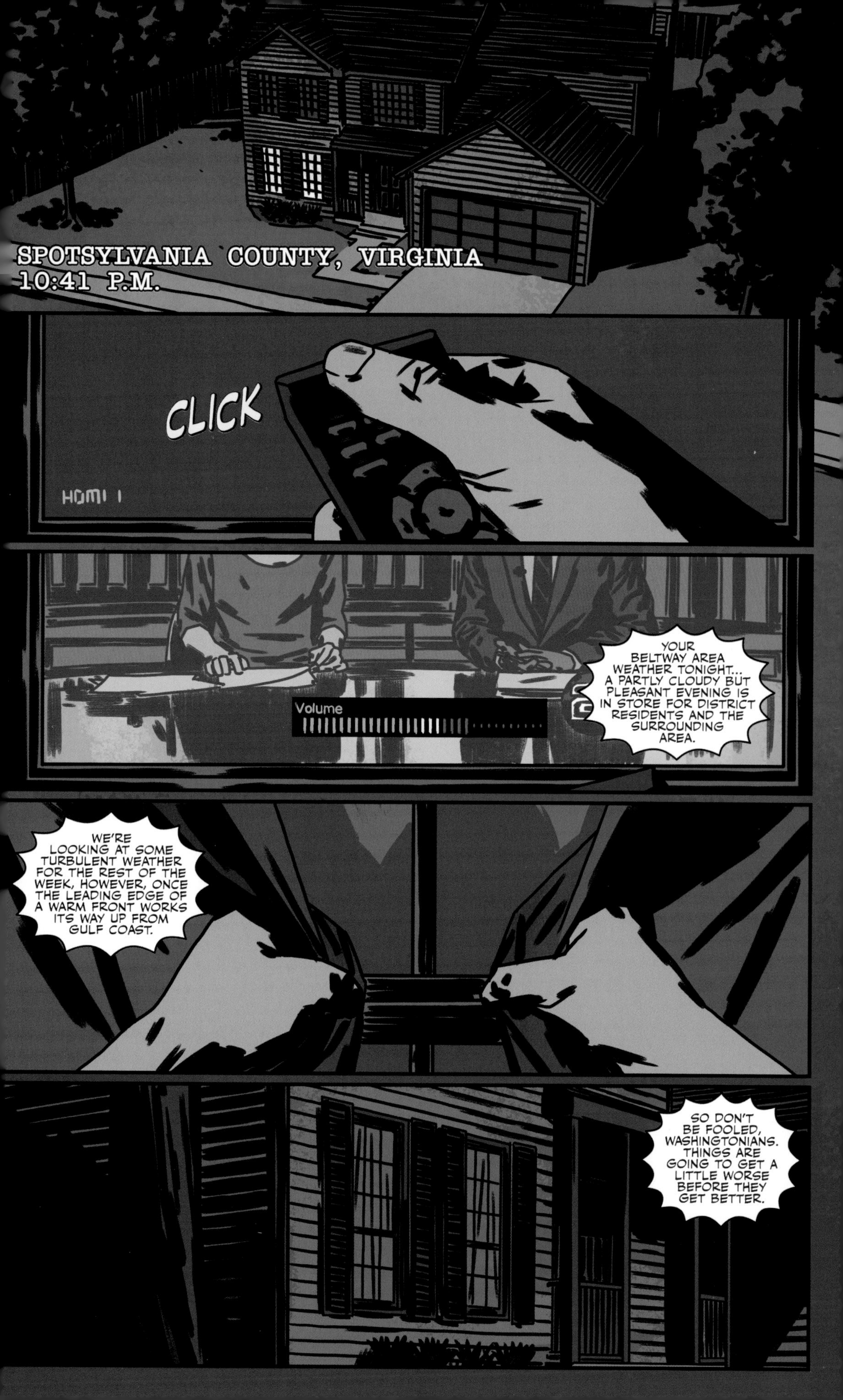
SPOTSYLVANIA COUNTY, VIRGINIA
10:41 P.M.
CLICK
HDMI 1
Volume
YOUR BELTWAY AREA WEATHER TONIGHT... A PARTLY CLOUDY BUT PLEASANT EVENING IS IN STORE FOR DISTRICT RESIDENTS AND THE SURROUNDING AREA.
WE'RE LOOKING AT SOME TURBULENT WEATHER FOR THE REST OF THE WEEK, HOWEVER, ONCE THE LEADING EDGE OF A WARM FRONT WORKS ITS WAY UP FROM GULF COAST.
SO DON'T BE FOOLED, WASHINGTONIANS. THINGS ARE GOING TO GET A LITTLE WORSE BEFORE THEY GET BETTER.

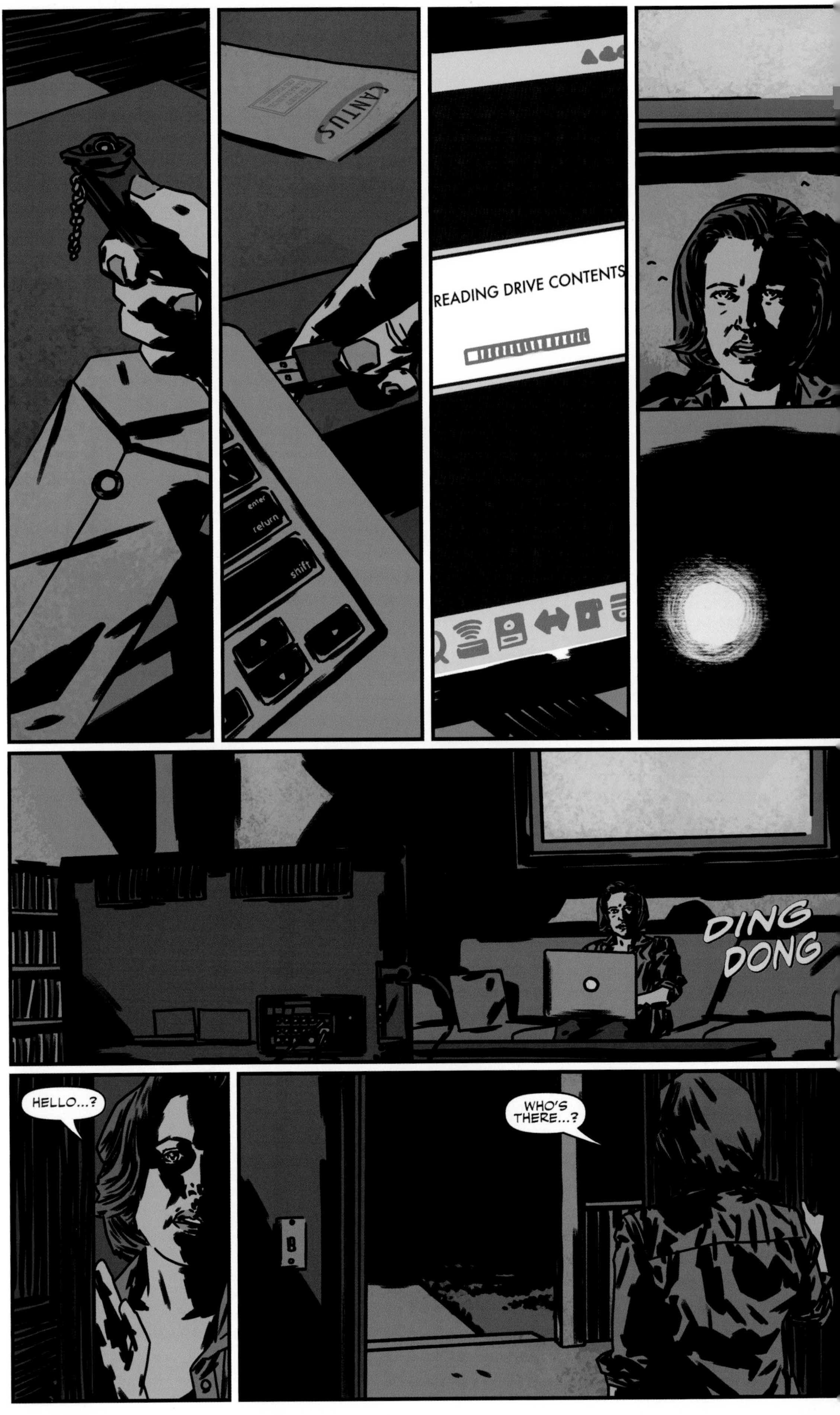
CANTUS
READING DRIVE CONTENTS
DING DONG
HELLO...?
WHO'S THERE...?

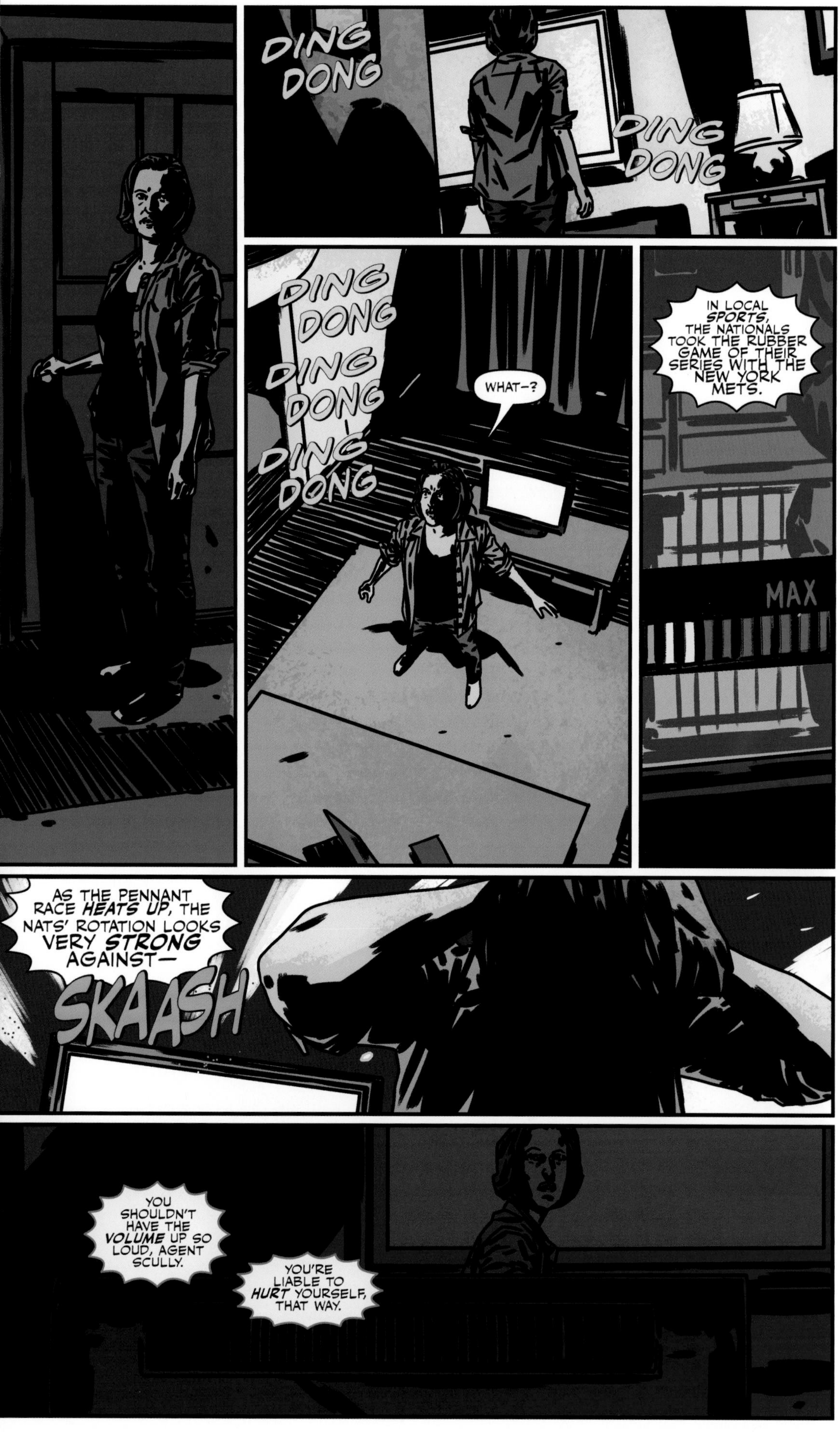
DING DONG
DING DONG
DING DONG
DING DONG
DING DONG
WHAT–?
IN LOCAL SPORTS, THE NATIONALS TOOK THE RUBBER GAME OF THEIR SERIES WITH THE NEW YORK METS.
MAX
AS THE PENNANT RACE HEATS UP, THE NATS' ROTATION LOOKS VERY STRONG AGAINST—
SKAASH
YOU SHOULDN'T HAVE THE VOLUME UP SO LOUD, AGENT SCULLY.
YOU'RE LIABLE TO HURT YOURSELF, THAT WAY.

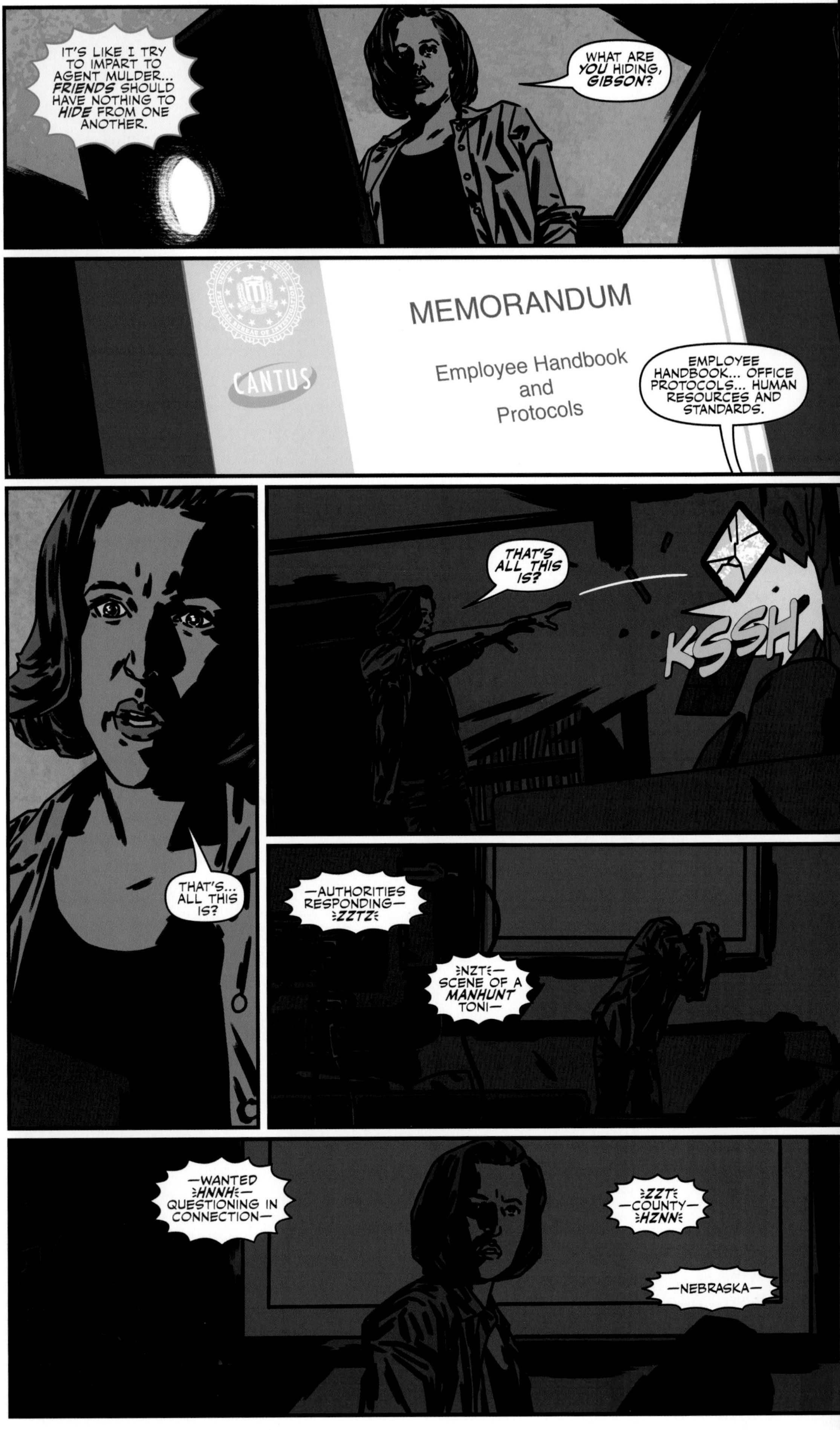
IT'S LIKE I TRY TO IMPART TO AGENT MULDER... FRIENDS SHOULD HAVE NOTHING TO HIDE FROM ONE ANOTHER.
WHAT ARE YOU HIDING, GIBSON?
MEMORANDUM
Employee Handbook and Protocols
CANTUS
EMPLOYEE HANDBOOK... OFFICE PROTOCOLS... HUMAN RESOURCES AND STANDARDS.
THAT'S... ALL THIS IS?
THAT'S ALL THIS IS?
KSSH
—AUTHORITIES RESPONDING— ZZTZ
NZT— SCENE OF A MANHUNT TONI—
—WANTED HNNH— QUESTIONING IN CONNECTION—
ZZT —COUNTY— HZNN
—NEBRASKA—

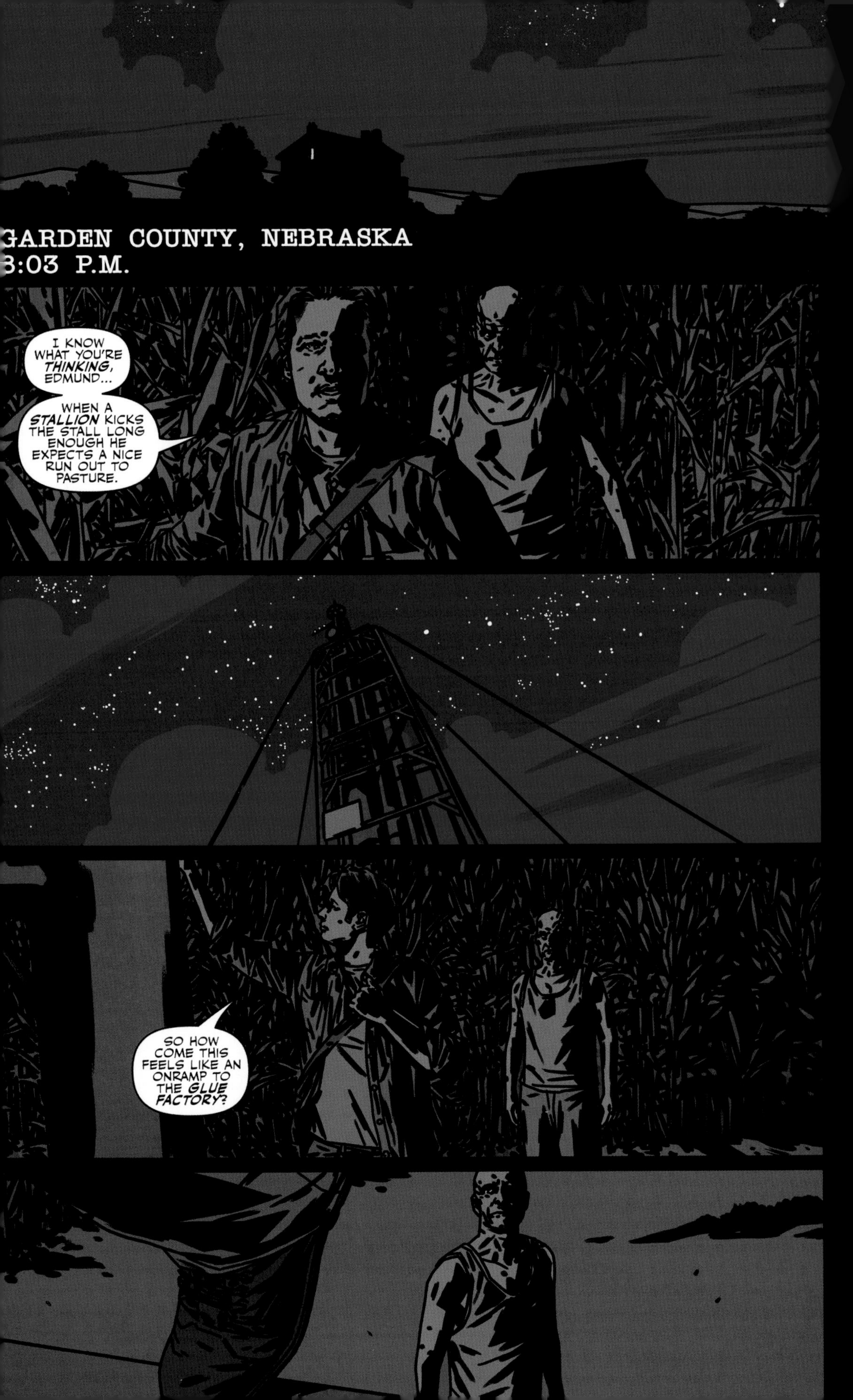
GARDEN COUNTY, NEBRASKA
3:03 P.M.
I KNOW WHAT YOU'RE THINKING, EDMUND...
WHEN A STALLION KICKS THE STALL LONG ENOUGH HE EXPECTS A NICE RUN OUT TO PASTURE.
SO HOW COME THIS FEELS LIKE AN ONRAMP TO THE GLUE FACTORY?

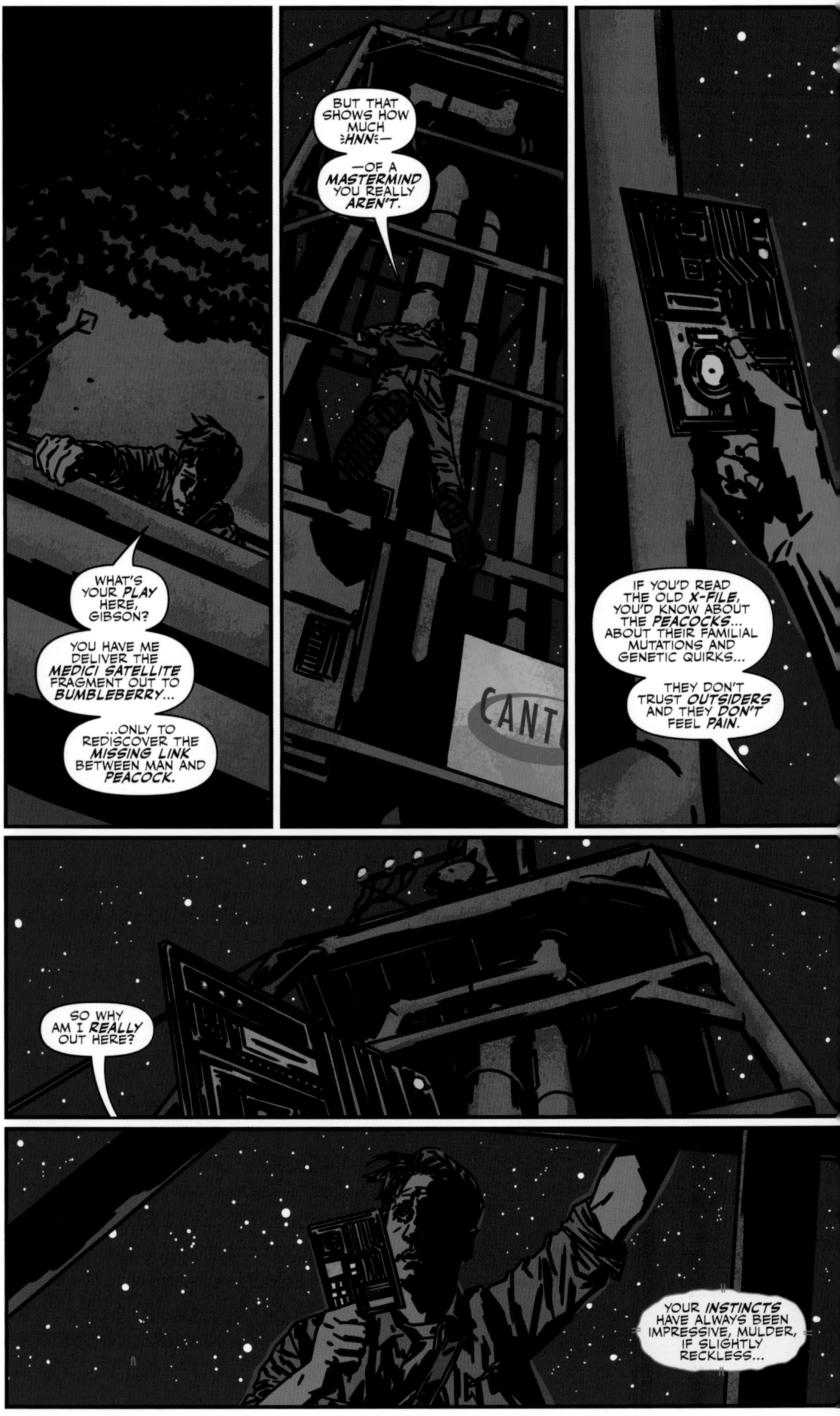
WHAT'S YOUR PLAY HERE, GIBSON?
YOU HAVE ME DELIVER THE MEDICI SATELLITE FRAGMENT OUT TO BUMBLEBERRY...
...ONLY TO REDISCOVER THE MISSING LINK BETWEEN MAN AND PEACOCK.
BUT THAT SHOWS HOW MUCH HNN—
—OF A MASTERMIND YOU REALLY AREN'T.
CANT
IF YOU'D READ THE OLD X-FILE, YOU'D KNOW ABOUT THE PEACOCKS... ABOUT THEIR FAMILIAL MUTATIONS AND GENETIC QUIRKS...
THEY DON'T TRUST OUTSIDERS AND THEY DON'T FEEL PAIN.
SO WHY AM I REALLY OUT HERE?
YOUR INSTINCTS HAVE ALWAYS BEEN IMPRESSIVE, MULDER, IF SLIGHTLY RECKLESS...

BY NOW YOU'VE *REALIZED* THIS IS AN *ANTENNA.* AND YOU'RE RIGHT TO THINK THAT I'VE BROUGHT YOU HERE SO THAT THE *MEDICI ARRAY* CAN CONTINUE THE WORK IT WAS *DESIGNED* TO.

BUT I'M *DISAPPOINTED* IN YOUR LACK OF *SELFLESSNESS,* MULDER.

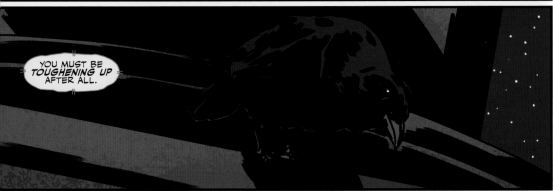

I CALCULATED YOU'D *SURELY* WANT TO FINALLY CLOSE SUCH A *GROTESQUE* EXAMPLE OF UNRESOLVED CASES LEFT TO FESTER DURING YOUR ORIGINAL RUN IN THE *X-FILES* DIVISION.

BUT HERE YOU ARE, OBSESSED WITH *MY* PLANS, AND PLAYING THE *GAME* LIKE YOU'RE FINALLY INTERESTED IN *WINNING* IT.

YOU MUST BE *TOUGHENING UP* AFTER ALL.

WHAT ARE YOU *RECEIVING* ON THIS THING, GIBSON?

WHAT'S *OUT* THERE THAT'S IN *CONTACT* WITH YOU?

NOTHING YOU NEED TO BE *CONCERNED* WITH, YET. I'VE BEEN *TRYING* TO PREPARE YOU, MULDER.

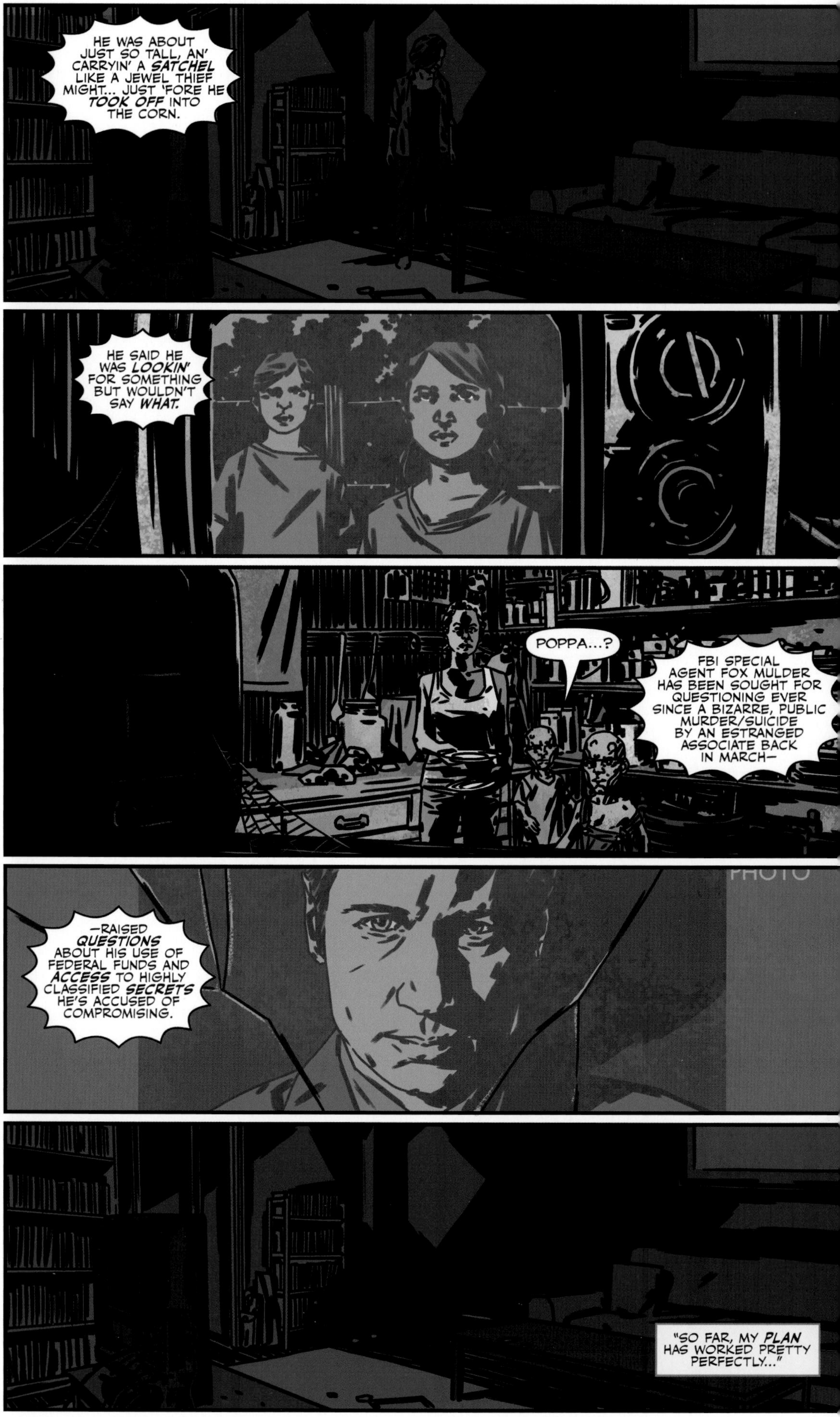
HE WAS ABOUT JUST SO TALL, AN' CARRYIN' A SATCHEL LIKE A JEWEL THIEF MIGHT... JUST 'FORE HE TOOK OFF INTO THE CORN.
HE SAID HE WAS LOOKIN' FOR SOMETHING BUT WOULDN'T SAY WHAT.
POPPA...?
FBI SPECIAL AGENT FOX MULDER HAS BEEN SOUGHT FOR QUESTIONING EVER SINCE A BIZARRE, PUBLIC MURDER/SUICIDE BY AN ESTRANGED ASSOCIATE BACK IN MARCH—
PHOTO
—RAISED QUESTIONS ABOUT HIS USE OF FEDERAL FUNDS AND ACCESS TO HIGHLY CLASSIFIED SECRETS HE'S ACCUSED OF COMPROMISING.
"SO FAR, MY PLAN HAS WORKED PRETTY PERFECTLY..."

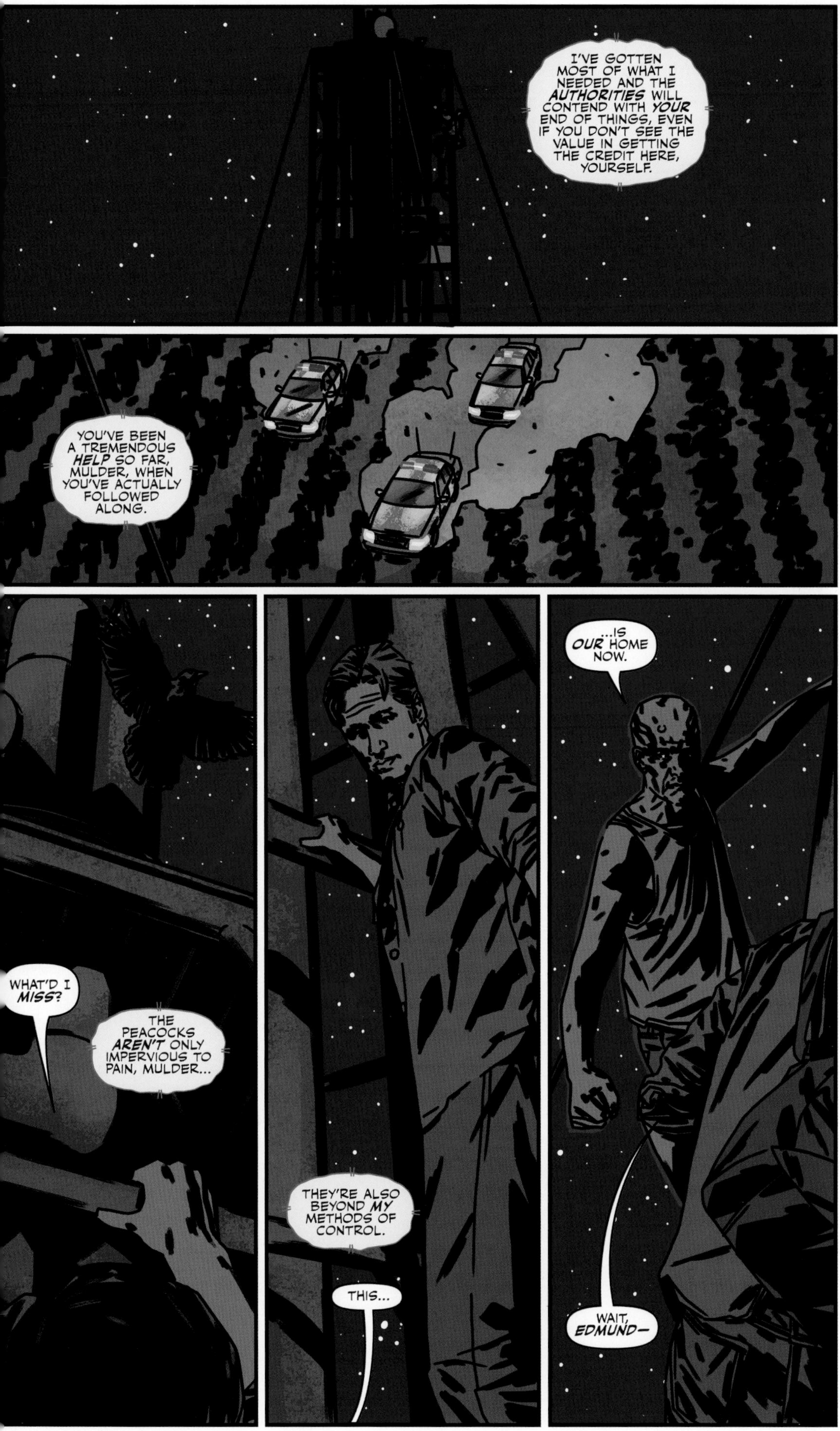
I'VE GOTTEN MOST OF WHAT I NEEDED AND THE *AUTHORITIES* WILL CONTEND WITH *YOUR* END OF THINGS, EVEN IF YOU DON'T SEE THE VALUE IN GETTING THE CREDIT HERE, YOURSELF.
YOU'VE BEEN A TREMENDOUS *HELP* SO FAR, MULDER, WHEN YOU'VE ACTUALLY FOLLOWED ALONG.
WHAT'D I *MISS*?
THE PEACOCKS *AREN'T* ONLY IMPERVIOUS TO PAIN, MULDER...
THEY'RE ALSO BEYOND *MY* METHODS OF CONTROL.
THIS...
...IS *OUR* HOME NOW.
WAIT, *EDMUND*—

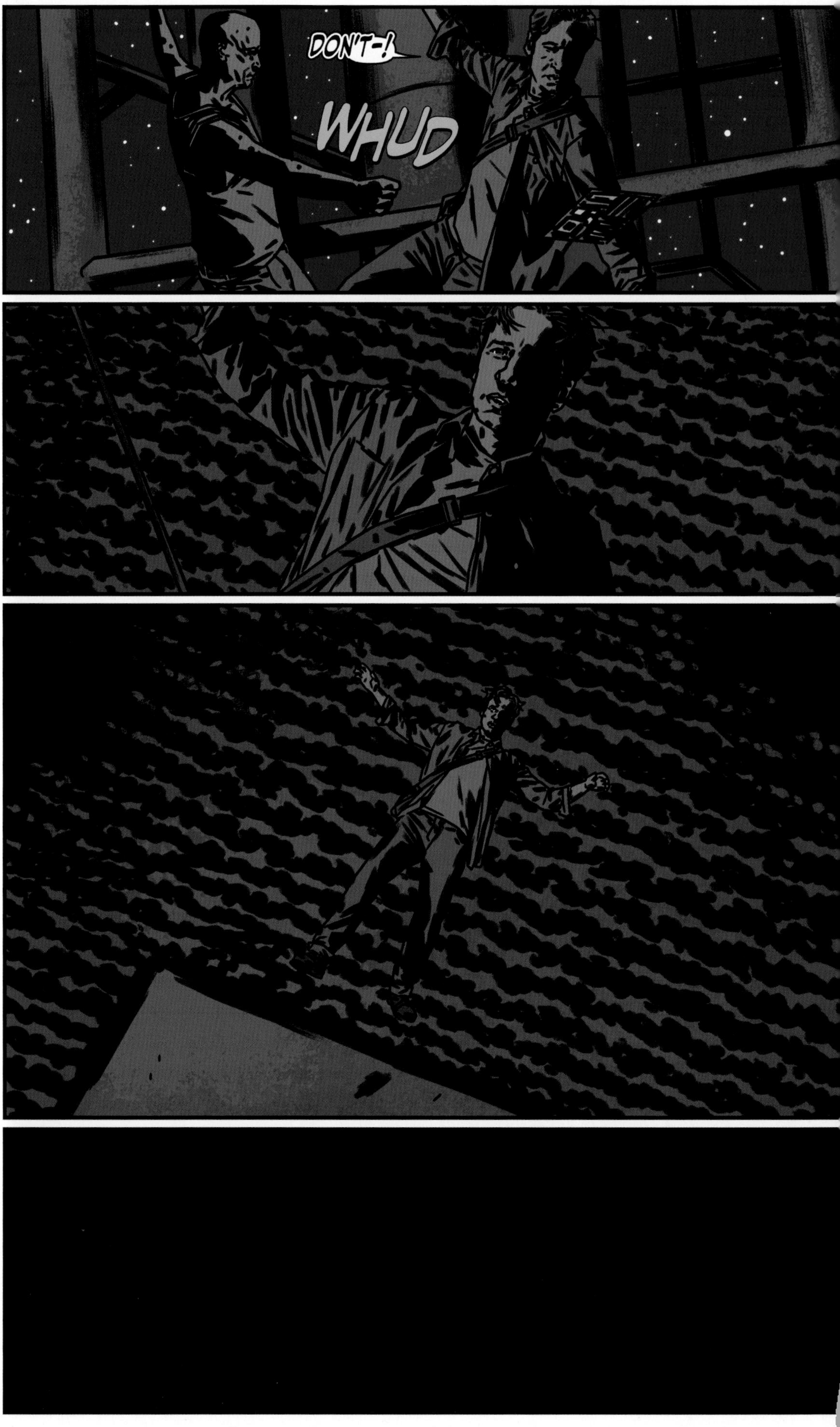
DON'T-!
WHUD

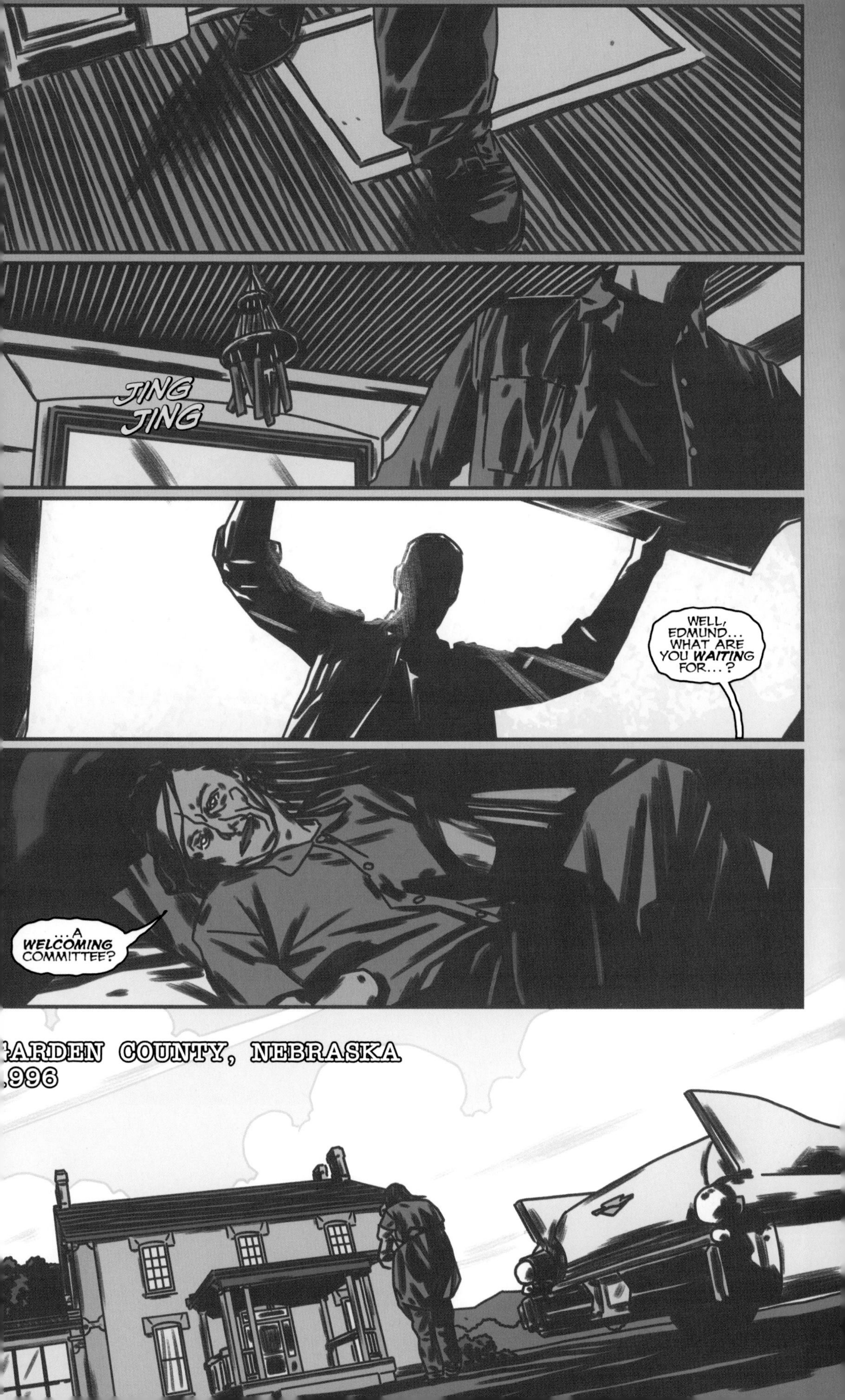
JING
JING
WELL, EDMUND... WHAT ARE YOU WAITING FOR...?
...A WELCOMING COMMITTEE?
ARDEN COUNTY, NEBRASKA
996

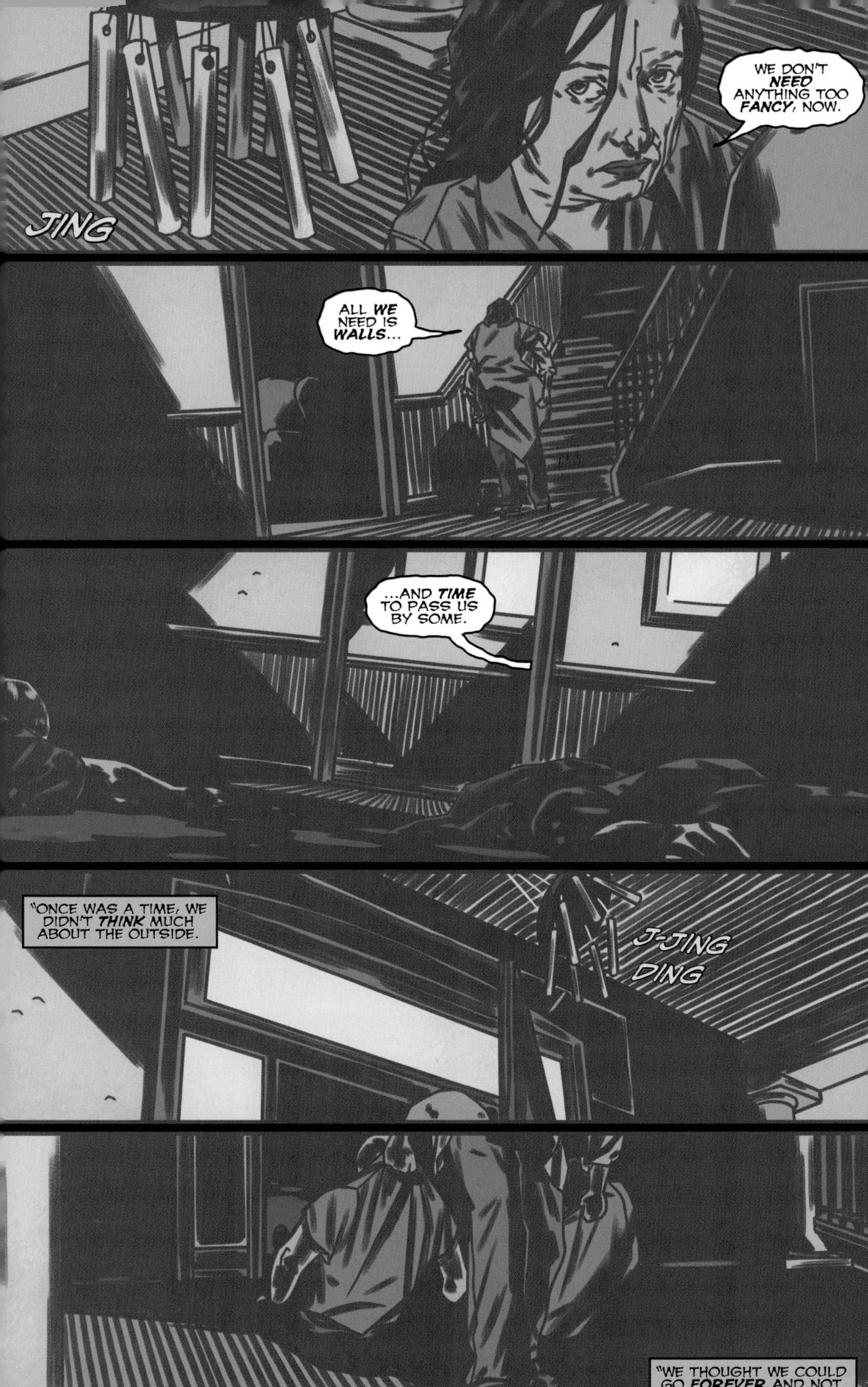
JING
WE DON'T NEED ANYTHING TOO FANCY, NOW.
ALL WE NEED IS WALLS...
...AND TIME TO PASS US BY SOME.
"ONCE WAS A TIME, WE DIDN'T THINK MUCH ABOUT THE OUTSIDE.
J-JING DING
"WE THOUGHT WE COULD GO FOREVER AND NOT FACE WHAT WOULD SOON COME FOR US."

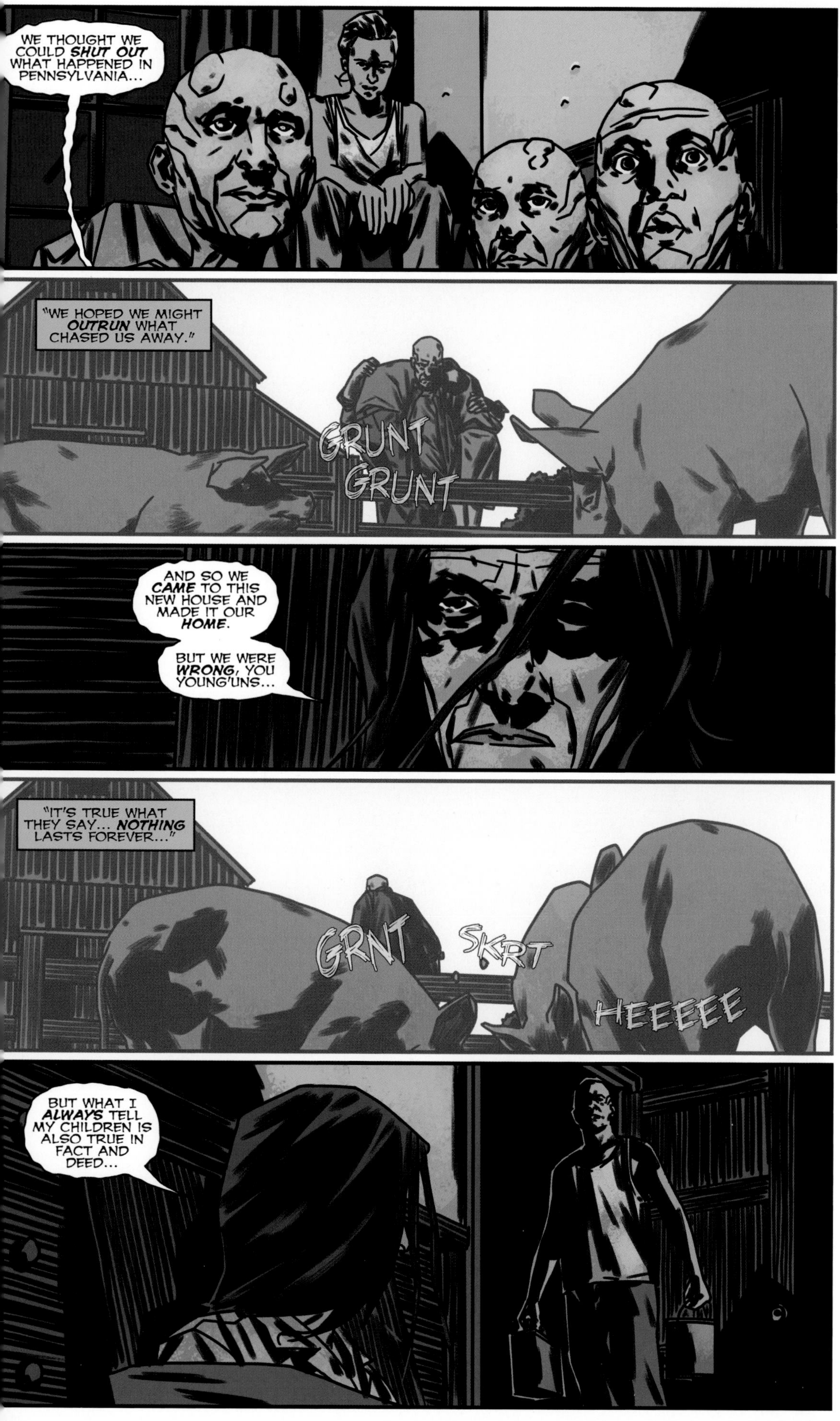
WE THOUGHT WE COULD SHUT OUT WHAT HAPPENED IN PENNSYLVANIA...
"WE HOPED WE MIGHT OUTRUN WHAT CHASED US AWAY."
GRUNT
GRUNT
AND SO WE CAME TO THIS NEW HOUSE AND MADE IT OUR HOME.
BUT WE WERE WRONG, YOU YOUNG'UNS...
"IT'S TRUE WHAT THEY SAY... NOTHING LASTS FOREVER..."
GRNT
SKRT
HEEEEEE
BUT WHAT I ALWAYS TELL MY CHILDREN IS ALSO TRUE IN FACT AND DEED...

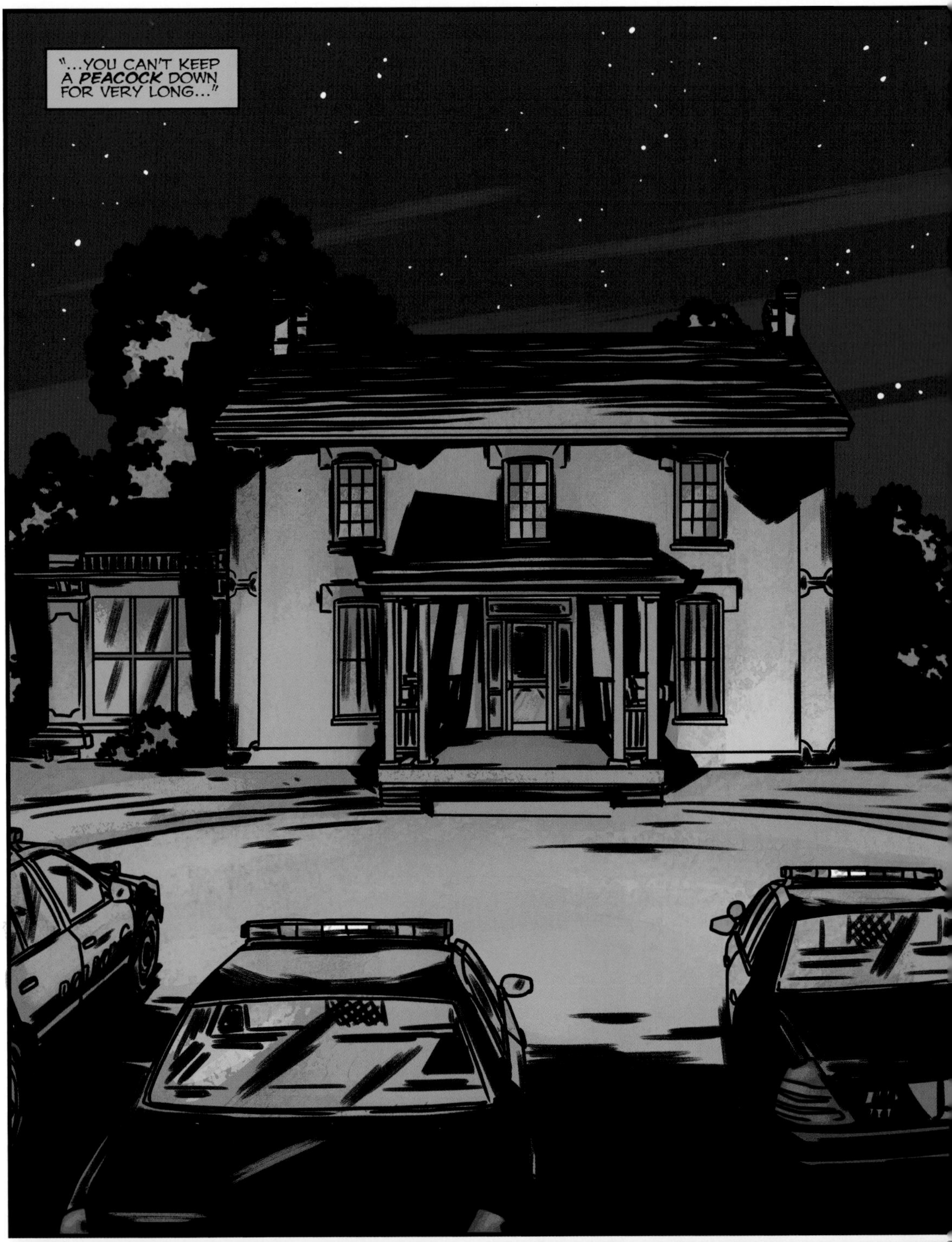
"...YOU CAN'T KEEP A PEACOCK DOWN FOR VERY LONG..."

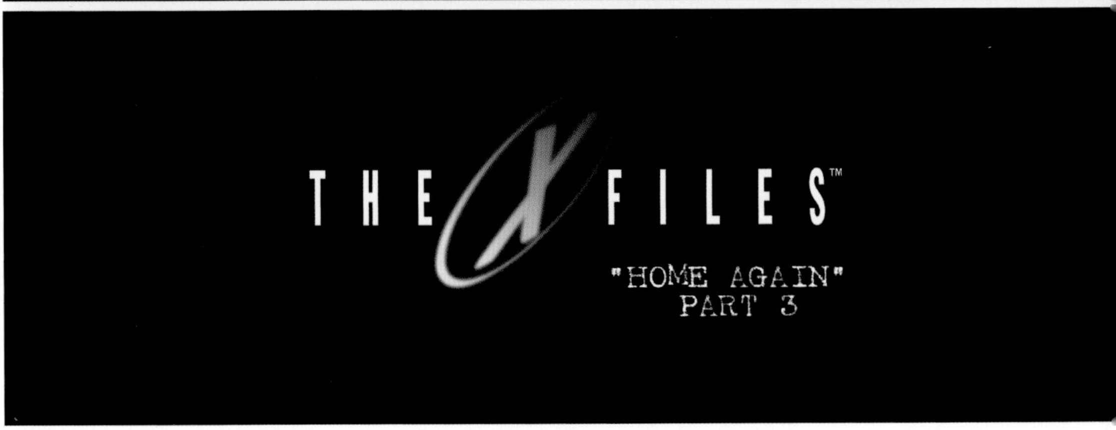
THE X FILES™
"HOME AGAIN"
PART 3

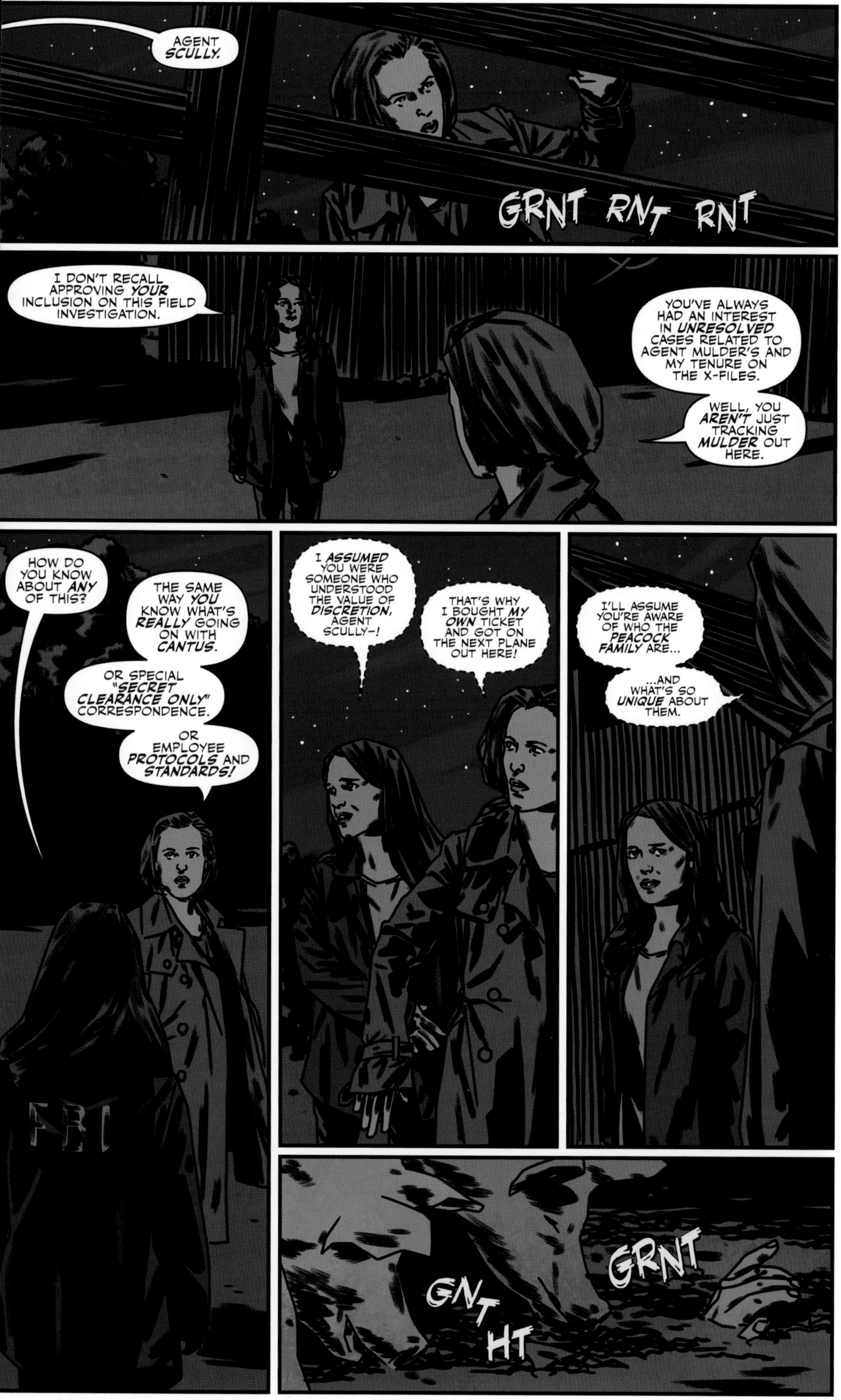
AGENT SCULLY.
GRNT RNT RNT
I DON'T RECALL APPROVING YOUR INCLUSION ON THIS FIELD INVESTIGATION.
YOU'VE ALWAYS HAD AN INTEREST IN UNRESOLVED CASES RELATED TO AGENT MULDER'S AND MY TENURE ON THE X-FILES.
WELL, YOU AREN'T JUST TRACKING MULDER OUT HERE.
HOW DO YOU KNOW ABOUT ANY OF THIS?
THE SAME WAY YOU KNOW WHAT'S REALLY GOING ON WITH CANTUS.
OR SPECIAL "SECRET CLEARANCE ONLY" CORRESPONDENCE.
OR EMPLOYEE PROTOCOLS AND STANDARDS!
FBI
I ASSUMED YOU WERE SOMEONE WHO UNDERSTOOD THE VALUE OF DISCRETION, AGENT SCULLY–!
THAT'S WHY I BOUGHT MY OWN TICKET AND GOT ON THE NEXT PLANE OUT HERE!
I'LL ASSUME YOU'RE AWARE OF WHO THE PEACOCK FAMILY ARE...
...AND WHAT'S SO UNIQUE ABOUT THEM.
GNT HT
GRNT

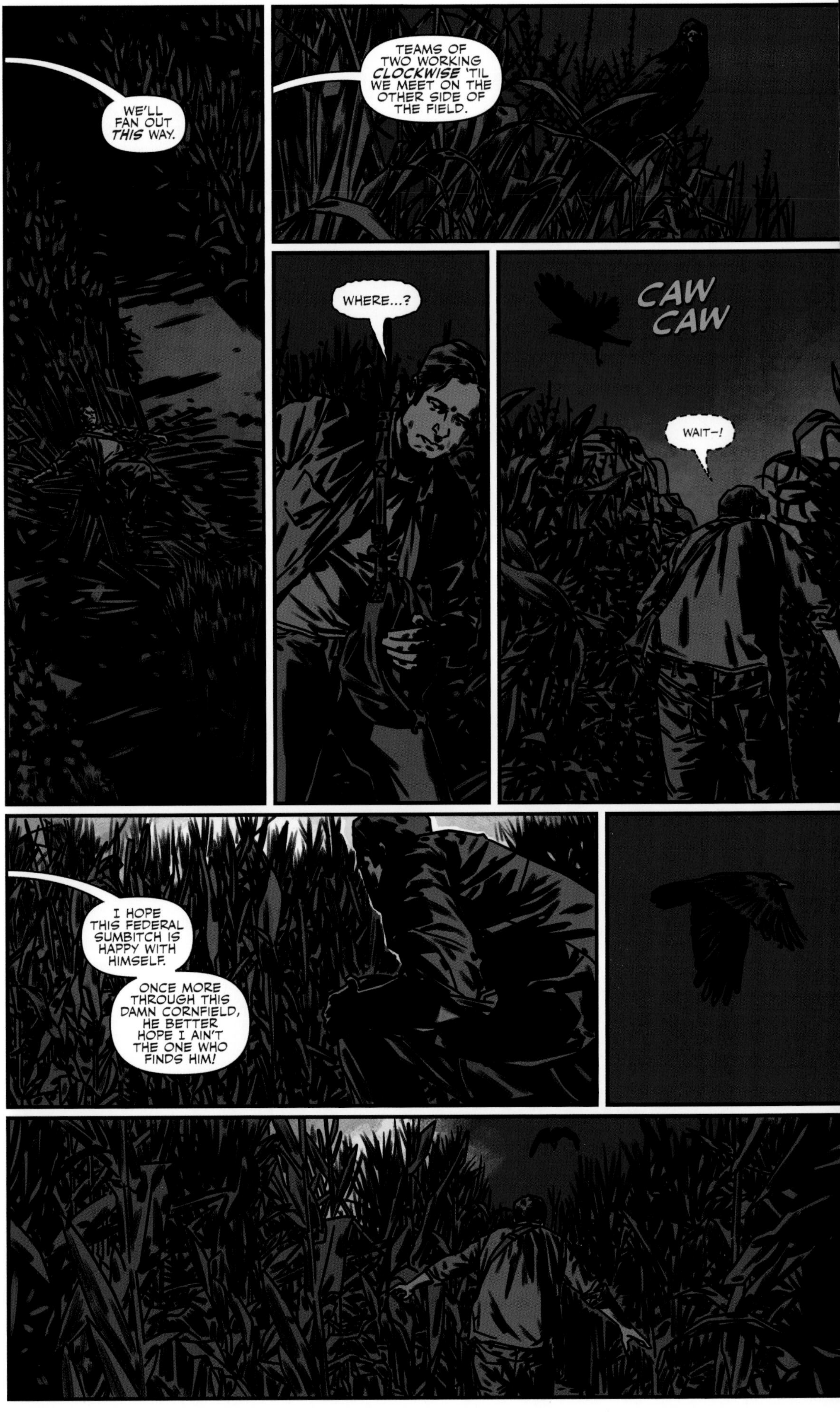
WE'LL FAN OUT THIS WAY.
TEAMS OF TWO WORKING CLOCKWISE 'TIL WE MEET ON THE OTHER SIDE OF THE FIELD.
WHERE...?
CAW CAW
WAIT-!
I HOPE THIS FEDERAL SUMBITCH IS HAPPY WITH HIMSELF.
ONCE MORE THROUGH THIS DAMN CORNFIELD, HE BETTER HOPE I AIN'T THE ONE WHO FINDS HIM!

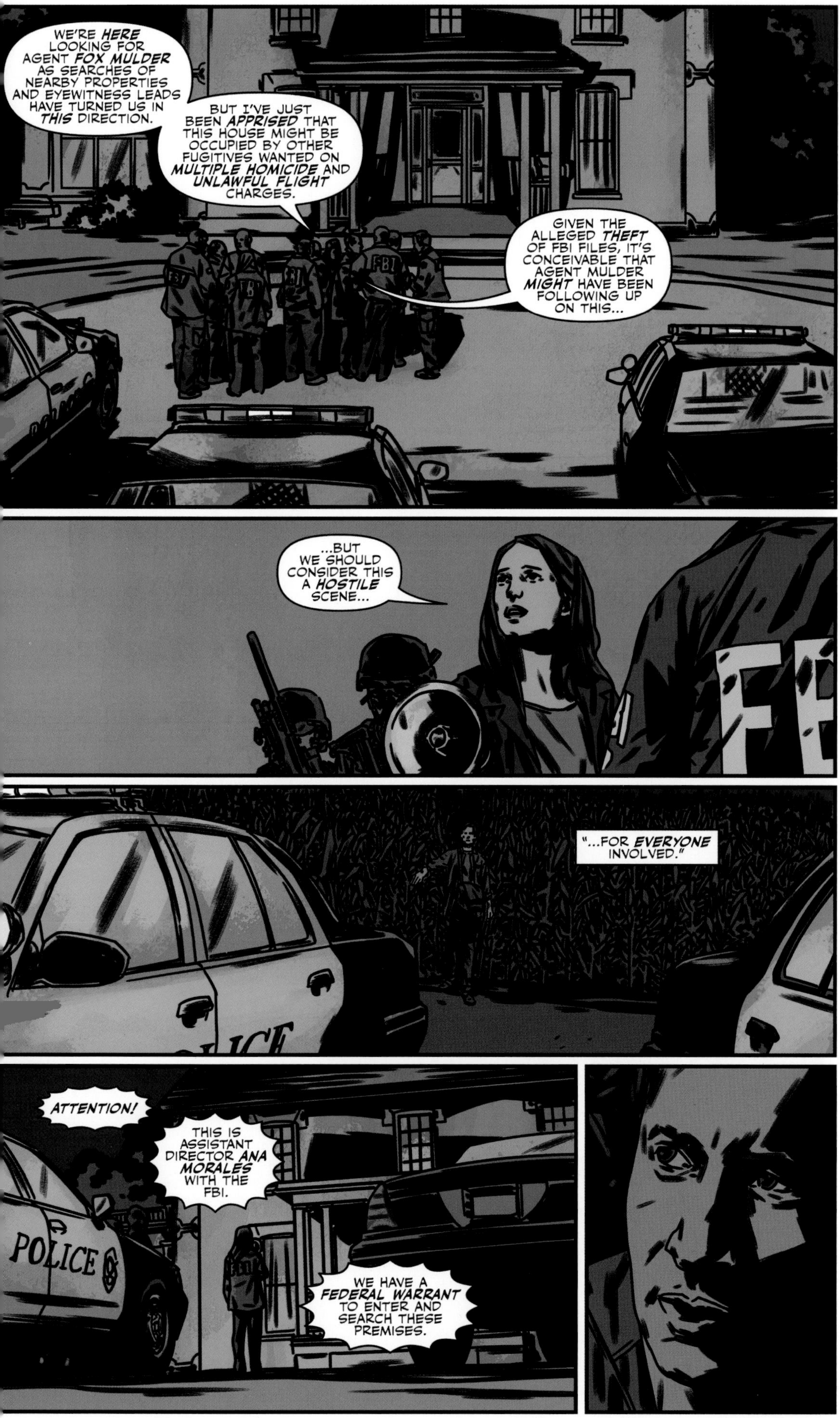
WE'RE HERE LOOKING FOR AGENT FOX MULDER AS SEARCHES OF NEARBY PROPERTIES AND EYEWITNESS LEADS HAVE TURNED US IN THIS DIRECTION.
BUT I'VE JUST BEEN APPRISED THAT THIS HOUSE MIGHT BE OCCUPIED BY OTHER FUGITIVES WANTED ON MULTIPLE HOMICIDE AND UNLAWFUL FLIGHT CHARGES.
GIVEN THE ALLEGED THEFT OF FBI FILES, IT'S CONCEIVABLE THAT AGENT MULDER MIGHT HAVE BEEN FOLLOWING UP ON THIS...
FBI
...BUT WE SHOULD CONSIDER THIS A HOSTILE SCENE...
FBI
"...FOR EVERYONE INVOLVED."
LICE
ATTENTION!
THIS IS ASSISTANT DIRECTOR ANA MORALES WITH THE FBI.
POLICE
WE HAVE A FEDERAL WARRANT TO ENTER AND SEARCH THESE PREMISES.

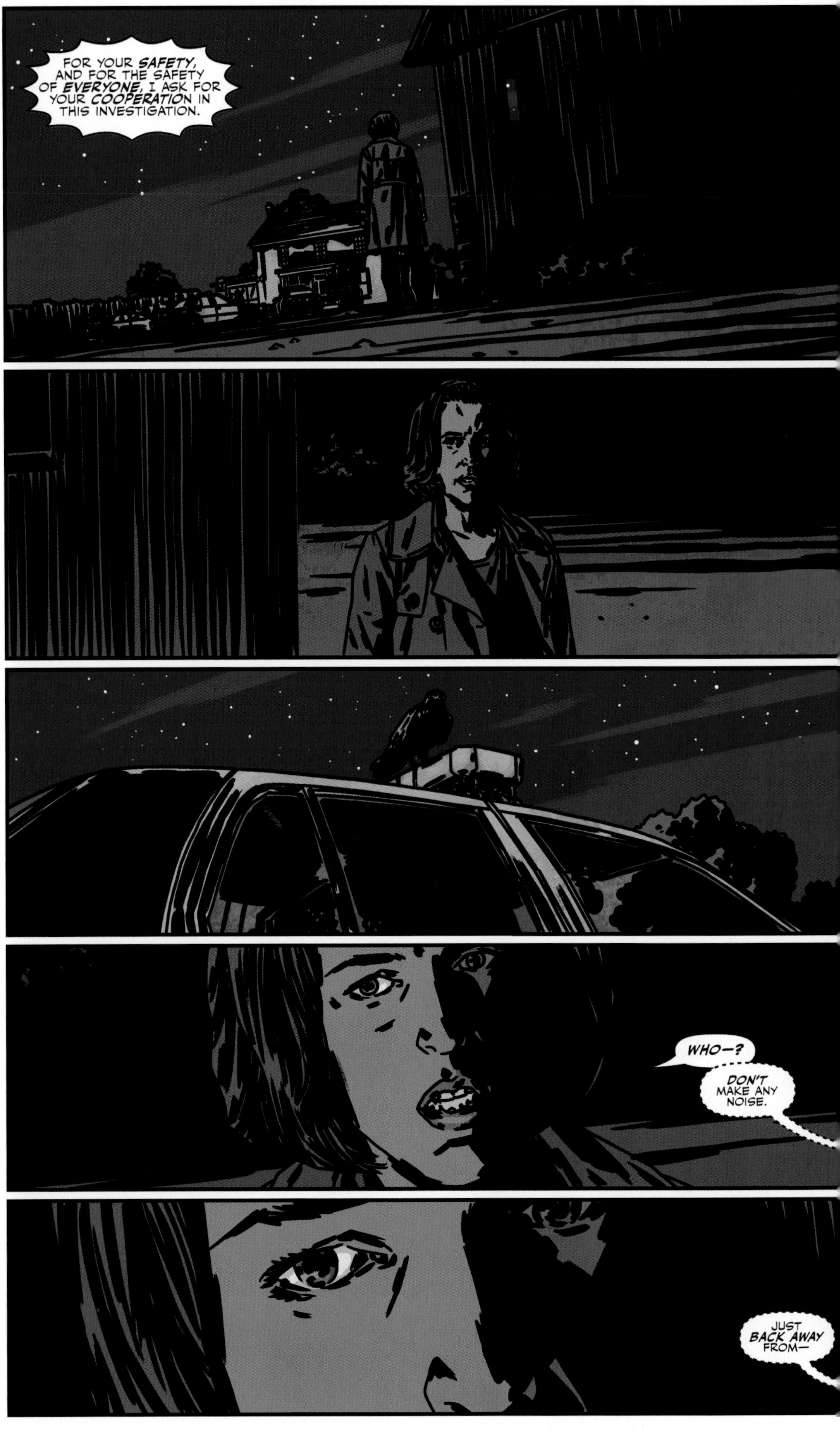
FOR YOUR SAFETY, AND FOR THE SAFETY OF EVERYONE, I ASK FOR YOUR COOPERATION IN THIS INVESTIGATION.
WHO—?
DON'T MAKE ANY NOISE.
JUST BACK AWAY FROM—

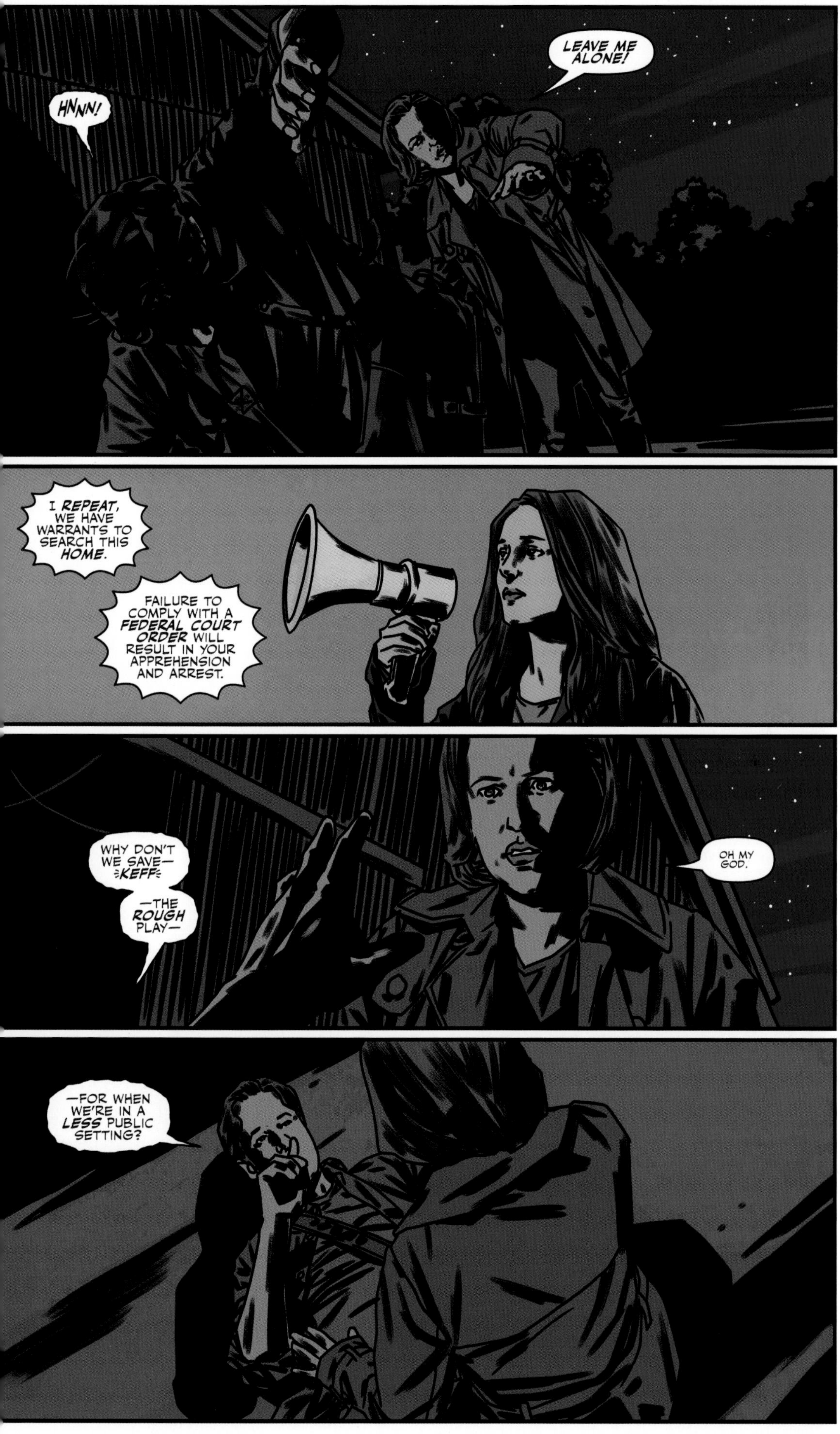
HNNN!
LEAVE ME ALONE!
I REPEAT, WE HAVE WARRANTS TO SEARCH THIS HOME.
FAILURE TO COMPLY WITH A FEDERAL COURT ORDER WILL RESULT IN YOUR APPREHENSION AND ARREST.
WHY DON'T WE SAVE— KEFF —THE ROUGH PLAY—
OH MY GOD.
—FOR WHEN WE'RE IN A LESS PUBLIC SETTING?

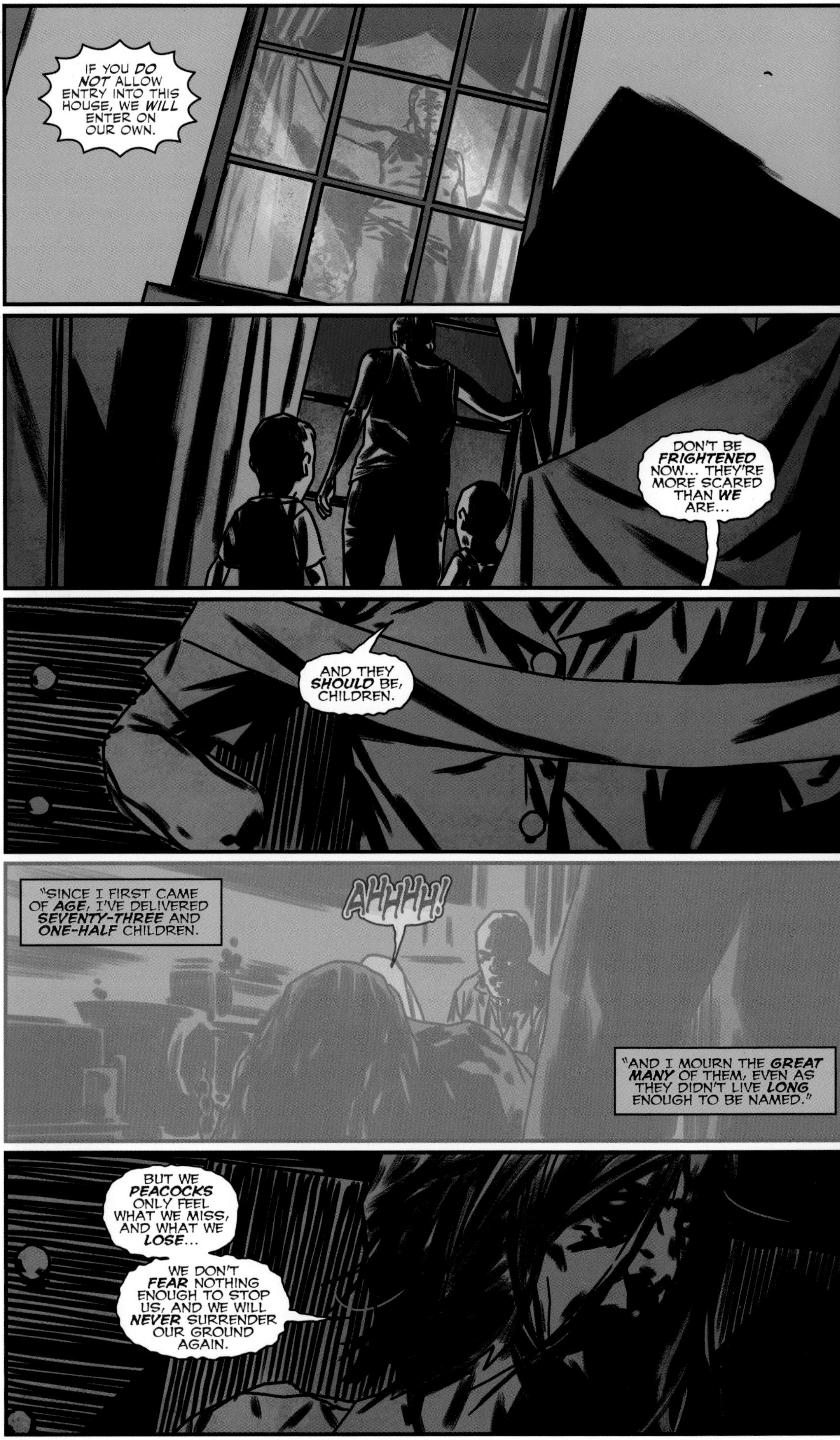
IF YOU DO NOT ALLOW ENTRY INTO THIS HOUSE, WE WILL ENTER ON OUR OWN.
DON'T BE FRIGHTENED NOW... THEY'RE MORE SCARED THAN WE ARE...
AND THEY SHOULD BE, CHILDREN.
"SINCE I FIRST CAME OF AGE, I'VE DELIVERED SEVENTY-THREE AND ONE-HALF CHILDREN.
AHHHH!
"AND I MOURN THE GREAT MANY OF THEM, EVEN AS THEY DIDN'T LIVE LONG ENOUGH TO BE NAMED."
BUT WE PEACOCKS ONLY FEEL WHAT WE MISS, AND WHAT WE LOSE...
WE DON'T FEAR NOTHING ENOUGH TO STOP US, AND WE WILL NEVER SURRENDER OUR GROUND AGAIN.

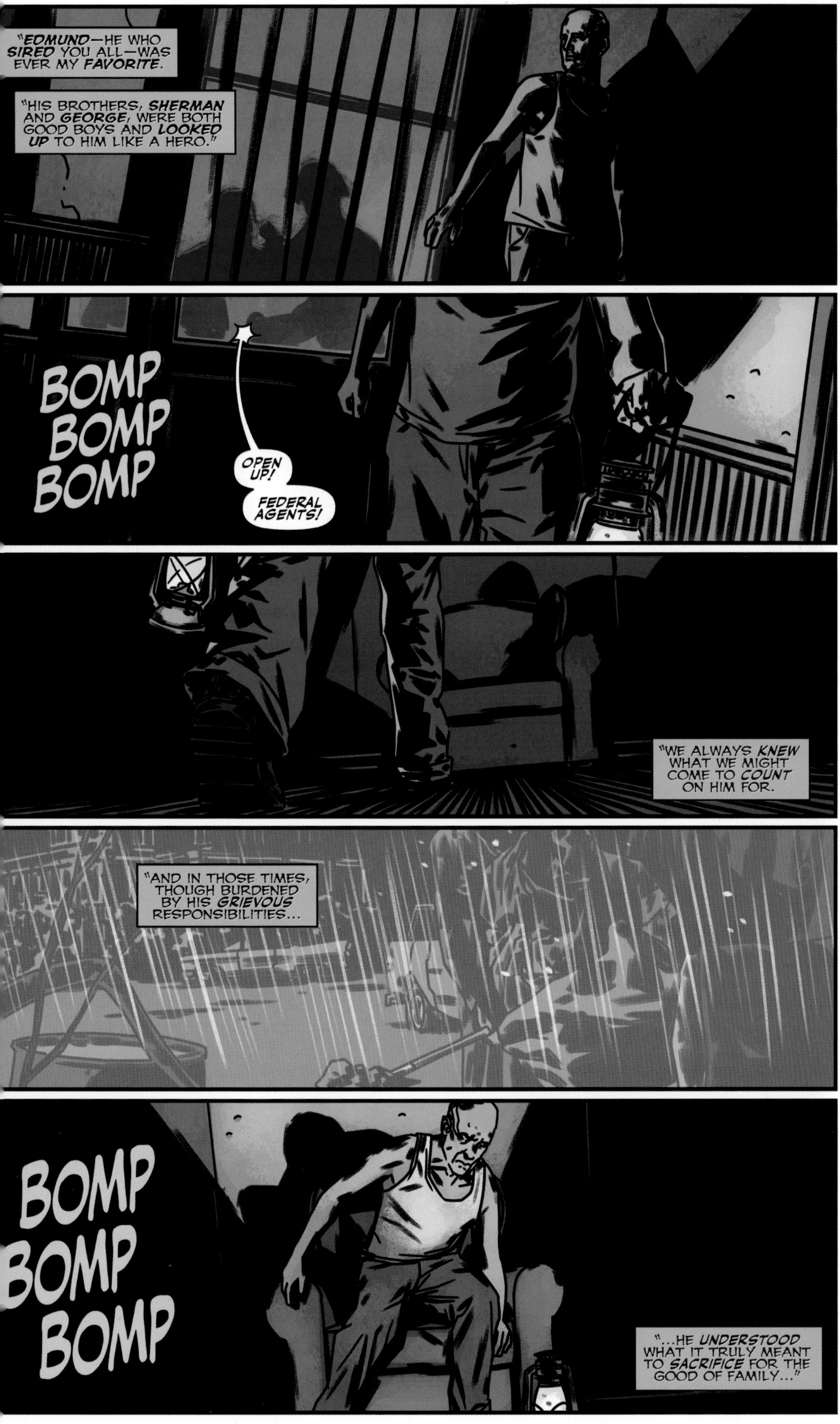
"EDMUND—HE WHO SIRED YOU ALL—WAS EVER MY FAVORITE.
"HIS BROTHERS, SHERMAN AND GEORGE, WERE BOTH GOOD BOYS AND LOOKED UP TO HIM LIKE A HERO."
BOMP BOMP BOMP
OPEN UP!
FEDERAL AGENTS!
"WE ALWAYS KNEW WHAT WE MIGHT COME TO COUNT ON HIM FOR.
"AND IN THOSE TIMES, THOUGH BURDENED BY HIS GRIEVOUS RESPONSIBILITIES...
BOMP BOMP BOMP
"...HE UNDERSTOOD WHAT IT TRULY MEANT TO SACRIFICE FOR THE GOOD OF FAMILY..."

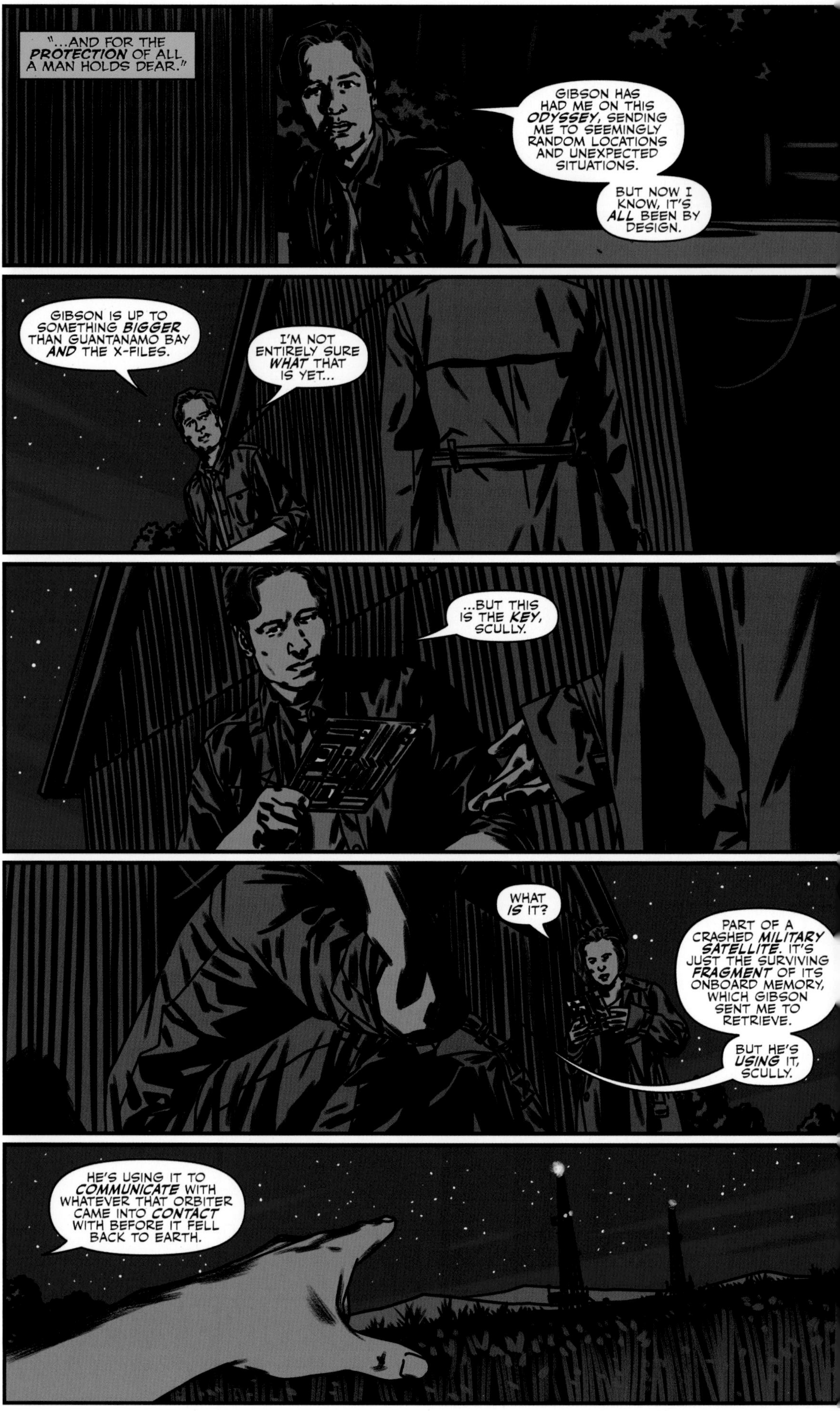
"...AND FOR THE PROTECTION OF ALL A MAN HOLDS DEAR."
GIBSON HAS HAD ME ON THIS ODYSSEY, SENDING ME TO SEEMINGLY RANDOM LOCATIONS AND UNEXPECTED SITUATIONS.
BUT NOW I KNOW, IT'S ALL BEEN BY DESIGN.
GIBSON IS UP TO SOMETHING BIGGER THAN GUANTANAMO BAY AND THE X-FILES.
I'M NOT ENTIRELY SURE WHAT THAT IS YET...
...BUT THIS IS THE KEY, SCULLY.
WHAT IS IT?
PART OF A CRASHED MILITARY SATELLITE. IT'S JUST THE SURVIVING FRAGMENT OF ITS ONBOARD MEMORY, WHICH GIBSON SENT ME TO RETRIEVE.
BUT HE'S USING IT, SCULLY.
HE'S USING IT TO COMMUNICATE WITH WHATEVER THAT ORBITER CAME INTO CONTACT WITH BEFORE IT FELL BACK TO EARTH.

WE NEED TO DIG UP EVERYTHING WE CAN ON THE *MEDICI-3* PROGRAM.

THAT AEROSPACE INDUSTRIALS AFFILIATED WITH THE *CANTUS GROUP* ARE BEHIND IT WON'T BE A SURPRISE, BUT IF WE CAN *EXPOSE* WHERE THE LINKS ARE BETWEEN THE ORGANIZATION'S TENDRILS AT THE DOJ AND THIS *OUTER SPACE COMMUNICATIONS* PROGRAM, WE CAN—

MULDER.

IT'S WHY HE BROUGHT ME *OUT* HERE, SCULLY.

MULDER, WHAT ABOUT THE *PEACOCKS?*

WHAT DO *THEY* HAVE TO DO WITH ANY OF THIS?

AN OLD *X-FILE* LEFT UNRESOLVED... A REAL *SHOCKER* OF A REVEAL FOR THE GENERAL PUBLIC...

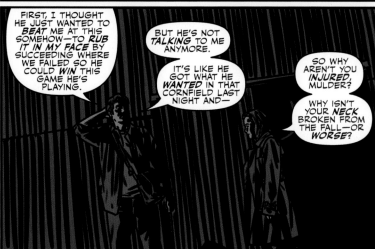

FIRST, I THOUGHT HE JUST WANTED TO *BEAT* ME AT THIS SOMEHOW—TO *RUB IT IN MY FACE* BY SUCCEEDING WHERE WE FAILED SO HE COULD *WIN* THIS GAME HE'S PLAYING.

BUT HE'S NOT *TALKING* TO ME ANYMORE.

IT'S LIKE HE GOT WHAT HE *WANTED* IN THAT CORNFIELD LAST NIGHT AND—

SO WHY AREN'T YOU *INJURED,* MULDER?

WHY ISN'T YOUR *NECK* BROKEN FROM THE FALL—OR *WORSE?*

MULDER, I *KNOW* HOW HARD IT IS TO *BELIEVE* SOME THINGS. YOU *KNOW* THAT.

BUT YOU NEED TO *CONSIDER* OTHER POSSIBILITIES HERE.

WHAT DO YOU MEAN?

GIBSON PRAISE TORE YOU DOWN AND TOOK *EVERYTHING* FROM YOU BEFORE HE FINALLY SENT YOU OUT TO RUN HIS *ERRANDS,* MULDER.

IT'S AT LEAST *CONCEIVABLE* THAT HE'S TRYING TO *REHABILITATE* YOU NOW, IF ONLY—

MY GOD, MULDER...

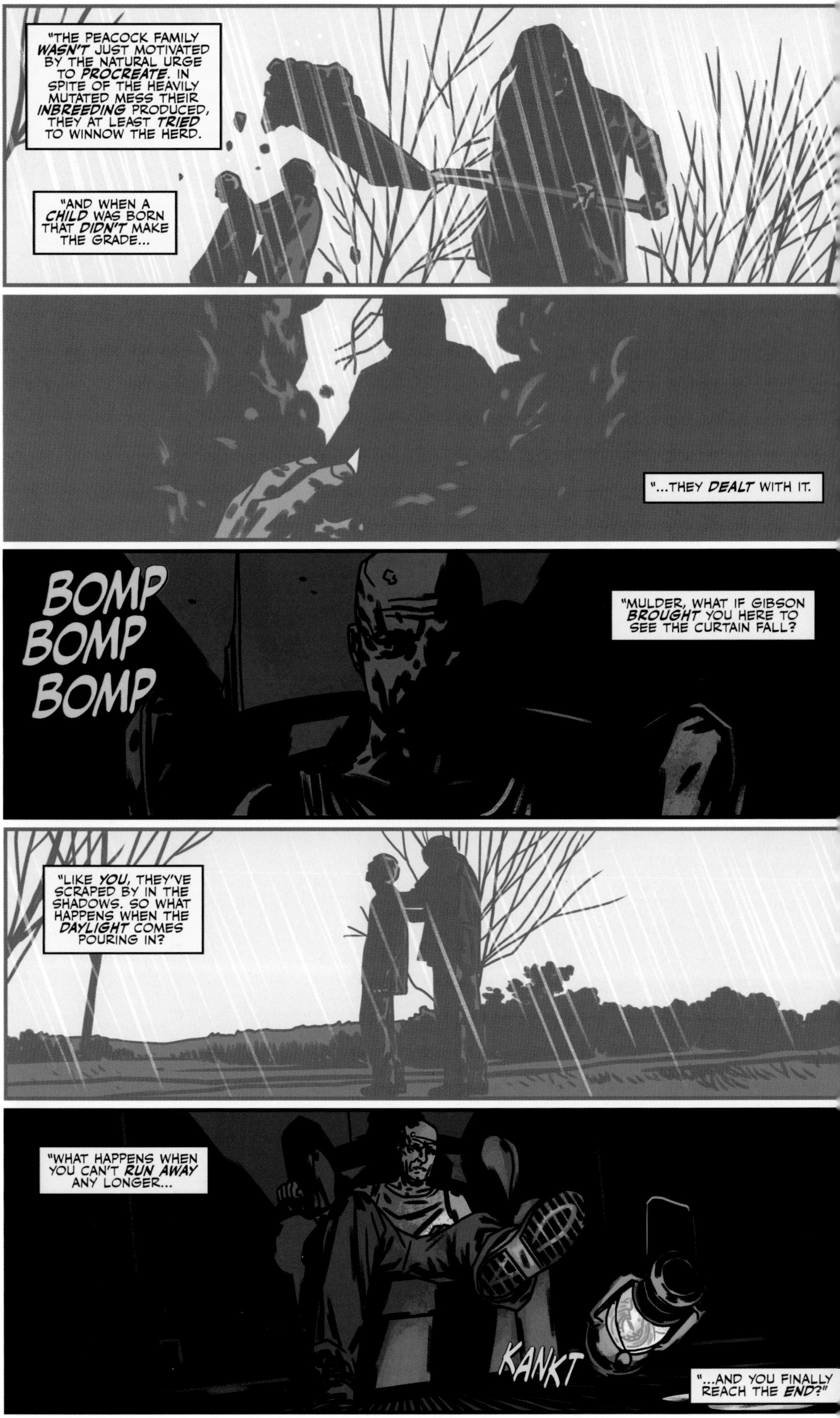
"THE PEACOCK FAMILY WASN'T JUST MOTIVATED BY THE NATURAL URGE TO PROCREATE. IN SPITE OF THE HEAVILY MUTATED MESS THEIR INBREEDING PRODUCED, THEY AT LEAST TRIED TO WINNOW THE HERD.
"AND WHEN A CHILD WAS BORN THAT DIDN'T MAKE THE GRADE...
"...THEY DEALT WITH IT.
BOMP BOMP BOMP
"MULDER, WHAT IF GIBSON BROUGHT YOU HERE TO SEE THE CURTAIN FALL?
"LIKE YOU, THEY'VE SCRAPED BY IN THE SHADOWS. SO WHAT HAPPENS WHEN THE DAYLIGHT COMES POURING IN?
"WHAT HAPPENS WHEN YOU CAN'T RUN AWAY ANY LONGER...
KANKT
"...AND YOU FINALLY REACH THE END?"

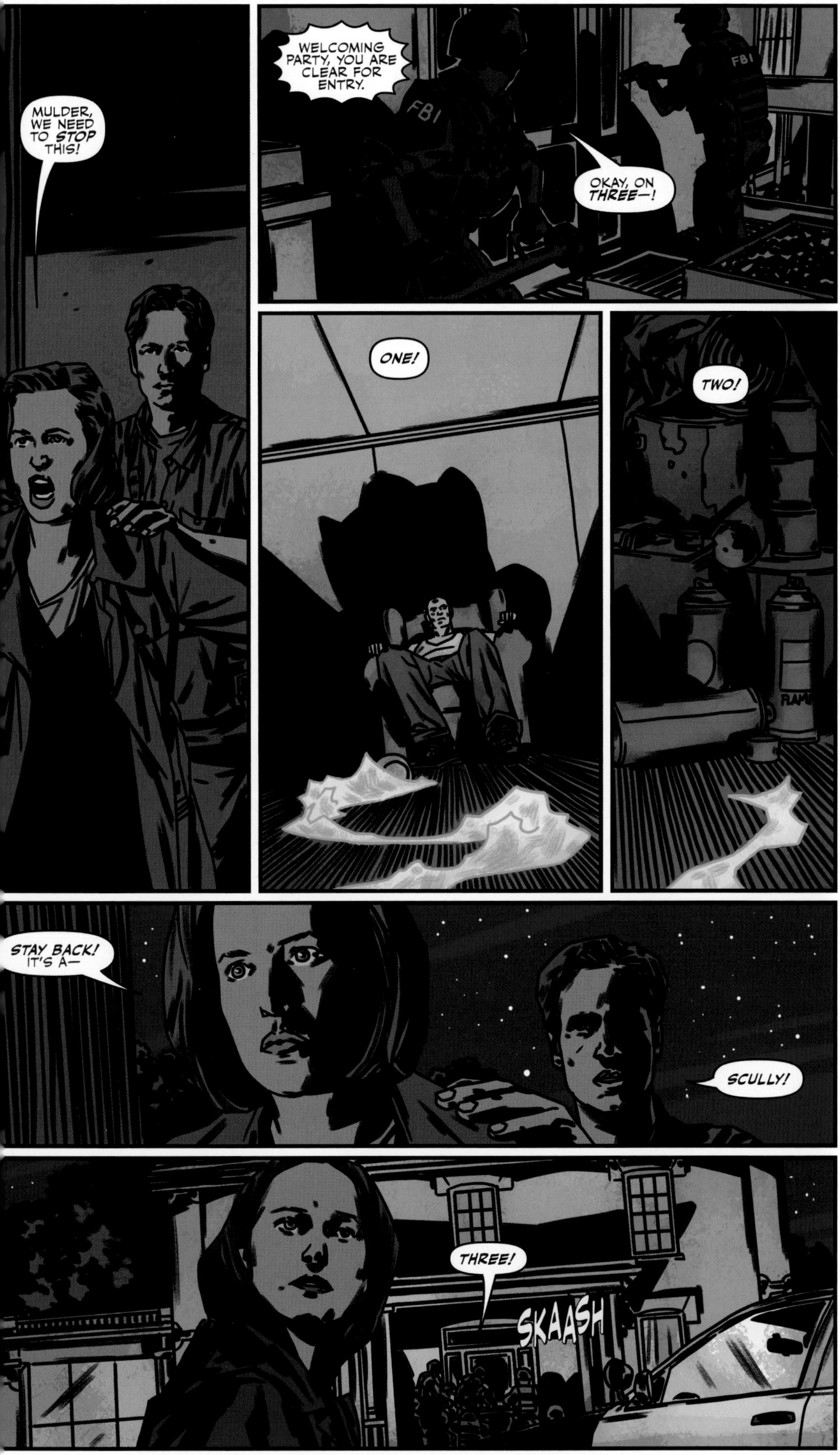
MULDER, WE NEED TO STOP THIS!
WELCOMING PARTY, YOU ARE CLEAR FOR ENTRY.
FBI
FBI
OKAY, ON THREE—!
ONE!
TWO!
STAY BACK! IT'S A—
SCULLY!
THREE!
SKAASH

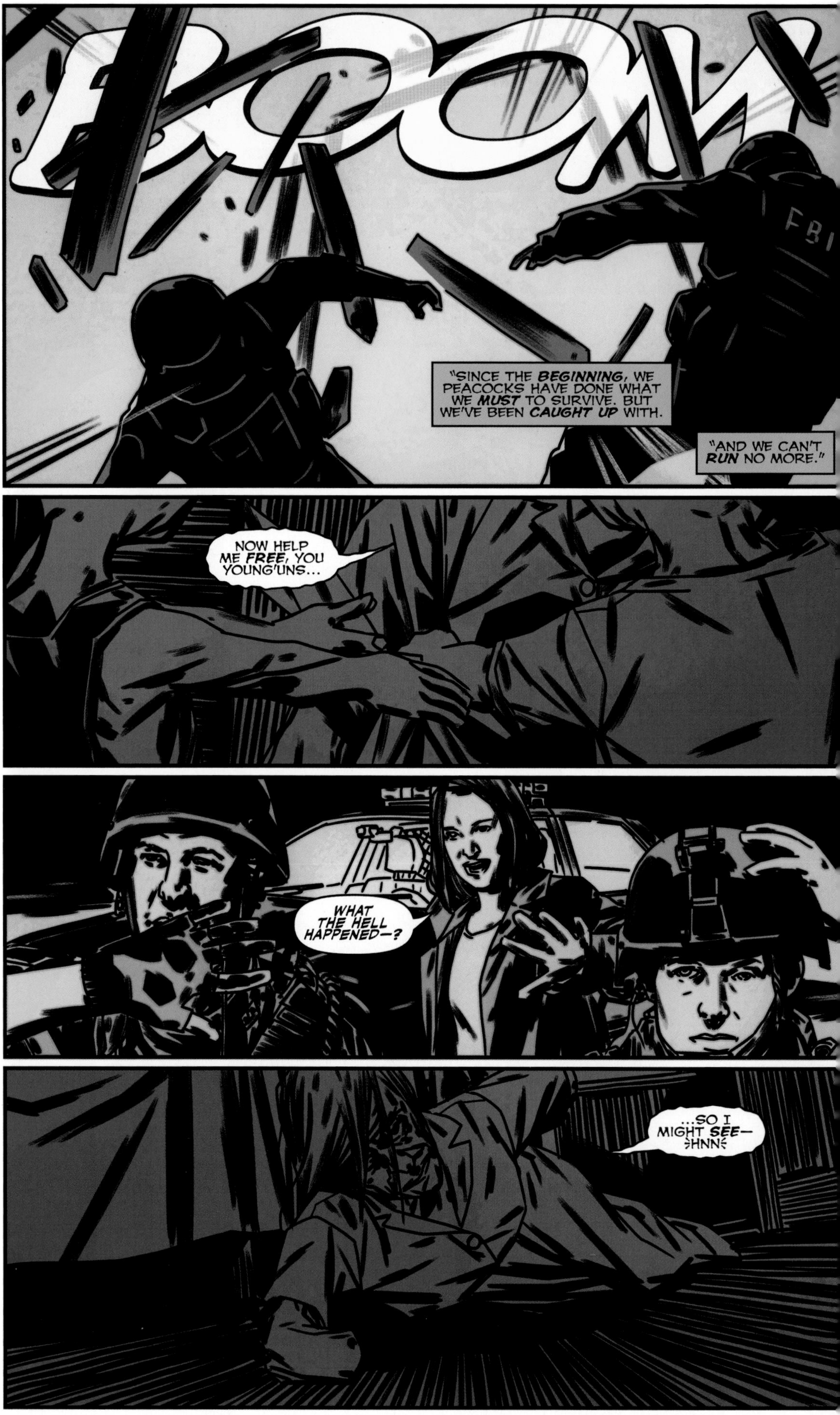
BOOM
FBI
"SINCE THE BEGINNING, WE PEACOCKS HAVE DONE WHAT WE MUST TO SURVIVE. BUT WE'VE BEEN CAUGHT UP WITH.
"AND WE CAN'T RUN NO MORE."
NOW HELP ME FREE, YOU YOUNG'UNS...
WHAT THE HELL HAPPENED—?
...SO I MIGHT SEE— HNN

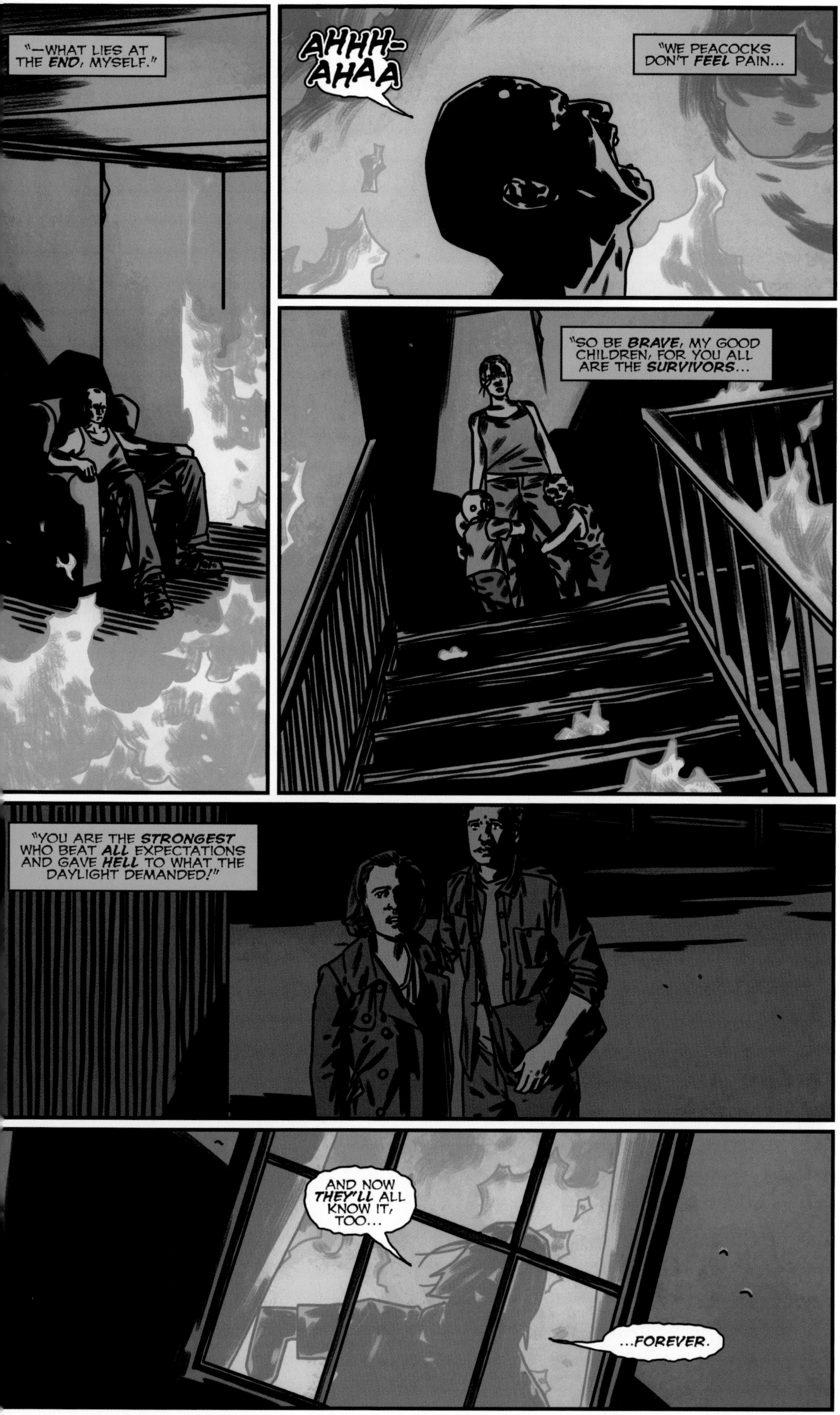
"—WHAT LIES AT THE END, MYSELF."
AHHH-AHAA
"WE PEACOCKS DON'T FEEL PAIN...
"SO BE BRAVE, MY GOOD CHILDREN, FOR YOU ALL ARE THE SURVIVORS...
"YOU ARE THE STRONGEST WHO BEAT ALL EXPECTATIONS AND GAVE HELL TO WHAT THE DAYLIGHT DEMANDED!"
AND NOW THEY'LL ALL KNOW IT, TOO...
...FOREVER.

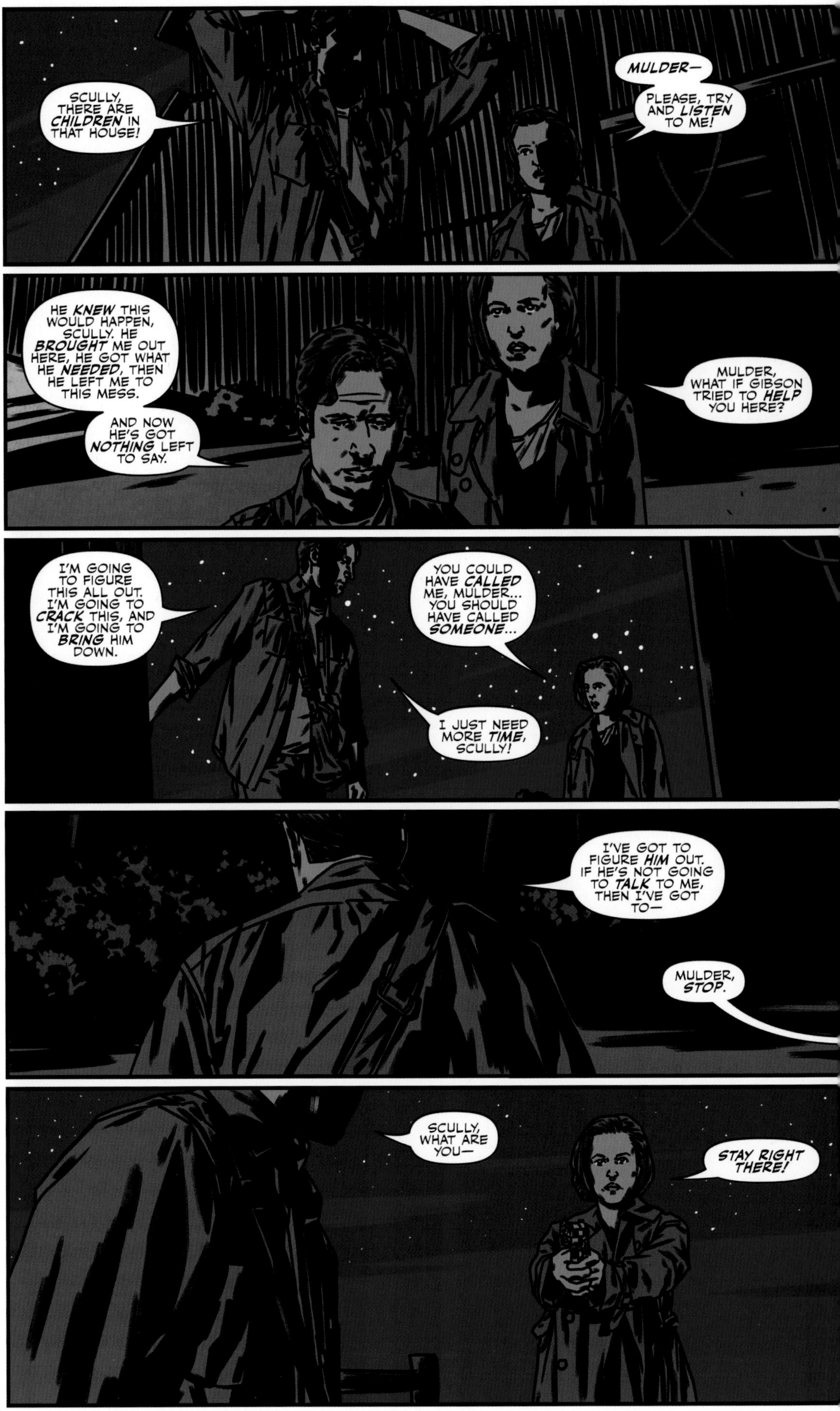
SCULLY, THERE ARE CHILDREN IN THAT HOUSE!
MULDER—
PLEASE, TRY AND LISTEN TO ME!
HE KNEW THIS WOULD HAPPEN, SCULLY. HE BROUGHT ME OUT HERE, HE GOT WHAT HE NEEDED, THEN HE LEFT ME TO THIS MESS.
AND NOW HE'S GOT NOTHING LEFT TO SAY.
MULDER, WHAT IF GIBSON TRIED TO HELP YOU HERE?
I'M GOING TO FIGURE THIS ALL OUT. I'M GOING TO CRACK THIS, AND I'M GOING TO BRING HIM DOWN.
YOU COULD HAVE CALLED ME, MULDER... YOU SHOULD HAVE CALLED SOMEONE...
I JUST NEED MORE TIME, SCULLY!
I'VE GOT TO FIGURE HIM OUT. IF HE'S NOT GOING TO TALK TO ME, THEN I'VE GOT TO—
MULDER, STOP.
SCULLY, WHAT ARE YOU—
STAY RIGHT THERE!

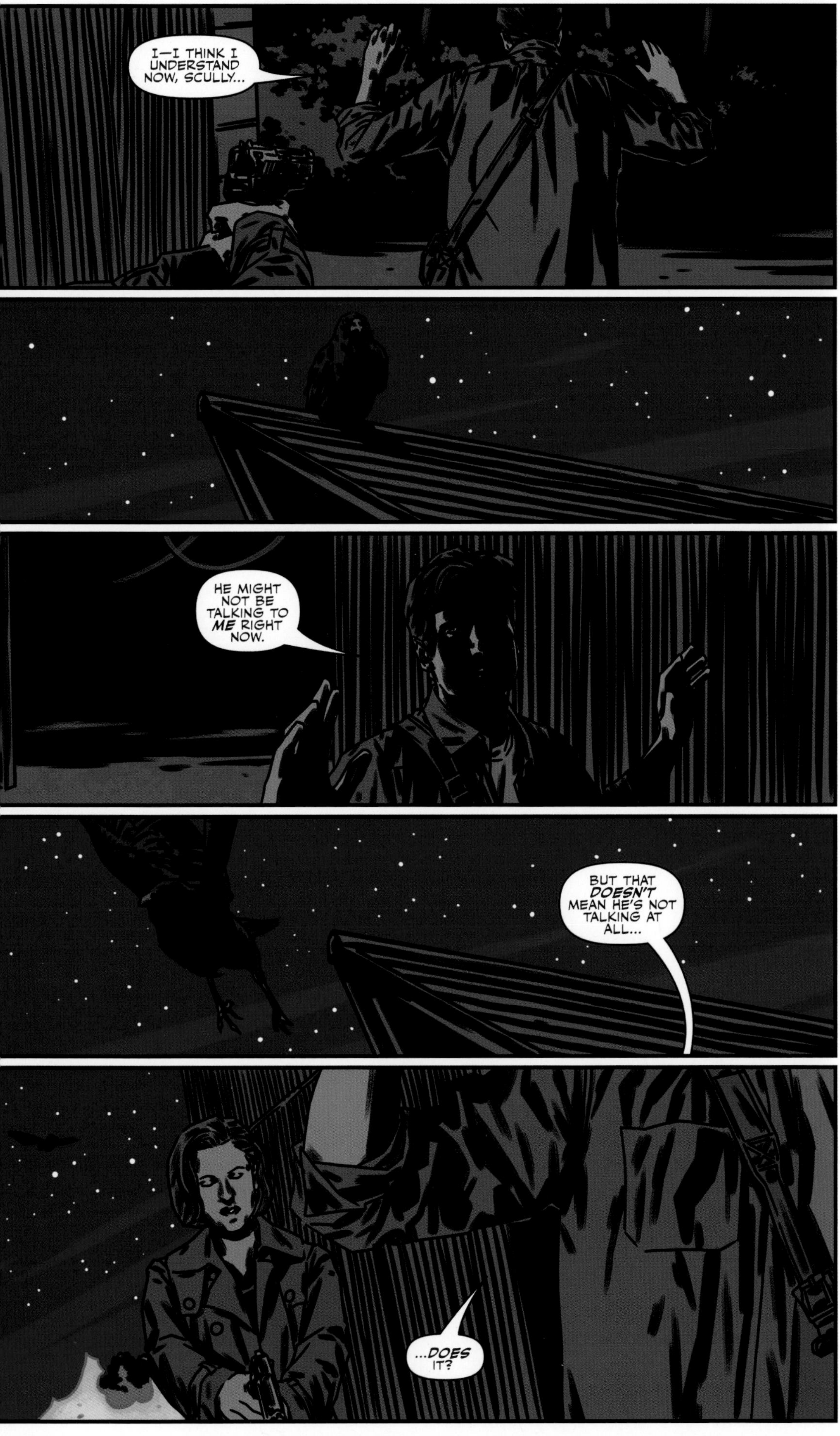
I—I THINK I UNDERSTAND NOW, SCULLY...
HE MIGHT NOT BE TALKING TO *ME* RIGHT NOW.
BUT THAT *DOESN'T* MEAN HE'S NOT TALKING AT ALL...
...*DOES* IT?

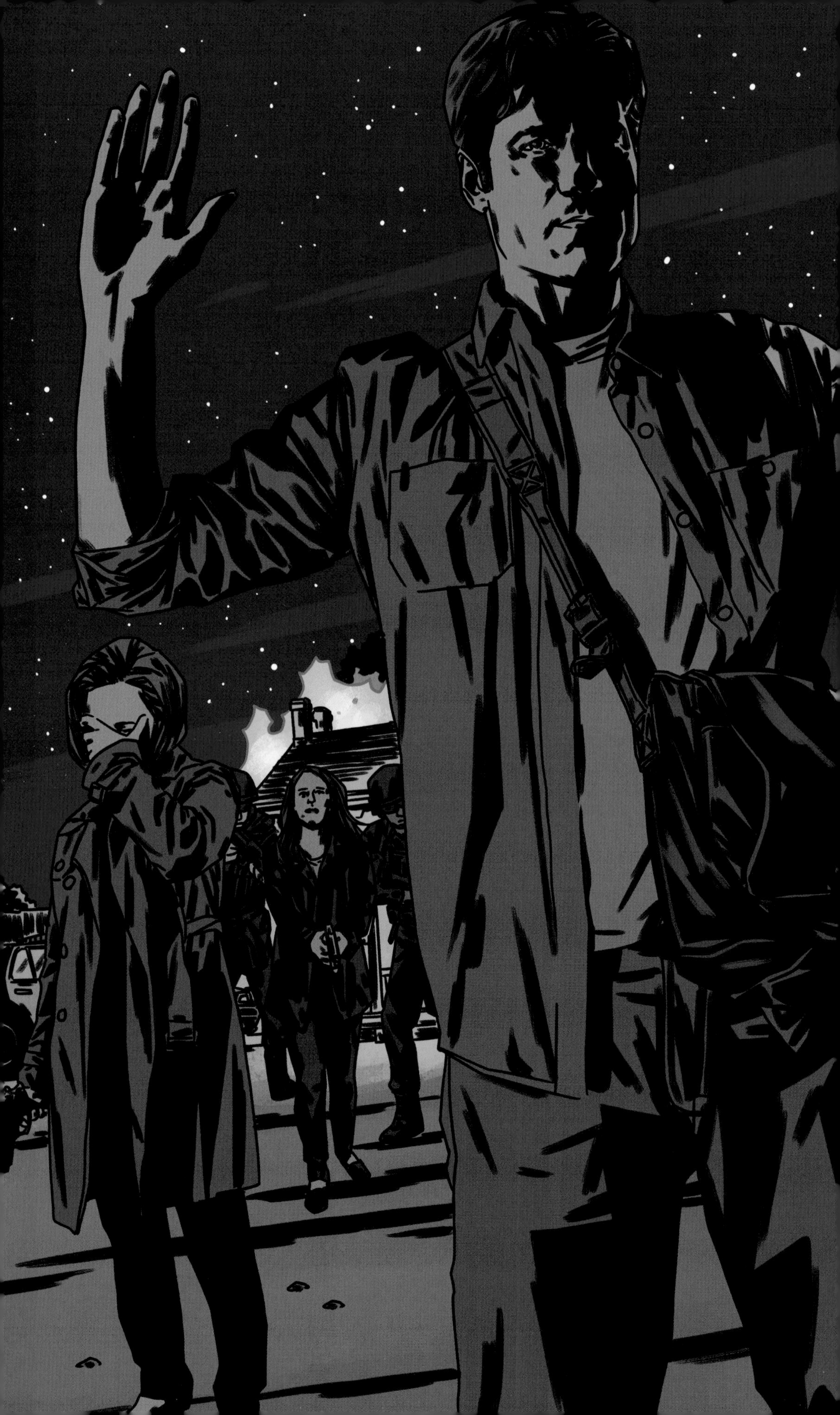

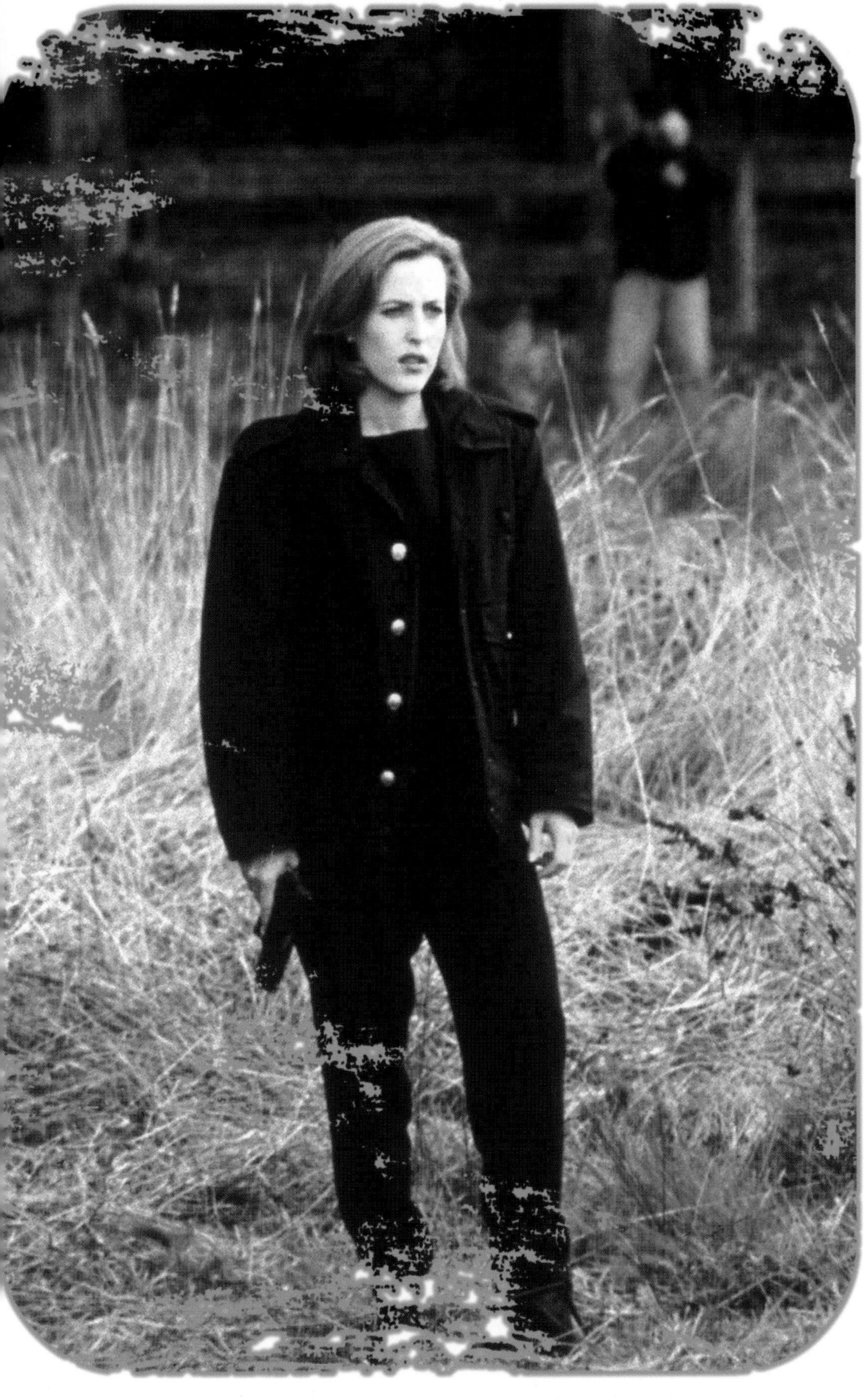

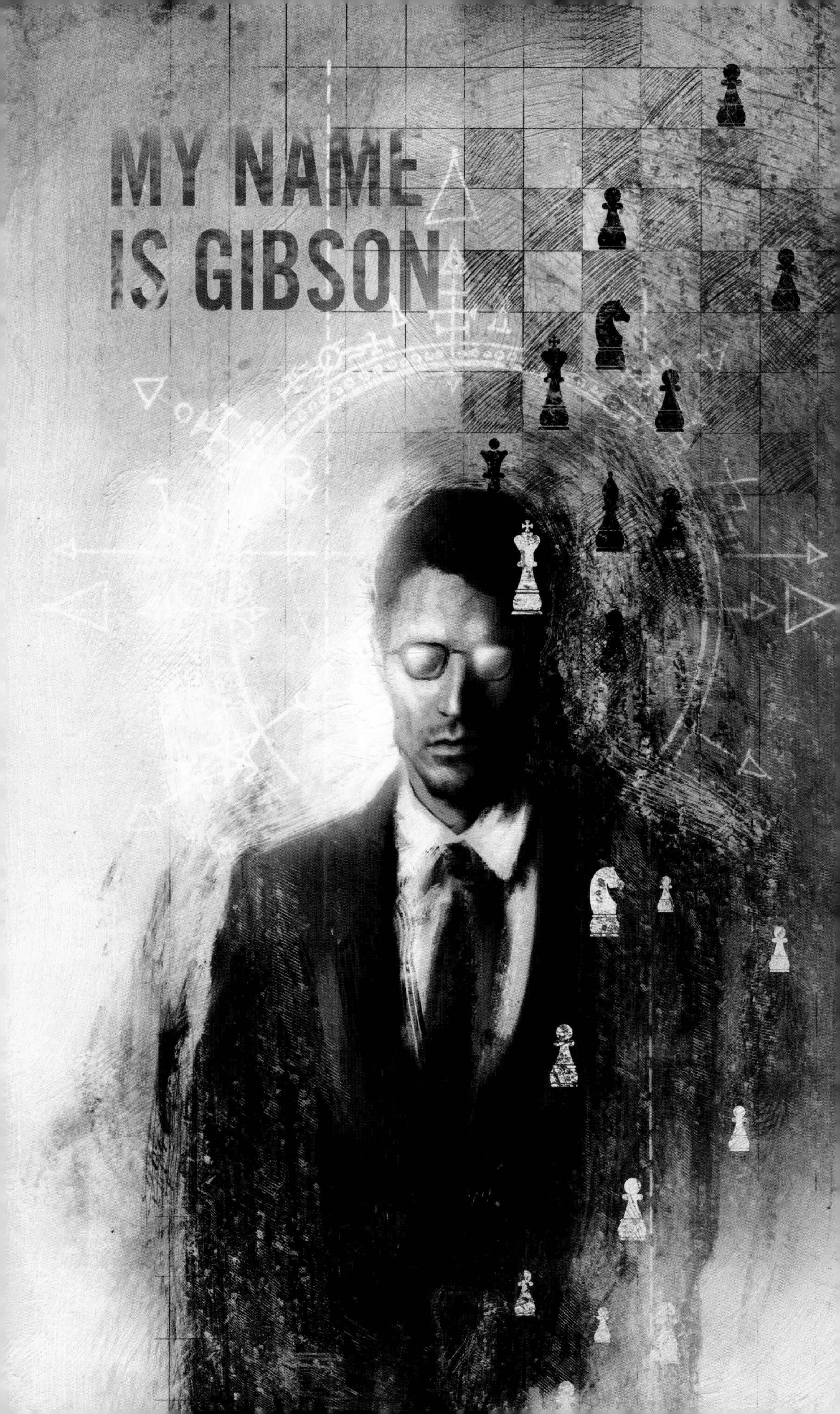
MY NAME
IS GIBSON

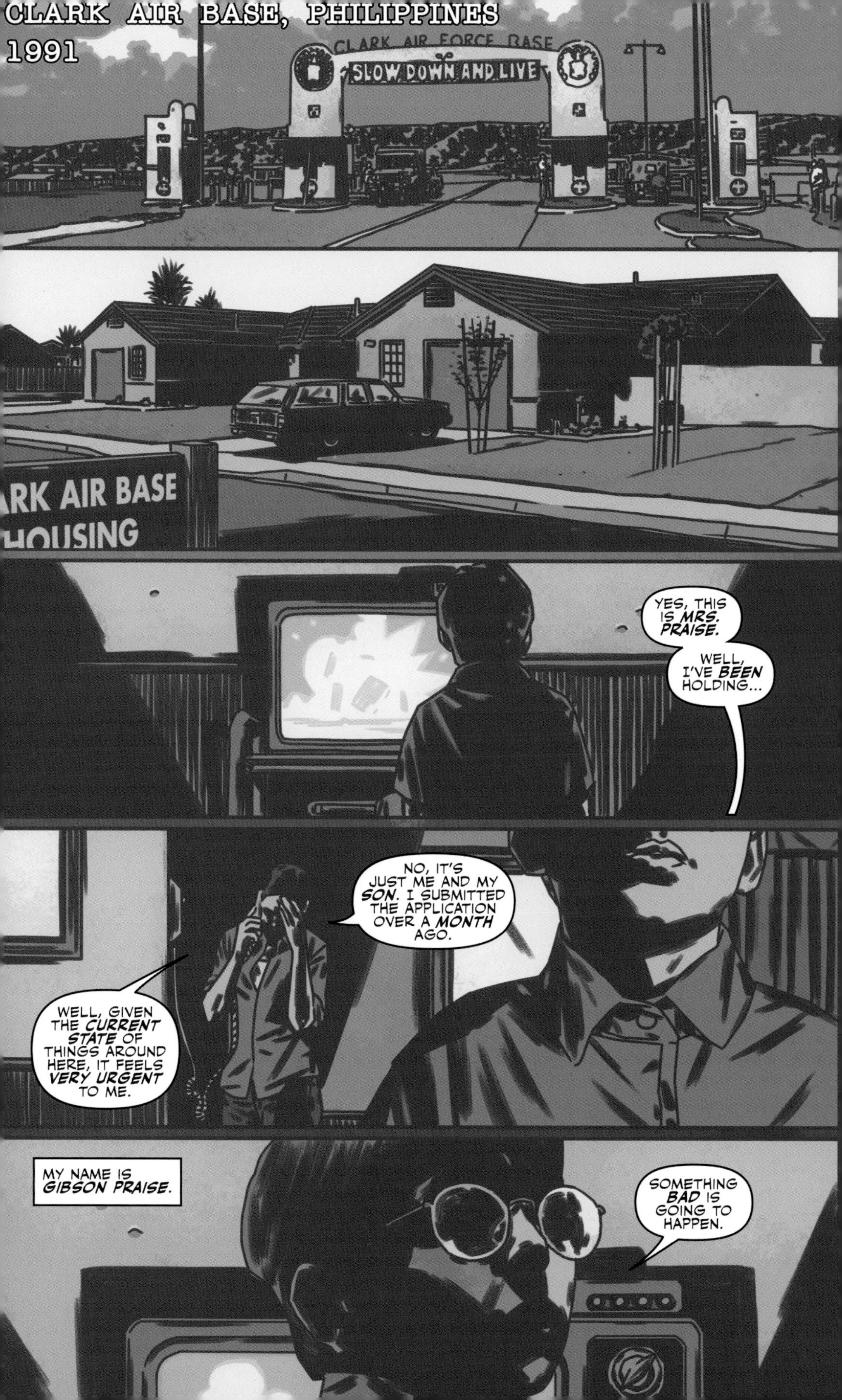
CLARK AIR BASE, PHILIPPINES
1991
CLARK AIR FORCE BASE
SLOW DOWN AND LIVE
RK AIR BASE
HOUSING
YES, THIS IS MRS. PRAISE.
WELL, I'VE BEEN HOLDING...
NO, IT'S JUST ME AND MY SON. I SUBMITTED THE APPLICATION OVER A MONTH AGO.
WELL, GIVEN THE CURRENT STATE OF THINGS AROUND HERE, IT FEELS VERY URGENT TO ME.
MY NAME IS GIBSON PRAISE.
SOMETHING BAD IS GOING TO HAPPEN.

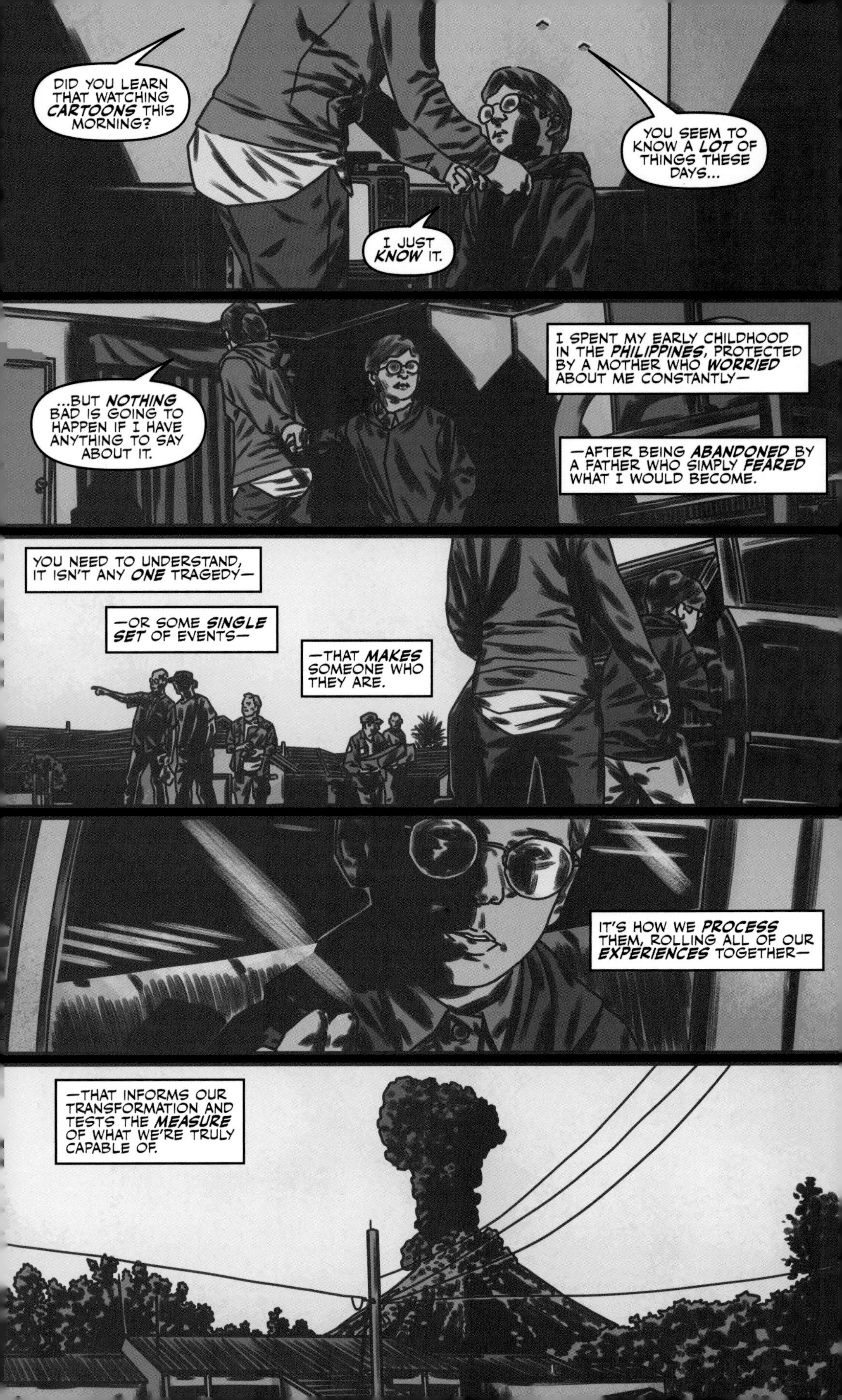
DID YOU LEARN THAT WATCHING CARTOONS THIS MORNING?
I JUST KNOW IT.
YOU SEEM TO KNOW A LOT OF THINGS THESE DAYS...
...BUT NOTHING BAD IS GOING TO HAPPEN IF I HAVE ANYTHING TO SAY ABOUT IT.
I SPENT MY EARLY CHILDHOOD IN THE PHILIPPINES, PROTECTED BY A MOTHER WHO WORRIED ABOUT ME CONSTANTLY—
—AFTER BEING ABANDONED BY A FATHER WHO SIMPLY FEARED WHAT I WOULD BECOME.
YOU NEED TO UNDERSTAND, IT ISN'T ANY ONE TRAGEDY—
—OR SOME SINGLE SET OF EVENTS—
—THAT MAKES SOMEONE WHO THEY ARE.
IT'S HOW WE PROCESS THEM, ROLLING ALL OF OUR EXPERIENCES TOGETHER—
—THAT INFORMS OUR TRANSFORMATION AND TESTS THE MEASURE OF WHAT WE'RE TRULY CAPABLE OF.

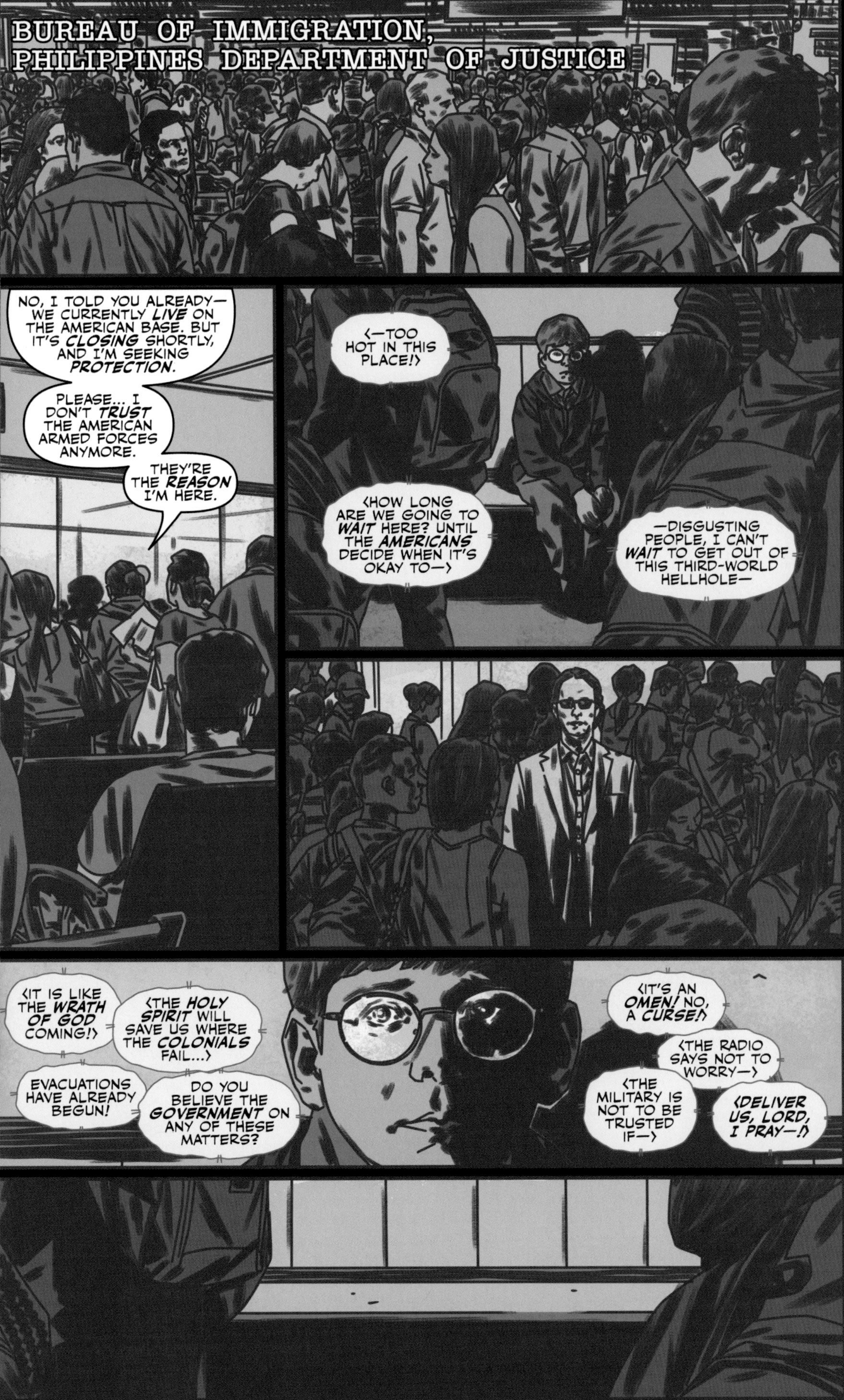

BUREAU OF IMMIGRATION, PHILIPPINES DEPARTMENT OF JUSTICE
NO, I TOLD YOU ALREADY— WE CURRENTLY *LIVE* ON THE AMERICAN BASE. BUT IT'S *CLOSING* SHORTLY, AND I'M SEEKING *PROTECTION*.
PLEASE... I DON'T *TRUST* THE AMERICAN ARMED FORCES ANYMORE.
THEY'RE THE *REASON* I'M HERE.
‹—TOO HOT IN THIS PLACE!›
‹HOW LONG ARE WE GOING TO *WAIT* HERE? UNTIL THE *AMERICANS* DECIDE WHEN IT'S OKAY TO—›
—DISGUSTING PEOPLE, I CAN'T *WAIT* TO GET OUT OF THIS THIRD-WORLD HELLHOLE—
‹IT IS LIKE THE *WRATH OF GOD* COMING!›
‹THE *HOLY SPIRIT* WILL SAVE US WHERE THE *COLONIALS* FAIL...›
EVACUATIONS HAVE ALREADY BEGUN!
DO YOU BELIEVE THE *GOVERNMENT* ON ANY OF THESE MATTERS?
‹IT'S AN *OMEN!* NO, A *CURSE!*›
‹THE RADIO SAYS NOT TO WORRY—›
‹THE MILITARY IS NOT TO BE TRUSTED IF—›
‹DELIVER US, LORD, I PRAY—!›

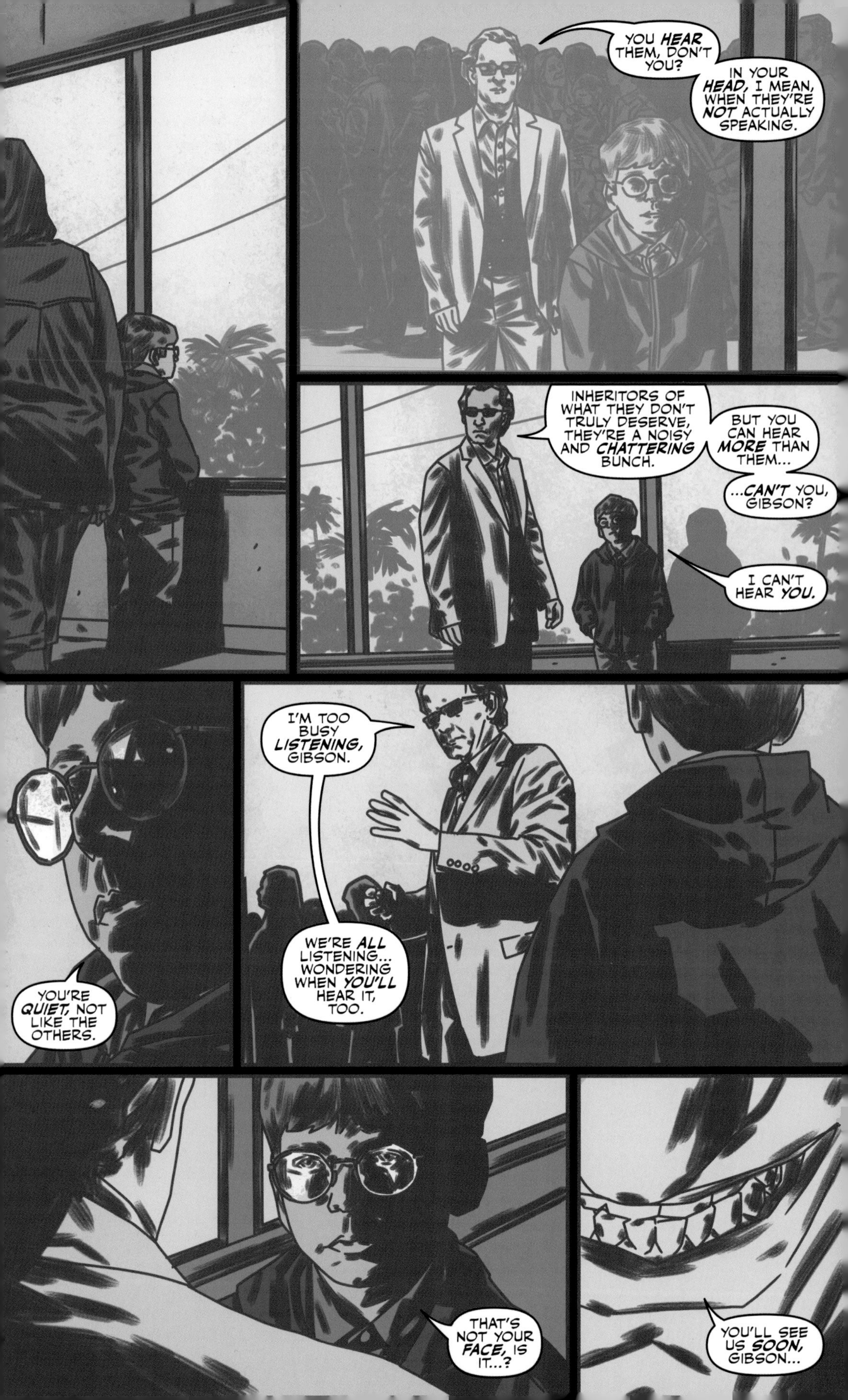
YOU HEAR THEM, DON'T YOU?
IN YOUR HEAD, I MEAN, WHEN THEY'RE NOT ACTUALLY SPEAKING.
INHERITORS OF WHAT THEY DON'T TRULY DESERVE, THEY'RE A NOISY AND CHATTERING BUNCH.
BUT YOU CAN HEAR MORE THAN THEM...
...CAN'T YOU, GIBSON?
I CAN'T HEAR YOU.
YOU'RE QUIET, NOT LIKE THE OTHERS.
I'M TOO BUSY LISTENING, GIBSON.
WE'RE ALL LISTENING... WONDERING WHEN YOU'LL HEAR IT, TOO.
THAT'S NOT YOUR FACE, IS IT...?
YOU'LL SEE US SOON, GIBSON...

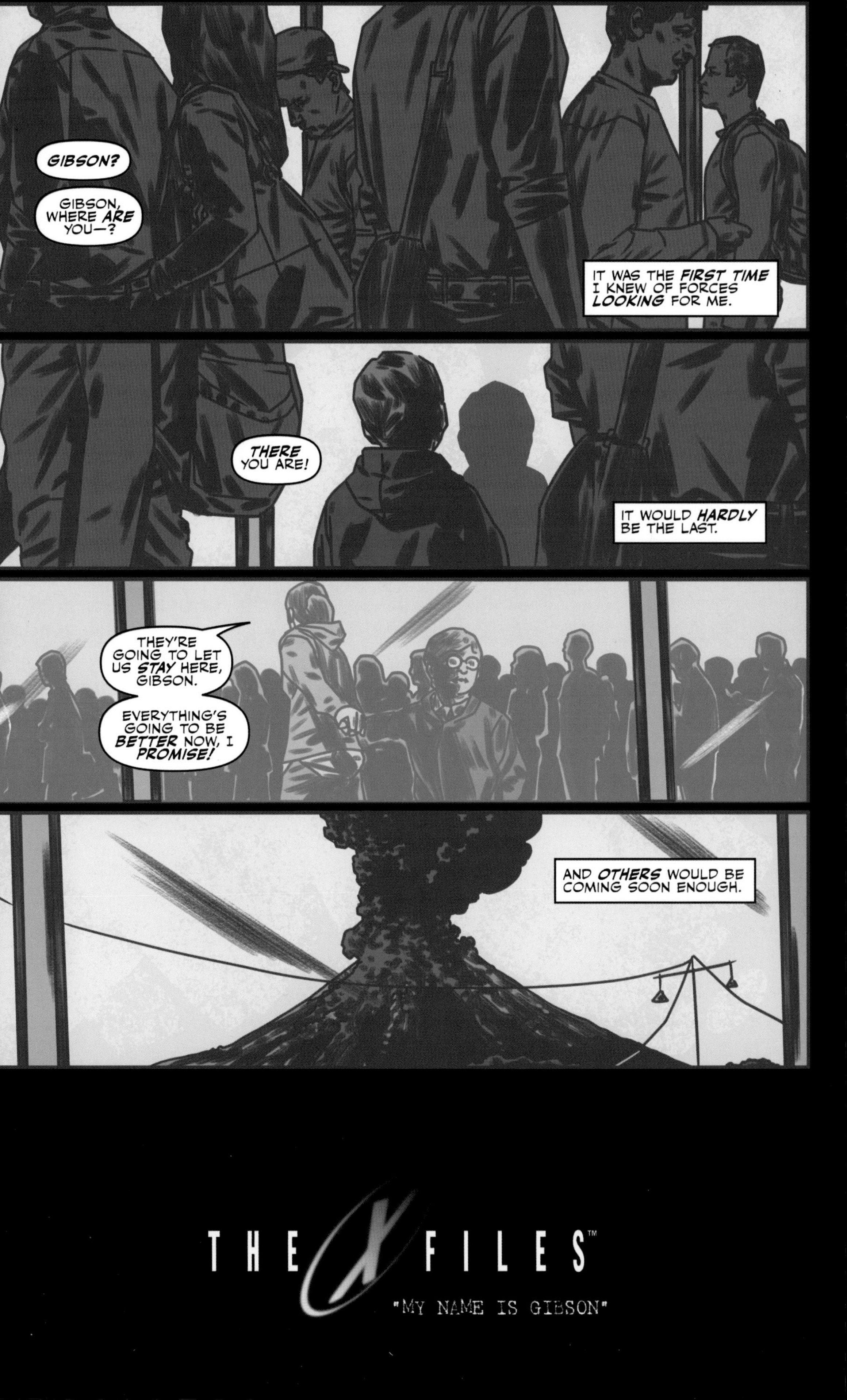
GIBSON?
GIBSON, WHERE ARE YOU—?
IT WAS THE FIRST TIME I KNEW OF FORCES LOOKING FOR ME.
THERE YOU ARE!
IT WOULD HARDLY BE THE LAST.
THEY'RE GOING TO LET US STAY HERE, GIBSON.
EVERYTHING'S GOING TO BE BETTER NOW, I PROMISE!
AND OTHERS WOULD BE COMING SOON ENOUGH.

THE X FILES™

"MY NAME IS GIBSON"

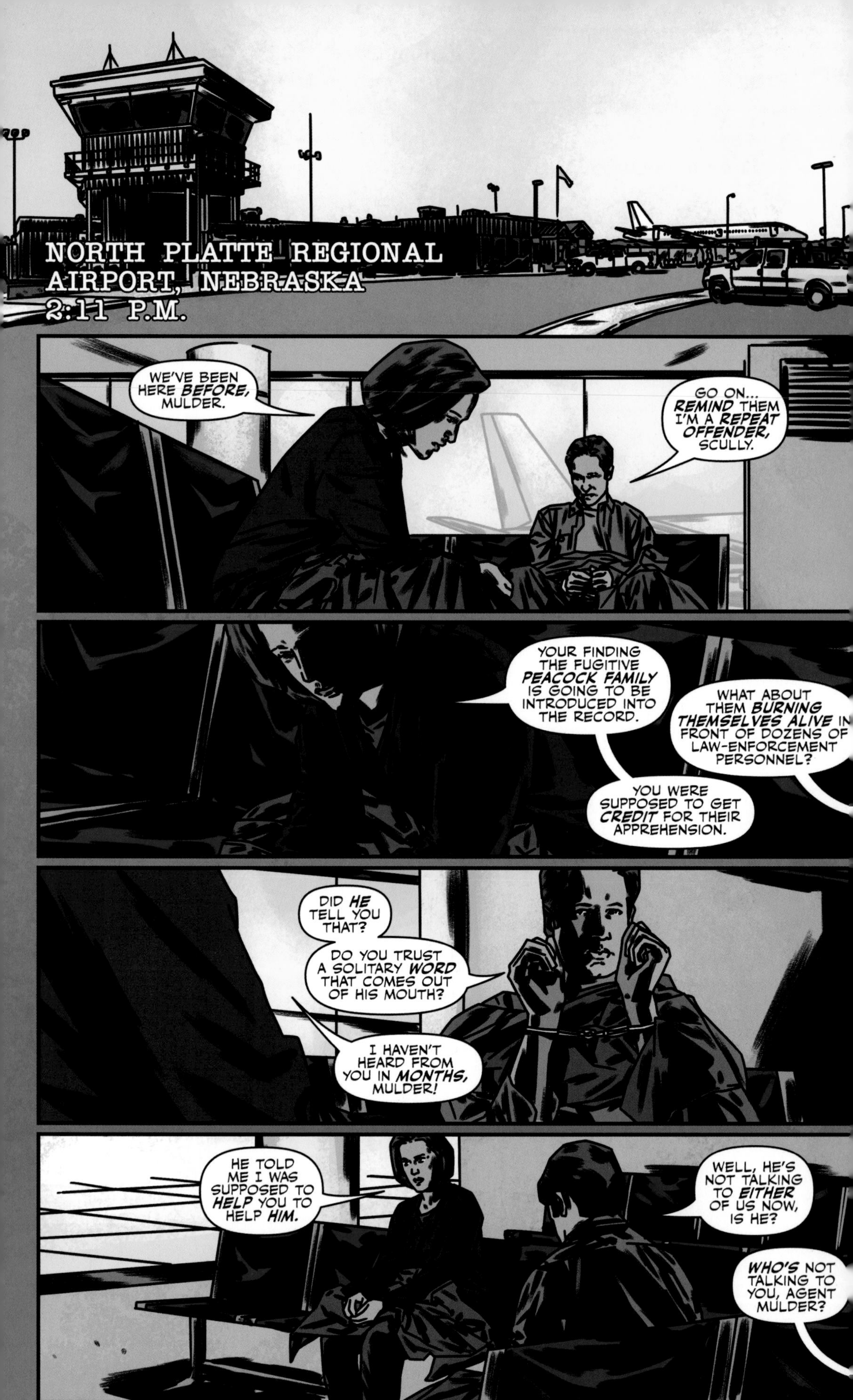
NORTH PLATTE REGIONAL AIRPORT, NEBRASKA 2:11 P.M.
WE'VE BEEN HERE BEFORE, MULDER.
GO ON... REMIND THEM I'M A REPEAT OFFENDER, SCULLY.
YOUR FINDING THE FUGITIVE PEACOCK FAMILY IS GOING TO BE INTRODUCED INTO THE RECORD.
YOU WERE SUPPOSED TO GET CREDIT FOR THEIR APPREHENSION.
WHAT ABOUT THEM BURNING THEMSELVES ALIVE IN FRONT OF DOZENS OF LAW-ENFORCEMENT PERSONNEL?
DID HE TELL YOU THAT?
DO YOU TRUST A SOLITARY WORD THAT COMES OUT OF HIS MOUTH?
I HAVEN'T HEARD FROM YOU IN MONTHS, MULDER!
HE TOLD ME I WAS SUPPOSED TO HELP YOU TO HELP HIM.
WELL, HE'S NOT TALKING TO EITHER OF US NOW, IS HE?
WHO'S NOT TALKING TO YOU, AGENT MULDER?

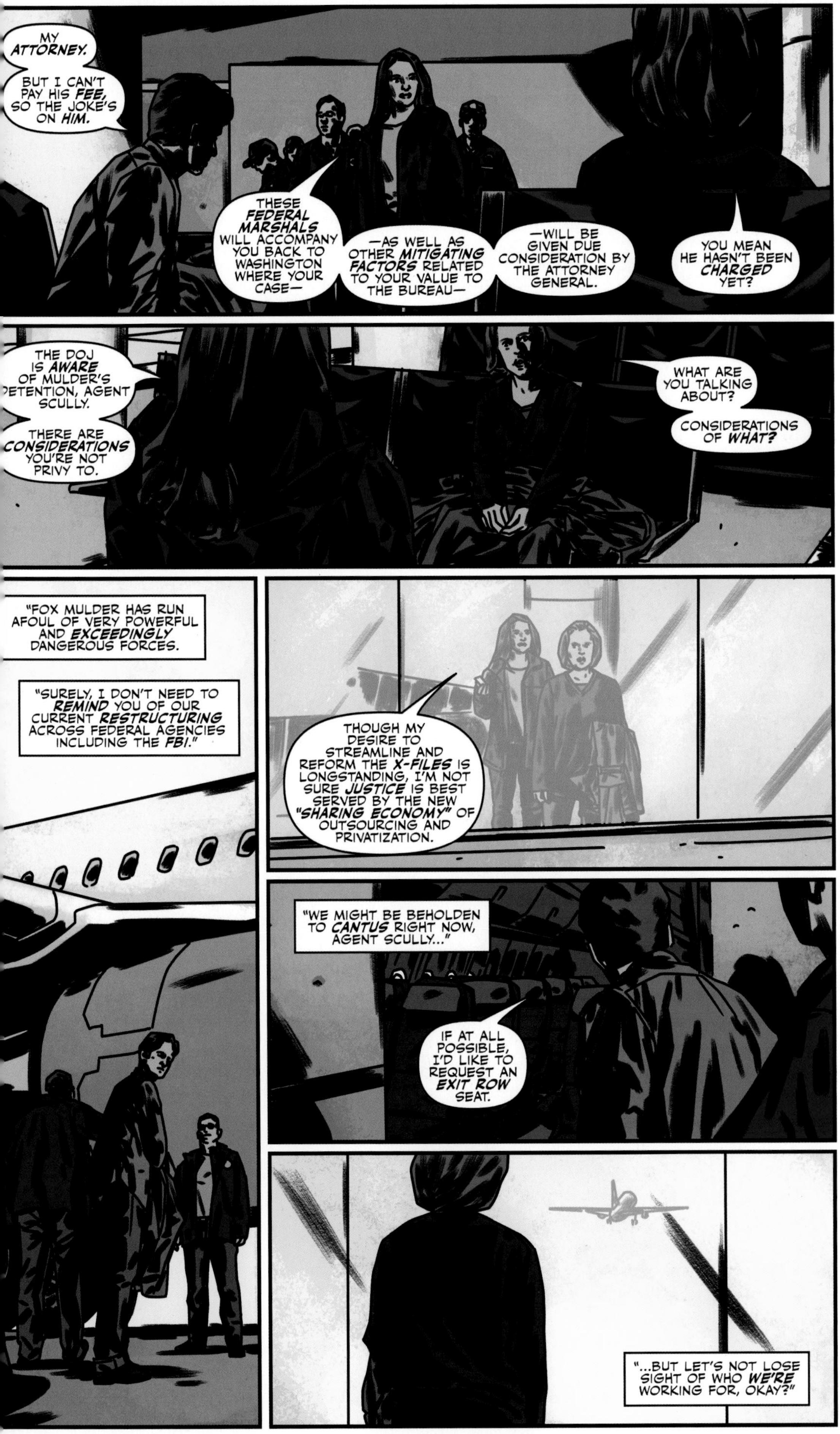
MY ATTORNEY.
BUT I CAN'T PAY HIS FEE, SO THE JOKE'S ON HIM.
THESE FEDERAL MARSHALS WILL ACCOMPANY YOU BACK TO WASHINGTON WHERE YOUR CASE—
—AS WELL AS OTHER MITIGATING FACTORS RELATED TO YOUR VALUE TO THE BUREAU—
—WILL BE GIVEN DUE CONSIDERATION BY THE ATTORNEY GENERAL.
YOU MEAN HE HASN'T BEEN CHARGED YET?
THE DOJ IS AWARE OF MULDER'S DETENTION, AGENT SCULLY.
THERE ARE CONSIDERATIONS YOU'RE NOT PRIVY TO.
WHAT ARE YOU TALKING ABOUT?
CONSIDERATIONS OF WHAT?
"FOX MULDER HAS RUN AFOUL OF VERY POWERFUL AND EXCEEDINGLY DANGEROUS FORCES.
"SURELY, I DON'T NEED TO REMIND YOU OF OUR CURRENT RESTRUCTURING ACROSS FEDERAL AGENCIES INCLUDING THE FBI."
THOUGH MY DESIRE TO STREAMLINE AND REFORM THE X-FILES IS LONGSTANDING, I'M NOT SURE JUSTICE IS BEST SERVED BY THE NEW "SHARING ECONOMY" OF OUTSOURCING AND PRIVATIZATION.
"WE MIGHT BE BEHOLDEN TO CANTUS RIGHT NOW, AGENT SCULLY..."
IF AT ALL POSSIBLE, I'D LIKE TO REQUEST AN EXIT ROW SEAT.
"...BUT LET'S NOT LOSE SIGHT OF WHO WE'RE WORKING FOR, OKAY?"

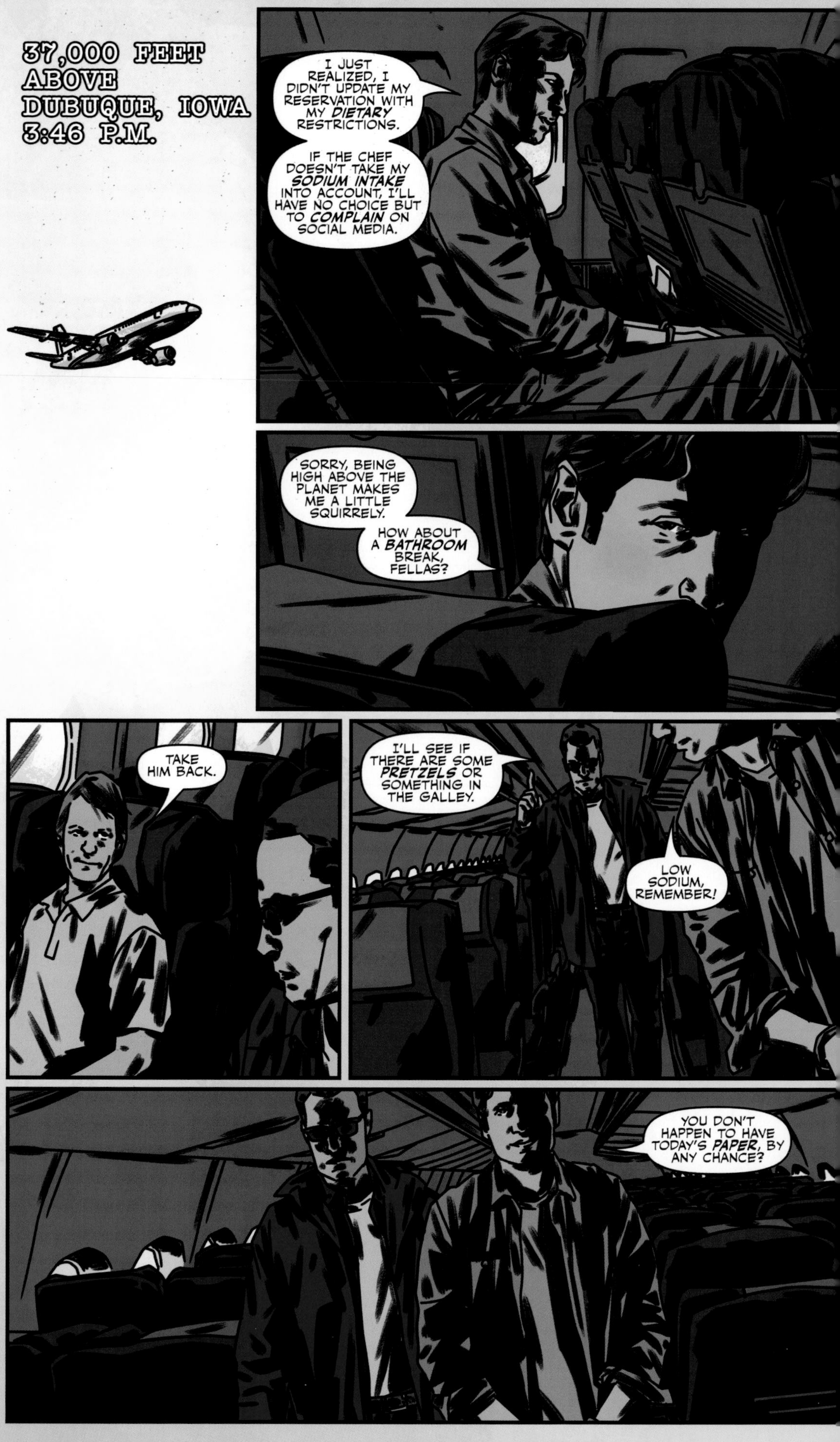
37,000 FEET ABOVE DUBUQUE, IOWA 3:46 P.M.
I JUST REALIZED, I DIDN'T UPDATE MY RESERVATION WITH MY DIETARY RESTRICTIONS.
IF THE CHEF DOESN'T TAKE MY SODIUM INTAKE INTO ACCOUNT, I'LL HAVE NO CHOICE BUT TO COMPLAIN ON SOCIAL MEDIA.
SORRY, BEING HIGH ABOVE THE PLANET MAKES ME A LITTLE SQUIRRELY.
HOW ABOUT A BATHROOM BREAK, FELLAS?
TAKE HIM BACK.
I'LL SEE IF THERE ARE SOME PRETZELS OR SOMETHING IN THE GALLEY.
LOW SODIUM, REMEMBER!
YOU DON'T HAPPEN TO HAVE TODAY'S PAPER, BY ANY CHANCE?

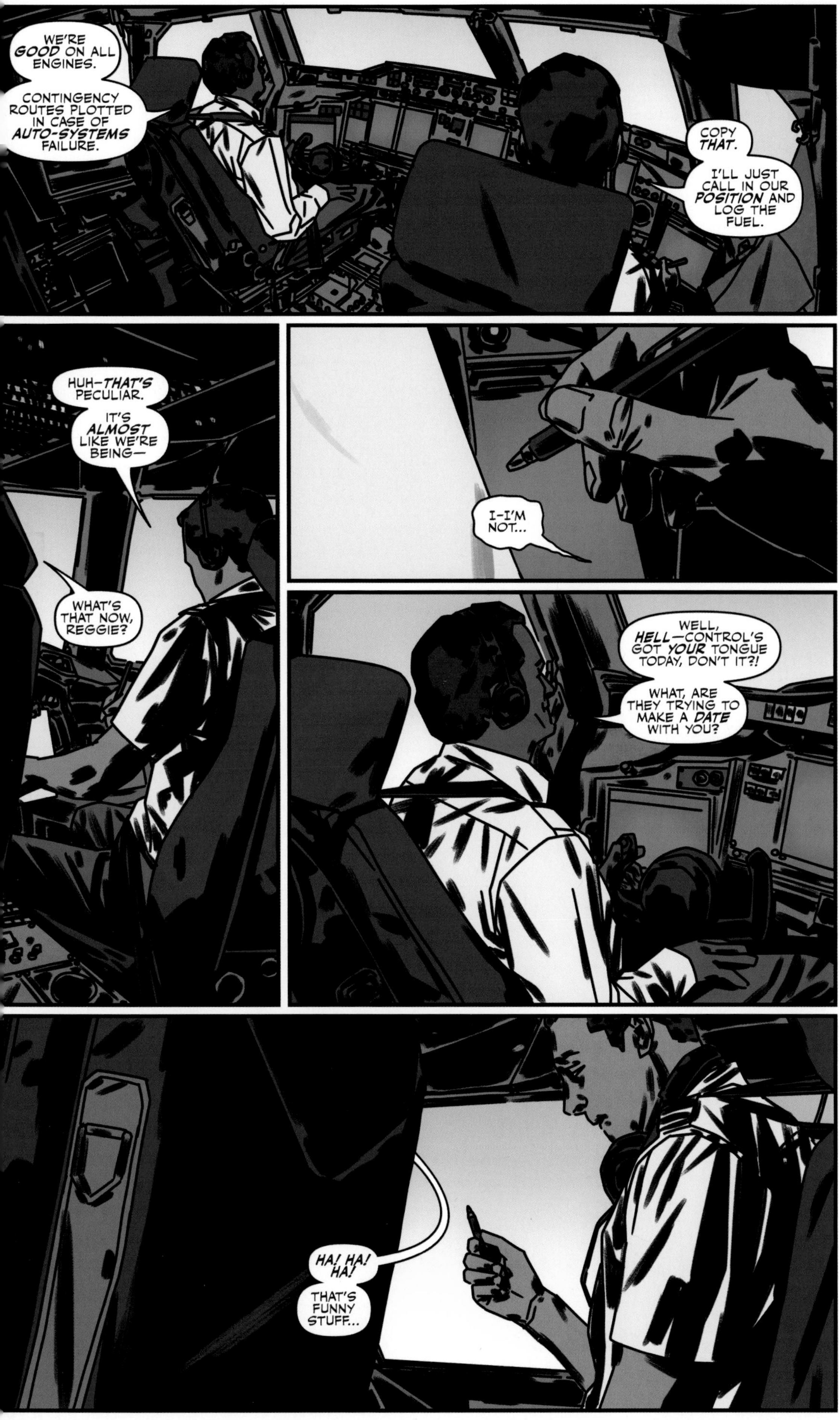
WE'RE GOOD ON ALL ENGINES.
CONTINGENCY ROUTES PLOTTED IN CASE OF AUTO-SYSTEMS FAILURE.
COPY THAT.
I'LL JUST CALL IN OUR POSITION AND LOG THE FUEL.
HUH—THAT'S PECULIAR.
IT'S ALMOST LIKE WE'RE BEING—
WHAT'S THAT NOW, REGGIE?
I-I'M NOT...
WELL, HELL—CONTROL'S GOT YOUR TONGUE TODAY, DON'T IT?!
WHAT, ARE THEY TRYING TO MAKE A DATE WITH YOU?
HA! HA! HA!
THAT'S FUNNY STUFF...

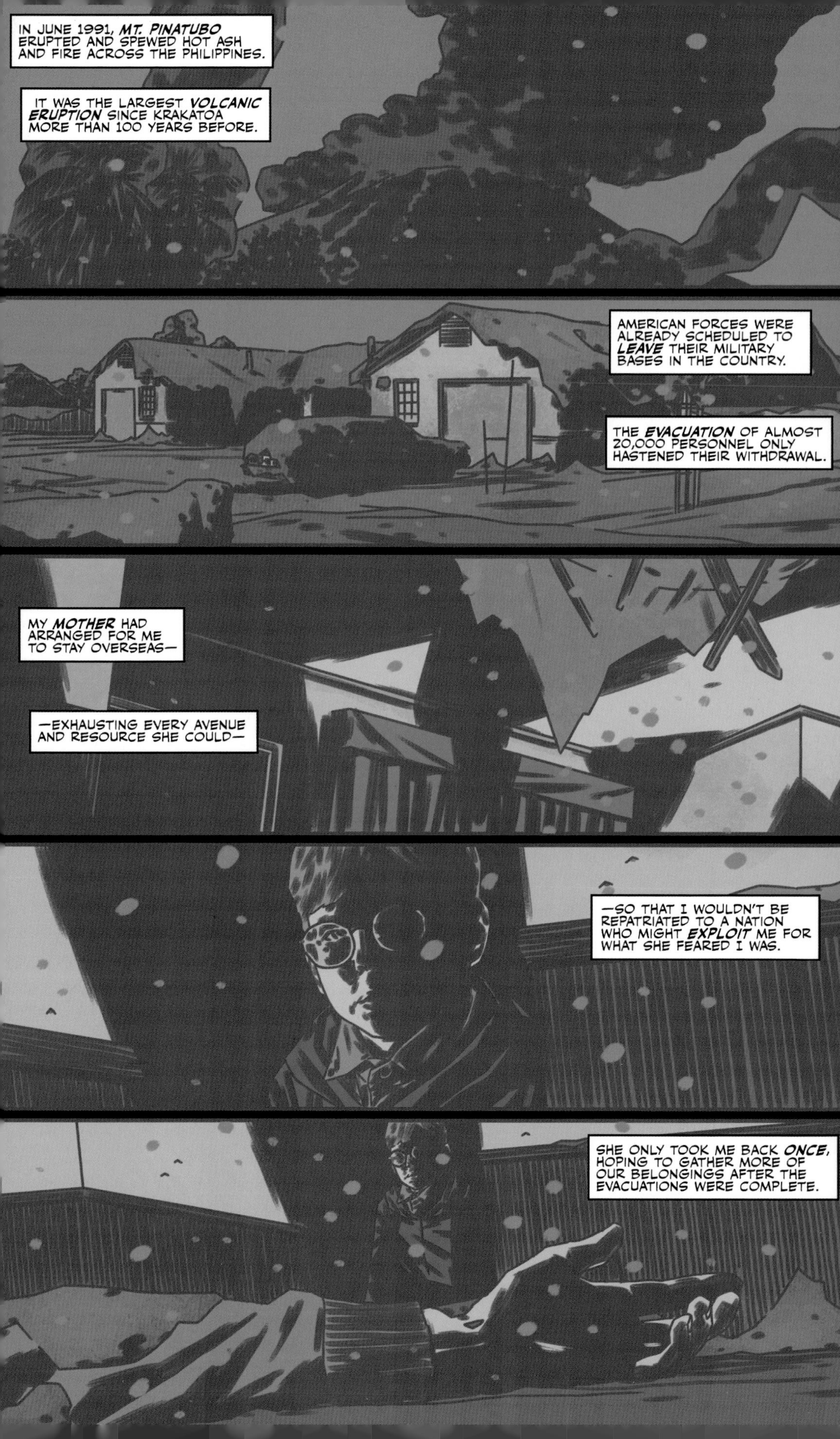
IN JUNE 1991, MT. PINATUBO ERUPTED AND SPEWED HOT ASH AND FIRE ACROSS THE PHILIPPINES.
IT WAS THE LARGEST VOLCANIC ERUPTION SINCE KRAKATOA MORE THAN 100 YEARS BEFORE.
AMERICAN FORCES WERE ALREADY SCHEDULED TO LEAVE THEIR MILITARY BASES IN THE COUNTRY.
THE EVACUATION OF ALMOST 20,000 PERSONNEL ONLY HASTENED THEIR WITHDRAWAL.
MY MOTHER HAD ARRANGED FOR ME TO STAY OVERSEAS—
—EXHAUSTING EVERY AVENUE AND RESOURCE SHE COULD—
—SO THAT I WOULDN'T BE REPATRIATED TO A NATION WHO MIGHT EXPLOIT ME FOR WHAT SHE FEARED I WAS.
SHE ONLY TOOK ME BACK ONCE, HOPING TO GATHER MORE OF OUR BELONGINGS AFTER THE EVACUATIONS WERE COMPLETE.

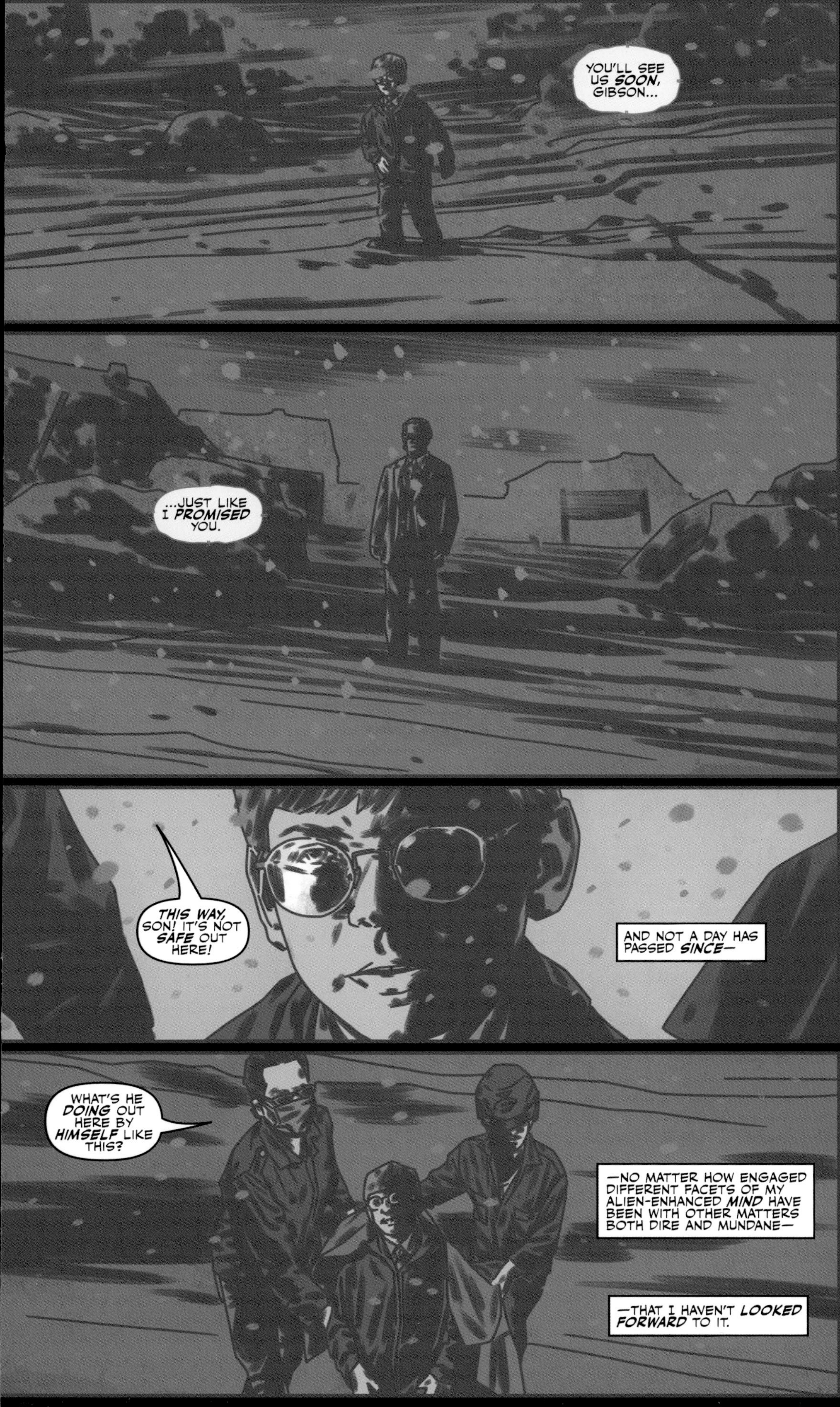
YOU'LL SEE US SOON, GIBSON...
...JUST LIKE I PROMISED YOU.
THIS WAY, SON! IT'S NOT SAFE OUT HERE!
AND NOT A DAY HAS PASSED SINCE—
WHAT'S HE DOING OUT HERE BY HIMSELF LIKE THIS?
—NO MATTER HOW ENGAGED DIFFERENT FACETS OF MY ALIEN-ENHANCED MIND HAVE BEEN WITH OTHER MATTERS BOTH DIRE AND MUNDANE—
—THAT I HAVEN'T LOOKED FORWARD TO IT.

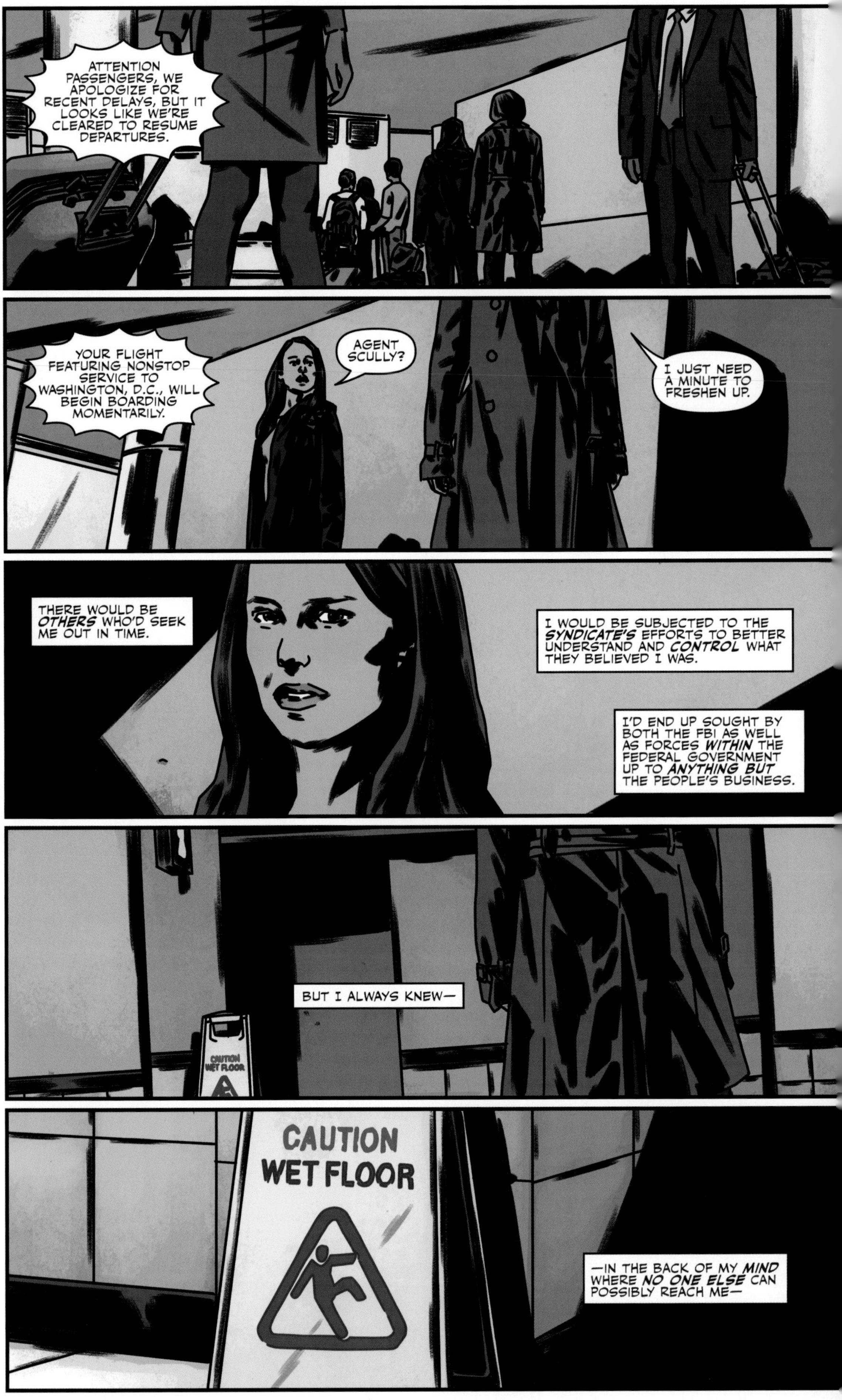
ATTENTION PASSENGERS, WE APOLOGIZE FOR RECENT DELAYS, BUT IT LOOKS LIKE WE'RE CLEARED TO RESUME DEPARTURES.
YOUR FLIGHT FEATURING NONSTOP SERVICE TO WASHINGTON, D.C., WILL BEGIN BOARDING MOMENTARILY.
AGENT SCULLY?
I JUST NEED A MINUTE TO FRESHEN UP.
THERE WOULD BE *OTHERS* WHO'D SEEK ME OUT IN TIME.
I WOULD BE SUBJECTED TO THE *SYNDICATE'S* EFFORTS TO BETTER UNDERSTAND AND *CONTROL* WHAT THEY BELIEVED I WAS.
I'D END UP SOUGHT BY BOTH THE FBI AS WELL AS FORCES *WITHIN* THE FEDERAL GOVERNMENT UP TO *ANYTHING BUT* THE PEOPLE'S BUSINESS.
BUT I ALWAYS KNEW—
CAUTION WET FLOOR
CAUTION WET FLOOR
—IN THE BACK OF MY *MIND* WHERE *NO ONE ELSE* CAN POSSIBLY REACH ME—

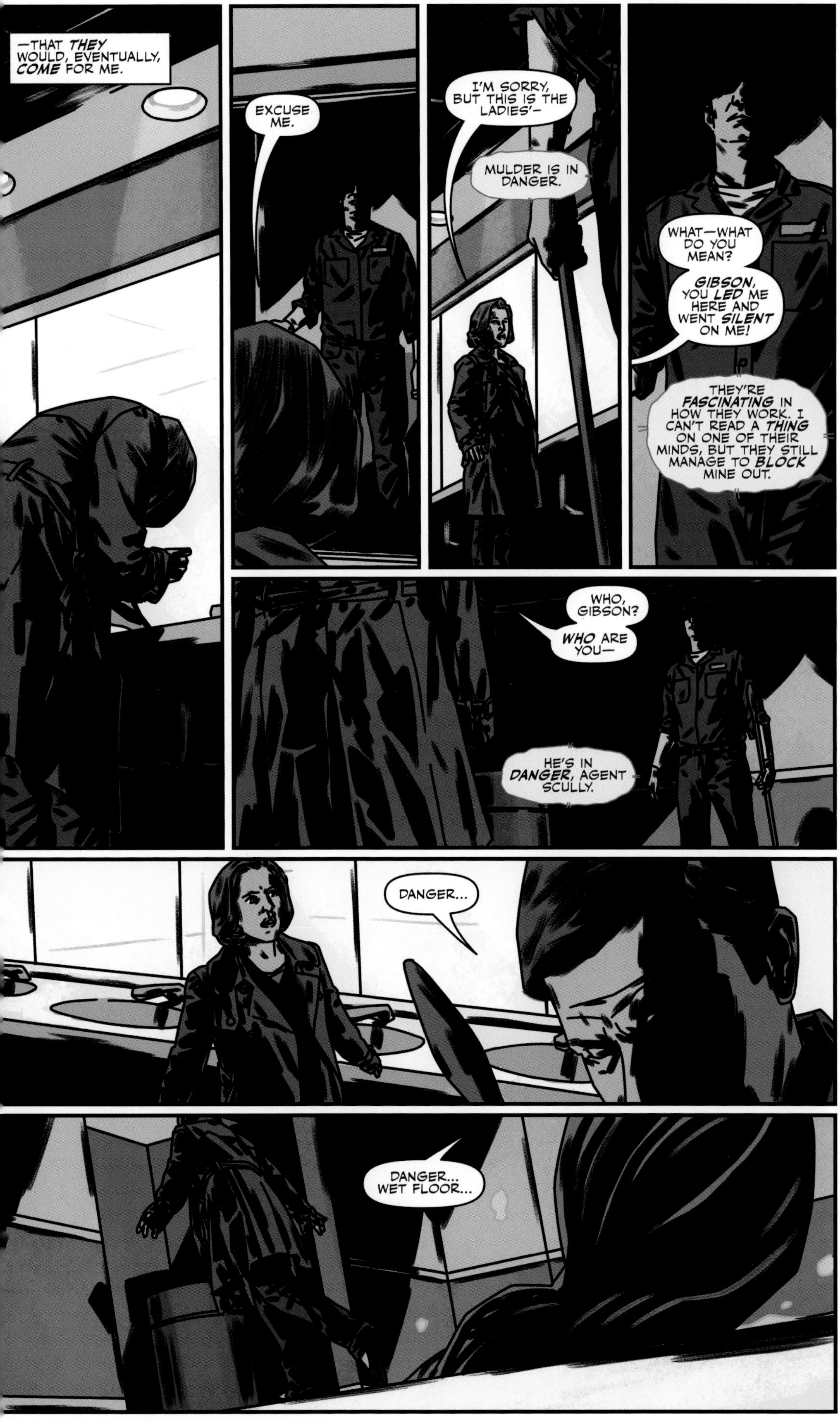
—THAT *THEY* WOULD, EVENTUALLY, *COME* FOR ME.
EXCUSE ME.
I'M SORRY, BUT THIS IS THE LADIES'—
MULDER IS IN DANGER.
WHAT—WHAT DO YOU MEAN?
GIBSON, YOU *LED* ME HERE AND WENT *SILENT* ON ME!
THEY'RE *FASCINATING* IN HOW THEY WORK. I CAN'T READ A *THING* ON ONE OF THEIR MINDS, BUT THEY STILL MANAGE TO *BLOCK* MINE OUT.
WHO, GIBSON?
WHO ARE YOU—
HE'S IN *DANGER*, AGENT SCULLY.
DANGER...
DANGER... WET FLOOR...

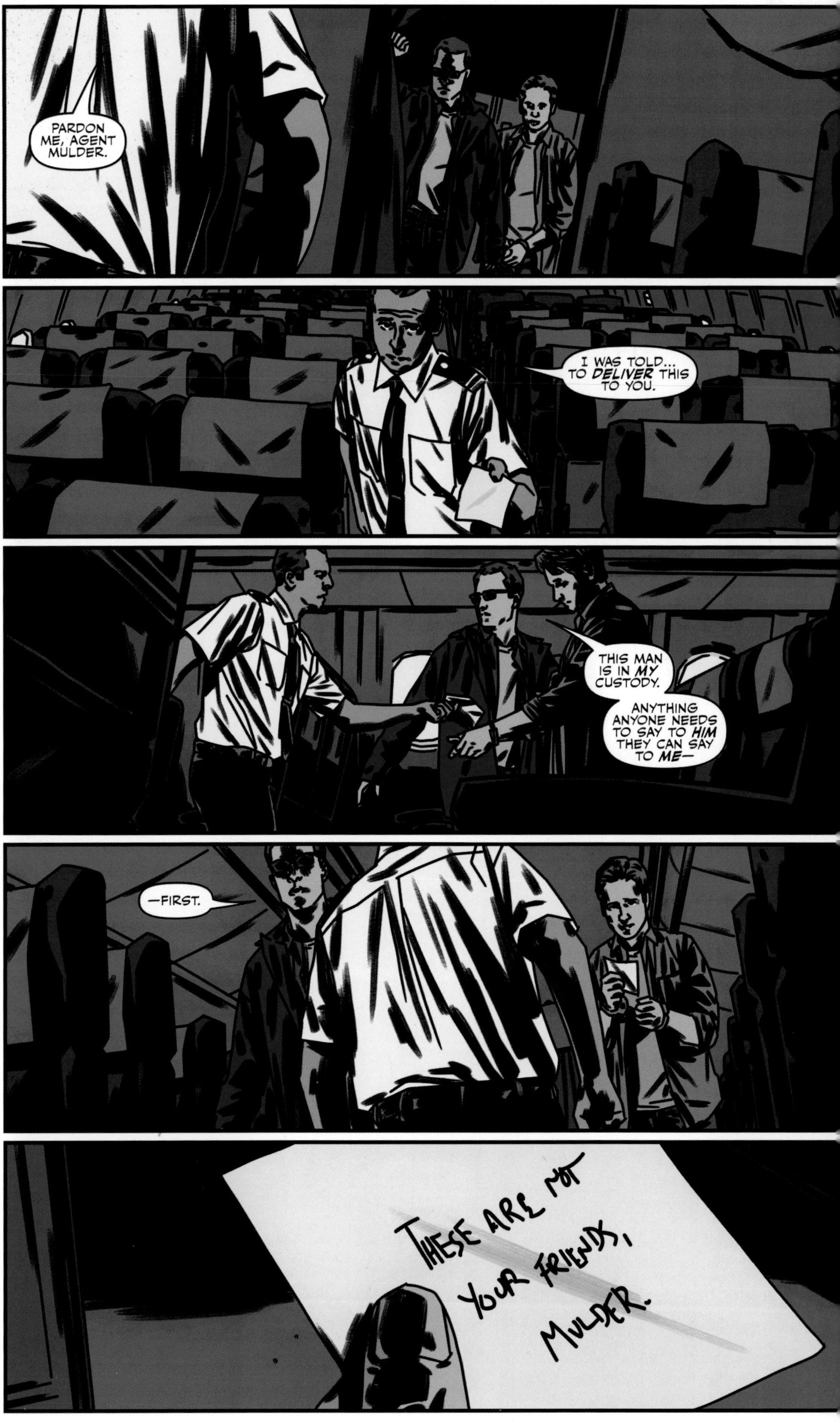
PARDON ME, AGENT MULDER.
I WAS TOLD... TO DELIVER THIS TO YOU.
THIS MAN IS IN MY CUSTODY.
ANYTHING ANYONE NEEDS TO SAY TO HIM THEY CAN SAY TO ME—
—FIRST.
THESE ARE NOT YOUR FRIENDS, MULDER.

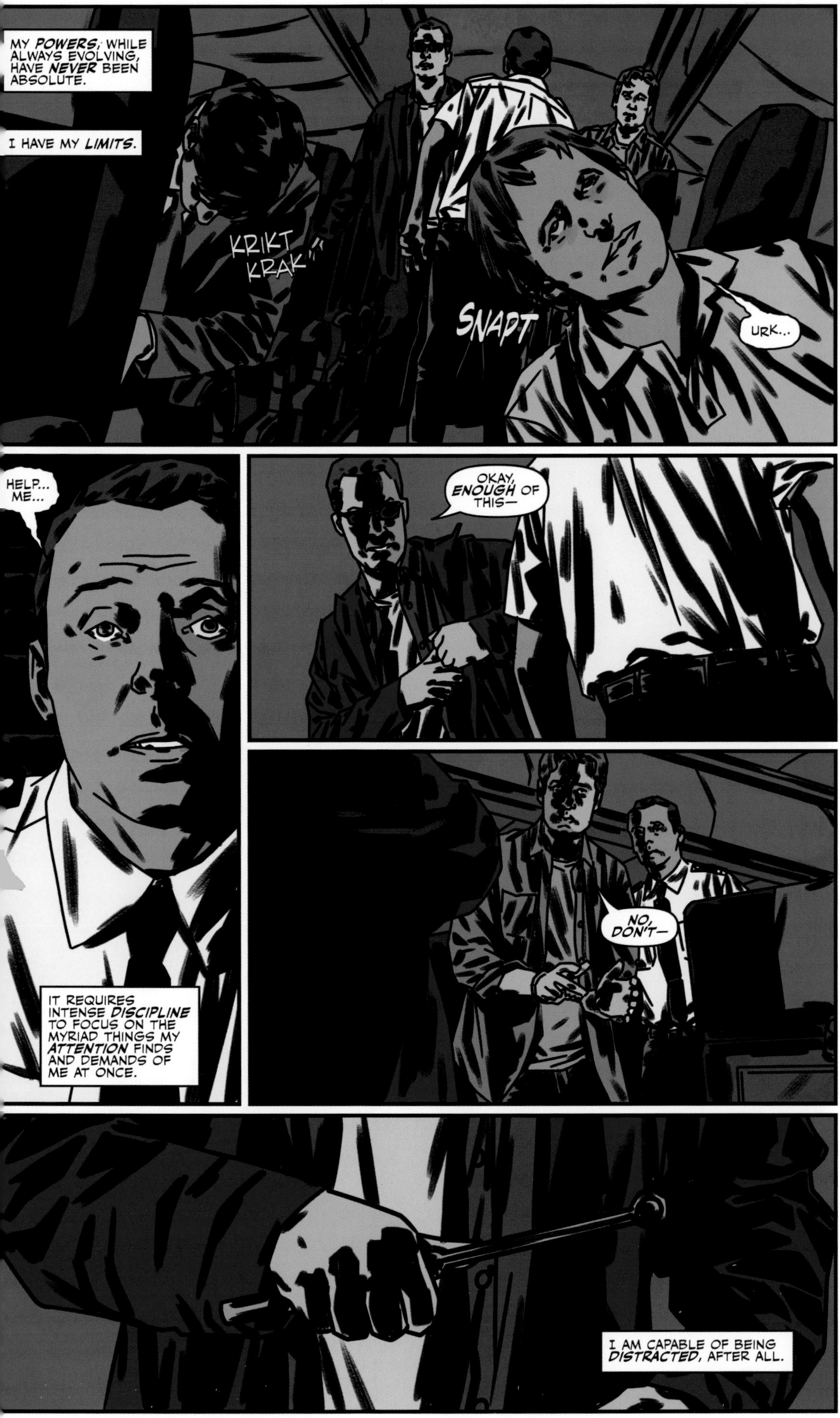

MY POWERS, WHILE ALWAYS EVOLVING, HAVE NEVER BEEN ABSOLUTE.
I HAVE MY LIMITS.
KRIKT KRAK
SNAPT
URK...
HELP... ME...
OKAY, ENOUGH OF THIS—
NO, DON'T—
IT REQUIRES INTENSE DISCIPLINE TO FOCUS ON THE MYRIAD THINGS MY ATTENTION FINDS AND DEMANDS OF ME AT ONCE.
I AM CAPABLE OF BEING DISTRACTED, AFTER ALL.

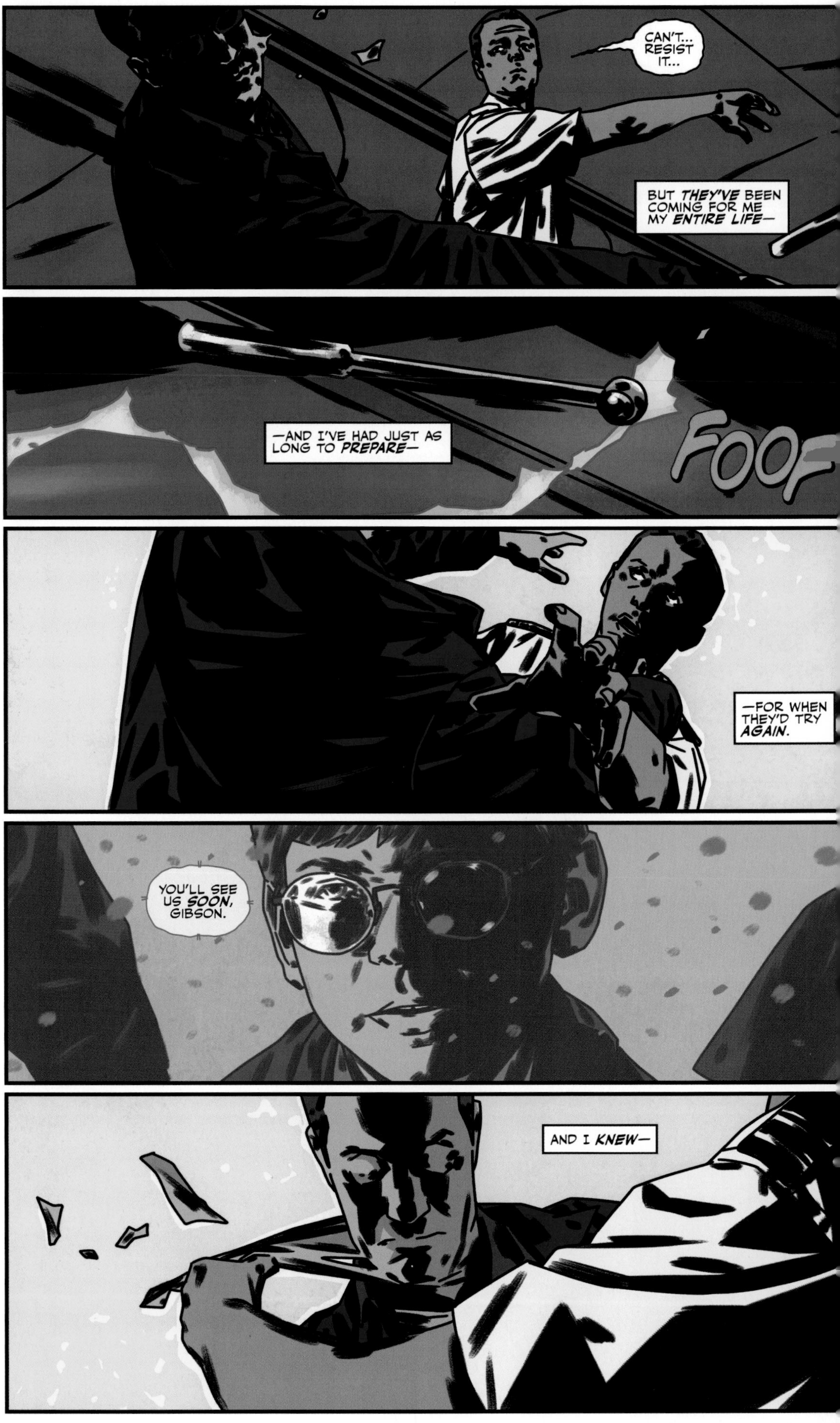
CAN'T... RESIST IT...
BUT *THEY'VE* BEEN COMING FOR ME MY *ENTIRE LIFE*—
—AND I'VE HAD JUST AS LONG TO *PREPARE*—
FOOF
—FOR WHEN THEY'D TRY *AGAIN*.
YOU'LL SEE US *SOON,* GIBSON.
AND I *KNEW*—

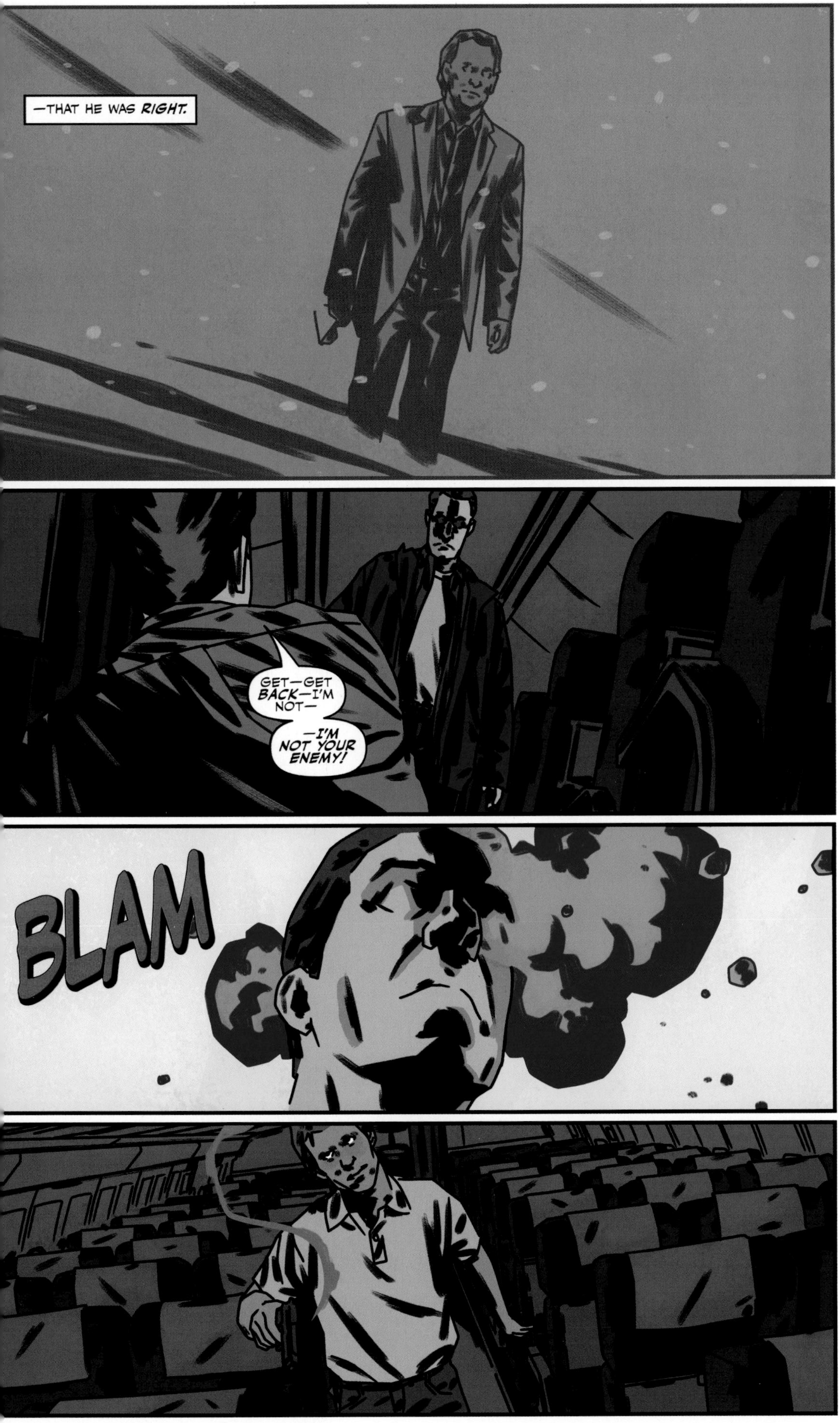
—THAT HE WAS *RIGHT.*
GET—GET *BACK*—I'M NOT—
—*I'M NOT YOUR ENEMY!*
BLAM

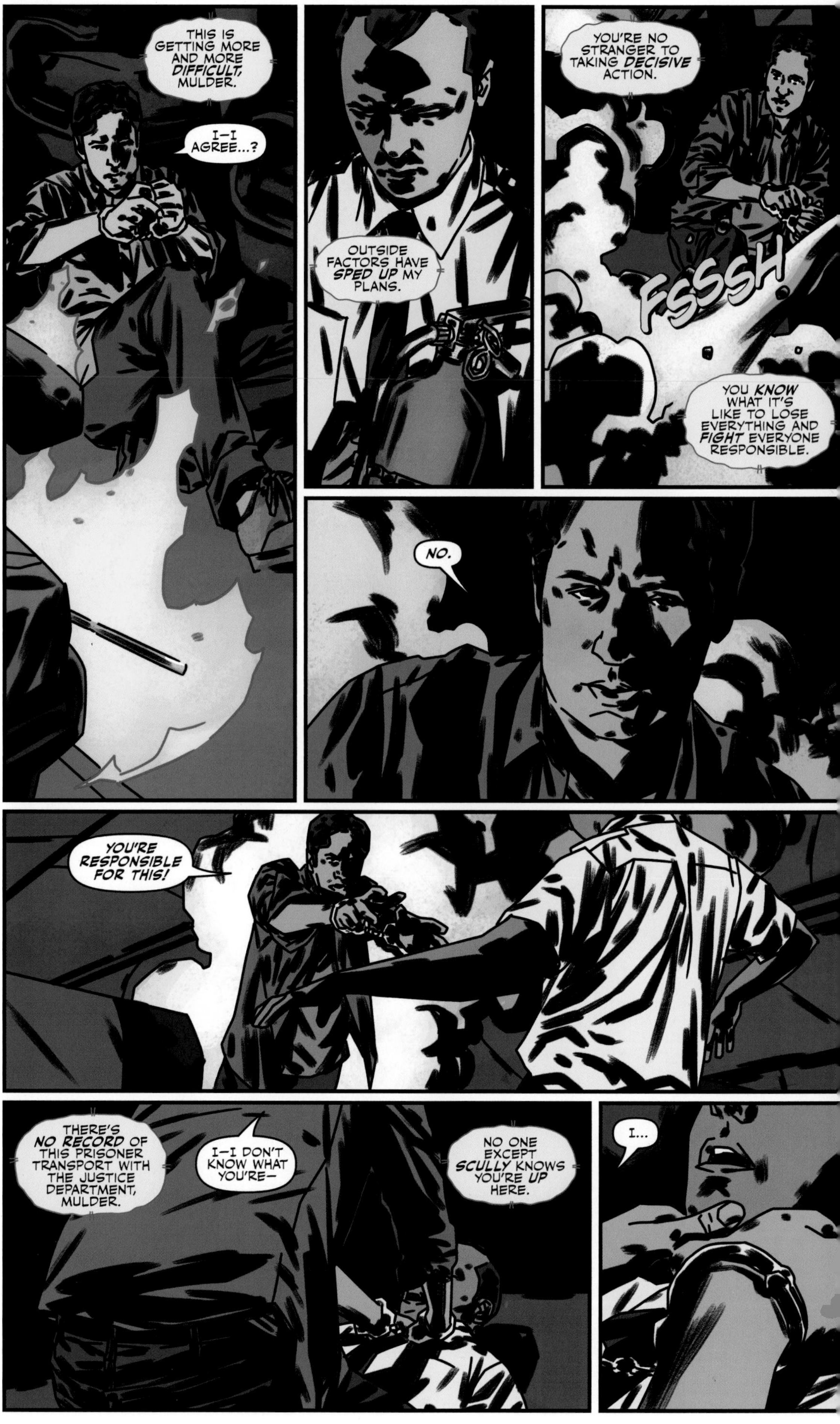

THIS IS GETTING MORE AND MORE DIFFICULT, MULDER.
I—I AGREE...?
OUTSIDE FACTORS HAVE SPED UP MY PLANS.
YOU'RE NO STRANGER TO TAKING DECISIVE ACTION.
FSSSH
YOU KNOW WHAT IT'S LIKE TO LOSE EVERYTHING AND FIGHT EVERYONE RESPONSIBLE.
NO.
YOU'RE RESPONSIBLE FOR THIS!
THERE'S NO RECORD OF THIS PRISONER TRANSPORT WITH THE JUSTICE DEPARTMENT, MULDER.
I—I DON'T KNOW WHAT YOU'RE—
NO ONE EXCEPT SCULLY KNOWS YOU'RE UP HERE.
I...

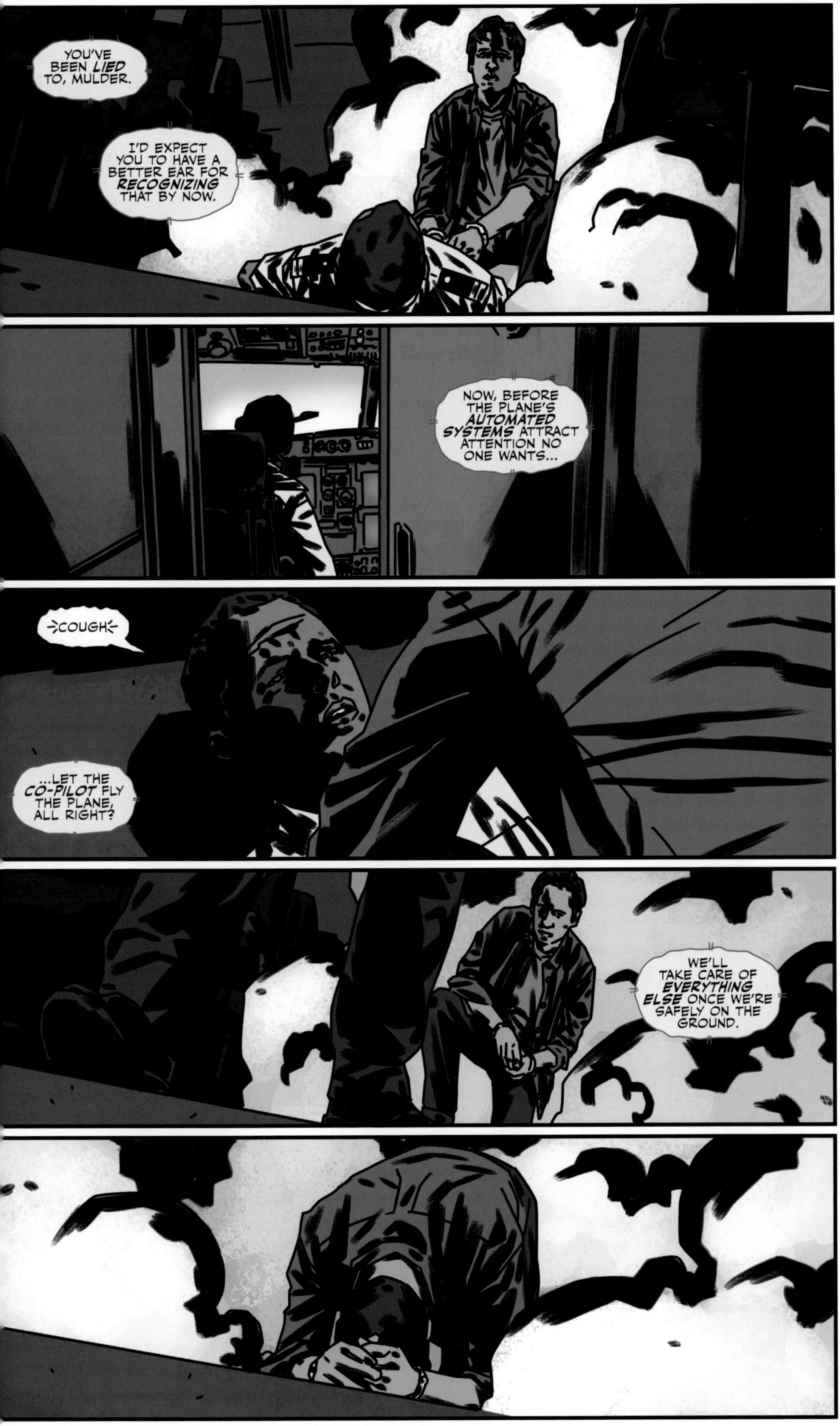
YOU'VE BEEN *LIED* TO, MULDER.
I'D EXPECT YOU TO HAVE A BETTER EAR FOR *RECOGNIZING* THAT BY NOW.
NOW, BEFORE THE PLANE'S *AUTOMATED SYSTEMS* ATTRACT ATTENTION NO ONE WANTS...
COUGH
...LET THE *CO-PILOT* FLY THE PLANE, ALL RIGHT?
WE'LL TAKE CARE OF *EVERYTHING ELSE* ONCE WE'RE SAFELY ON THE GROUND.

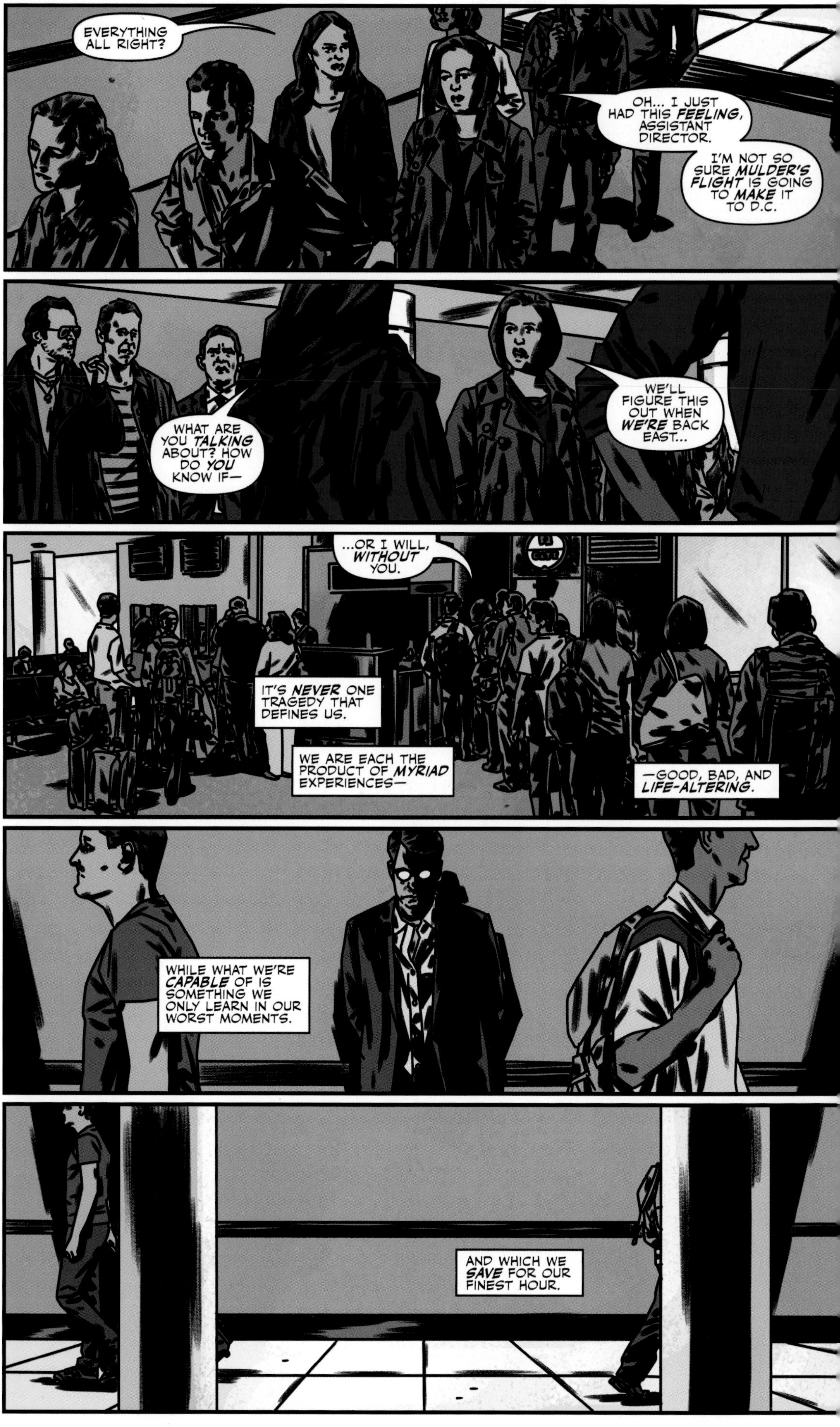
EVERYTHING ALL RIGHT?
OH... I JUST HAD THIS FEELING, ASSISTANT DIRECTOR.
I'M NOT SO SURE MULDER'S FLIGHT IS GOING TO MAKE IT TO D.C.
WHAT ARE YOU TALKING ABOUT? HOW DO YOU KNOW IF—
WE'LL FIGURE THIS OUT WHEN WE'RE BACK EAST...
...OR I WILL, WITHOUT YOU.
IT'S NEVER ONE TRAGEDY THAT DEFINES US.
WE ARE EACH THE PRODUCT OF MYRIAD EXPERIENCES—
—GOOD, BAD, AND LIFE-ALTERING.
WHILE WHAT WE'RE CAPABLE OF IS SOMETHING WE ONLY LEARN IN OUR WORST MOMENTS.
AND WHICH WE SAVE FOR OUR FINEST HOUR.

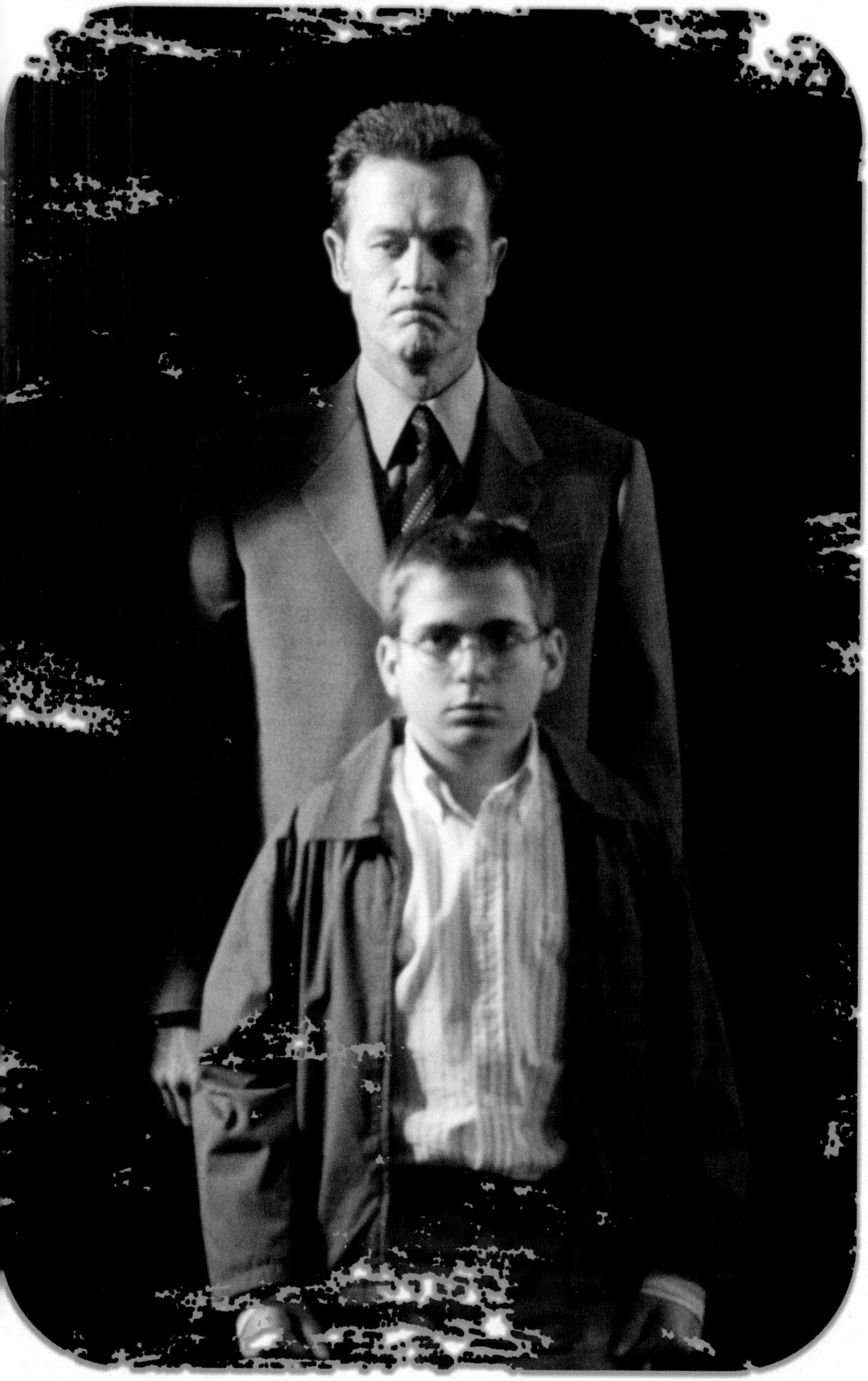

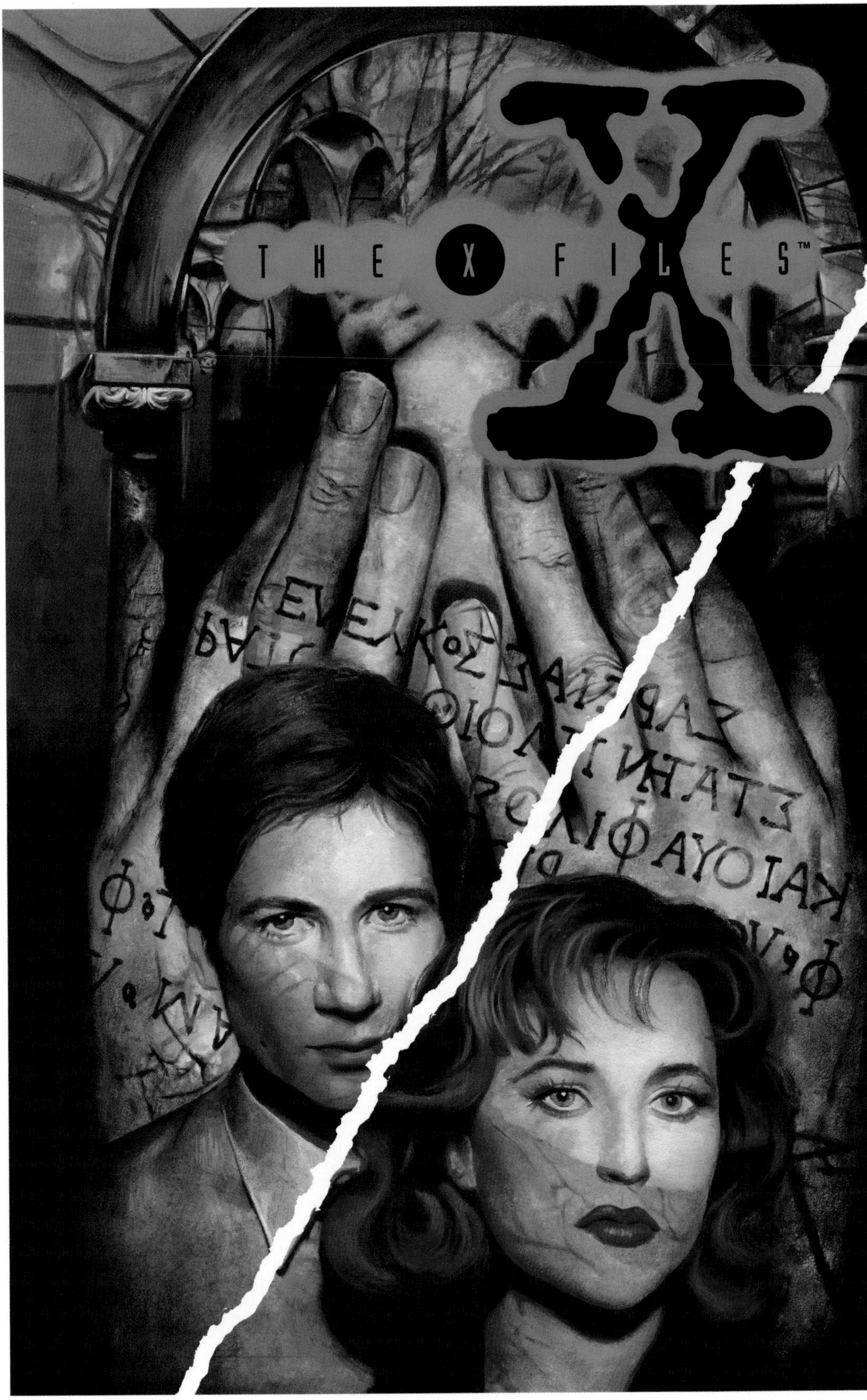
THE X FILES™

Art by Miran Kim

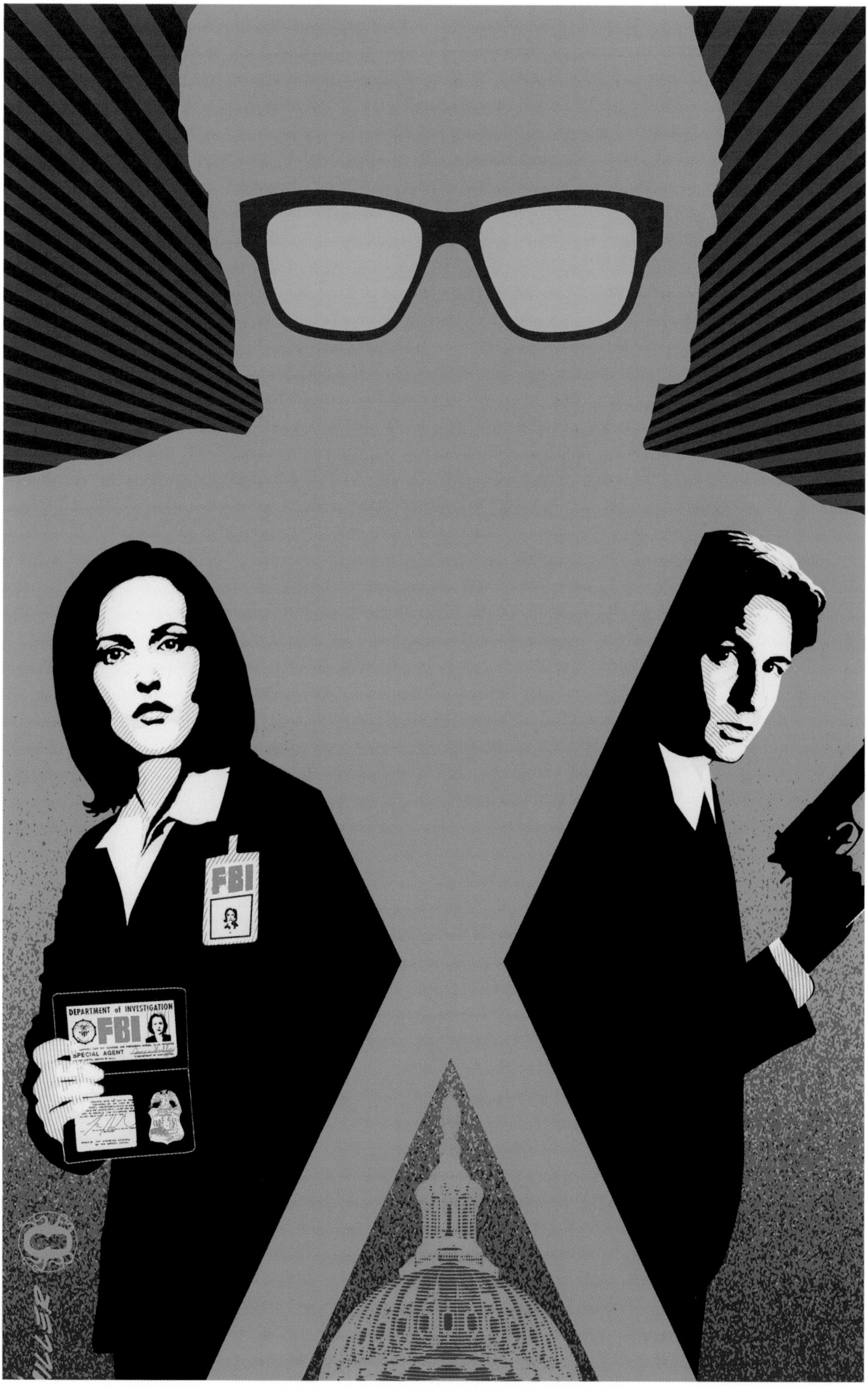
FBI
DEPARTMENT of INVESTIGATION
FBI
SPECIAL AGENT

Art by Brian Miller

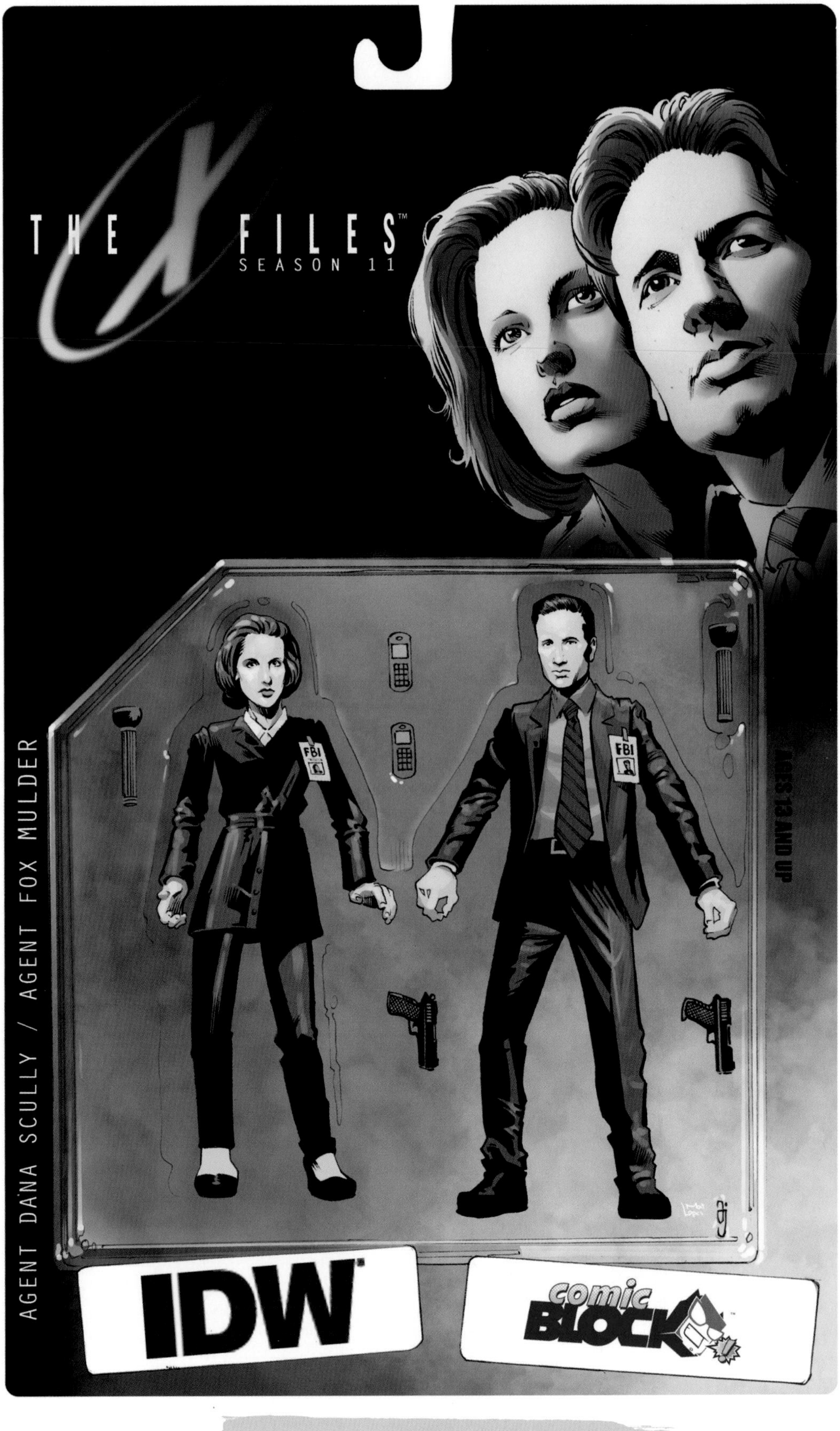
THE X FILES™
SEASON 11
AGENT DANA SCULLY / AGENT FOX MULDER
AGES 13 AND UP
FBI
FBI
IDW
comic
BLOCK

Art by Andrew Currie, Colors by Mat Lopes

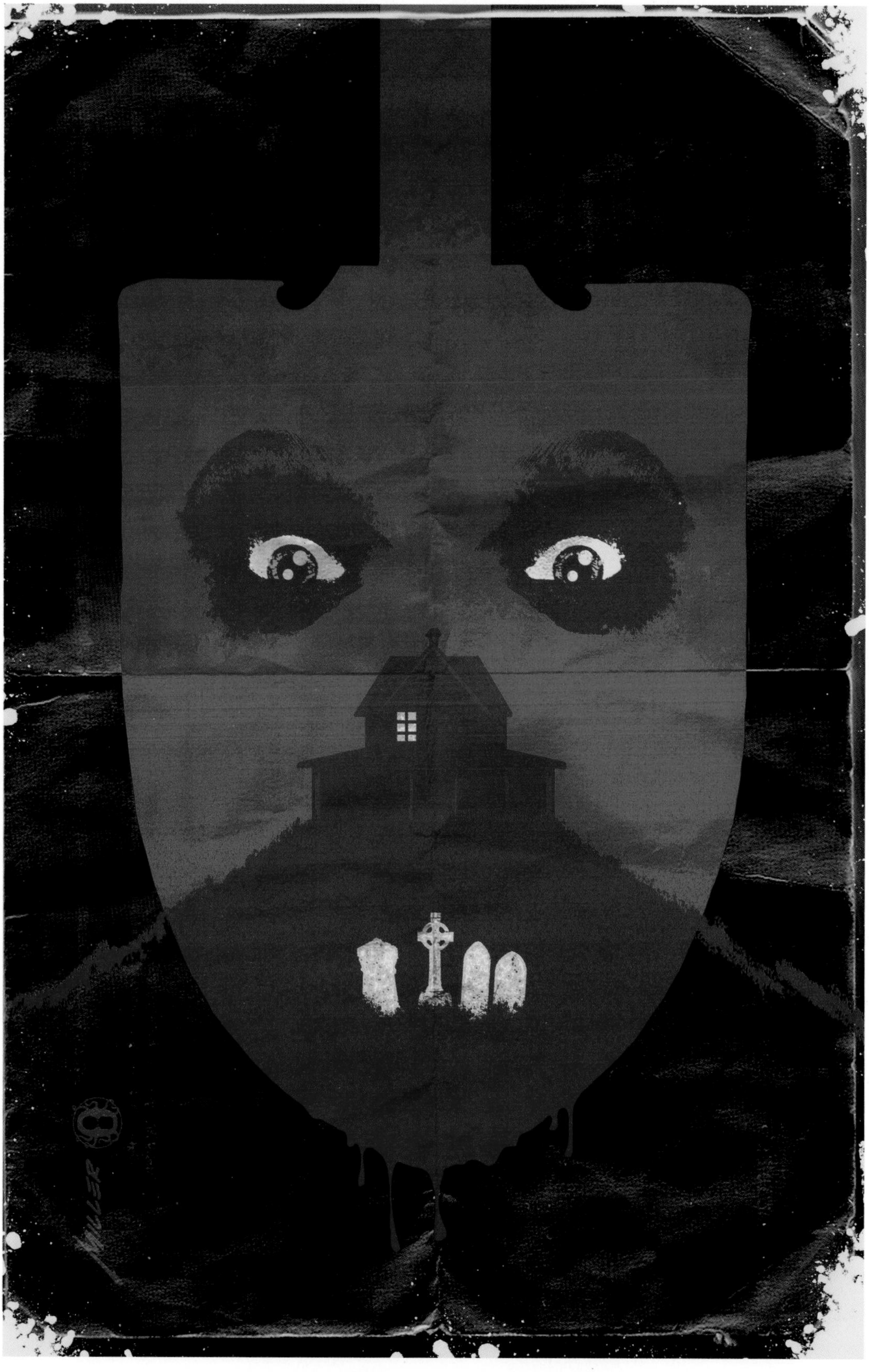
MILLER

Art by Brian Miller

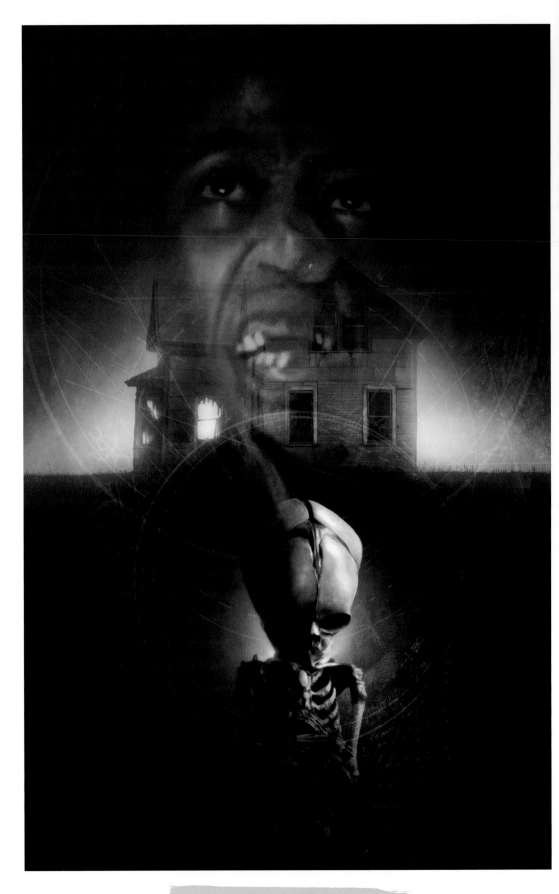

Art by Menton3

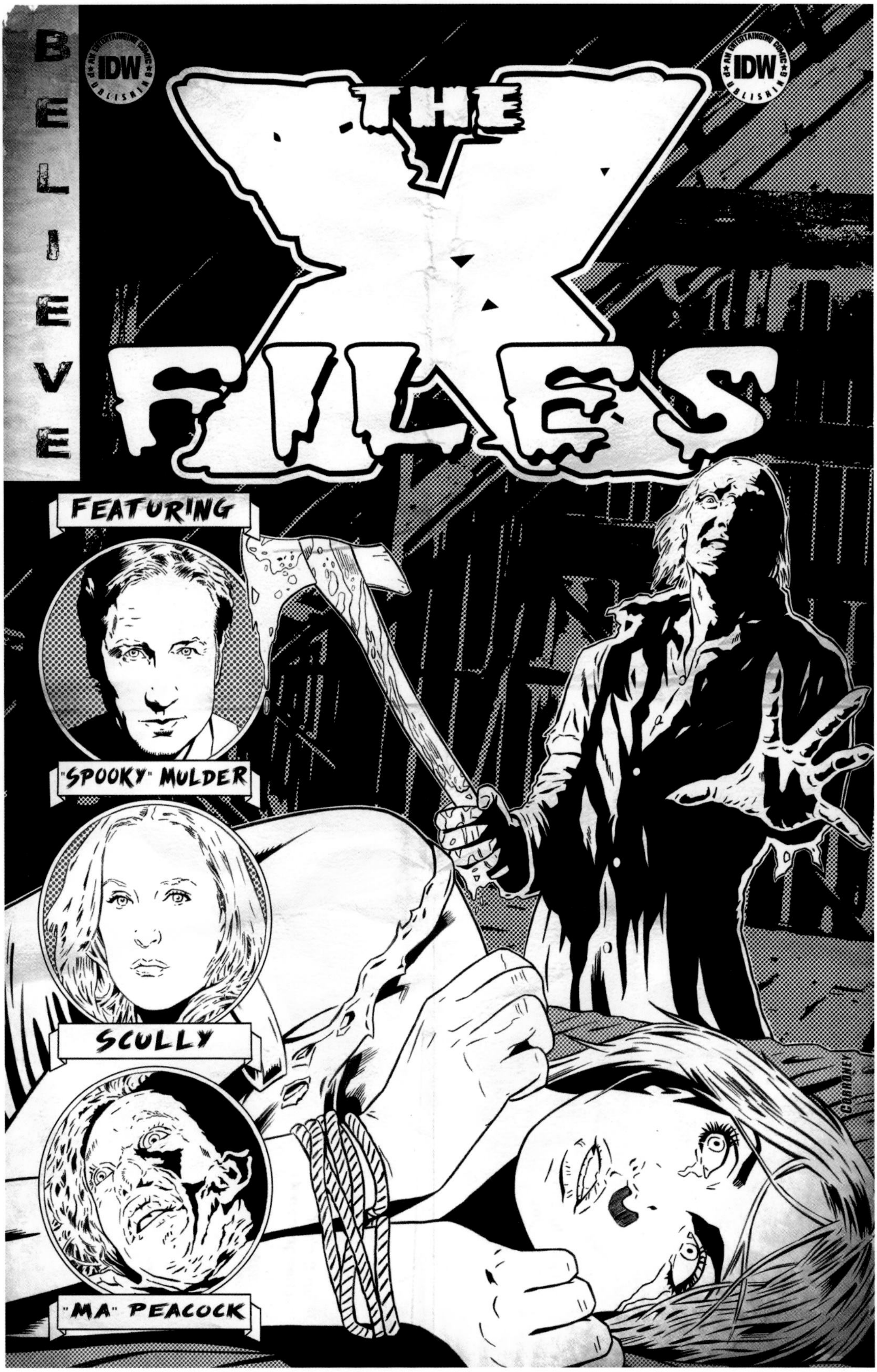
BELIEVE
IDW
IDW
THE X FILES
FEATURING
"SPOOKY" MULDER
SCULLY
"MA" PEACOCK
CORRONEY

Art by Joe Corroney

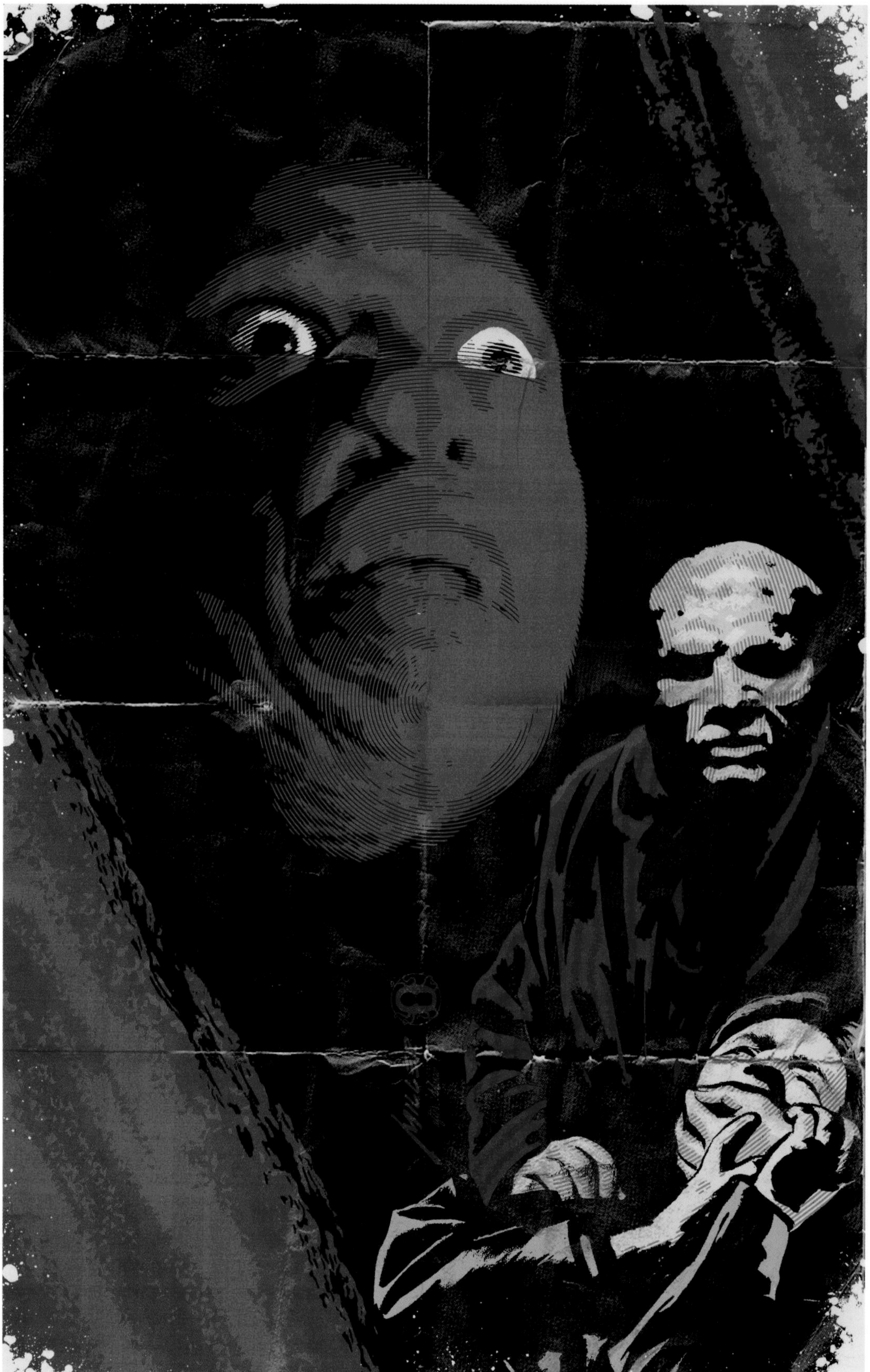

Art by Brian Miller

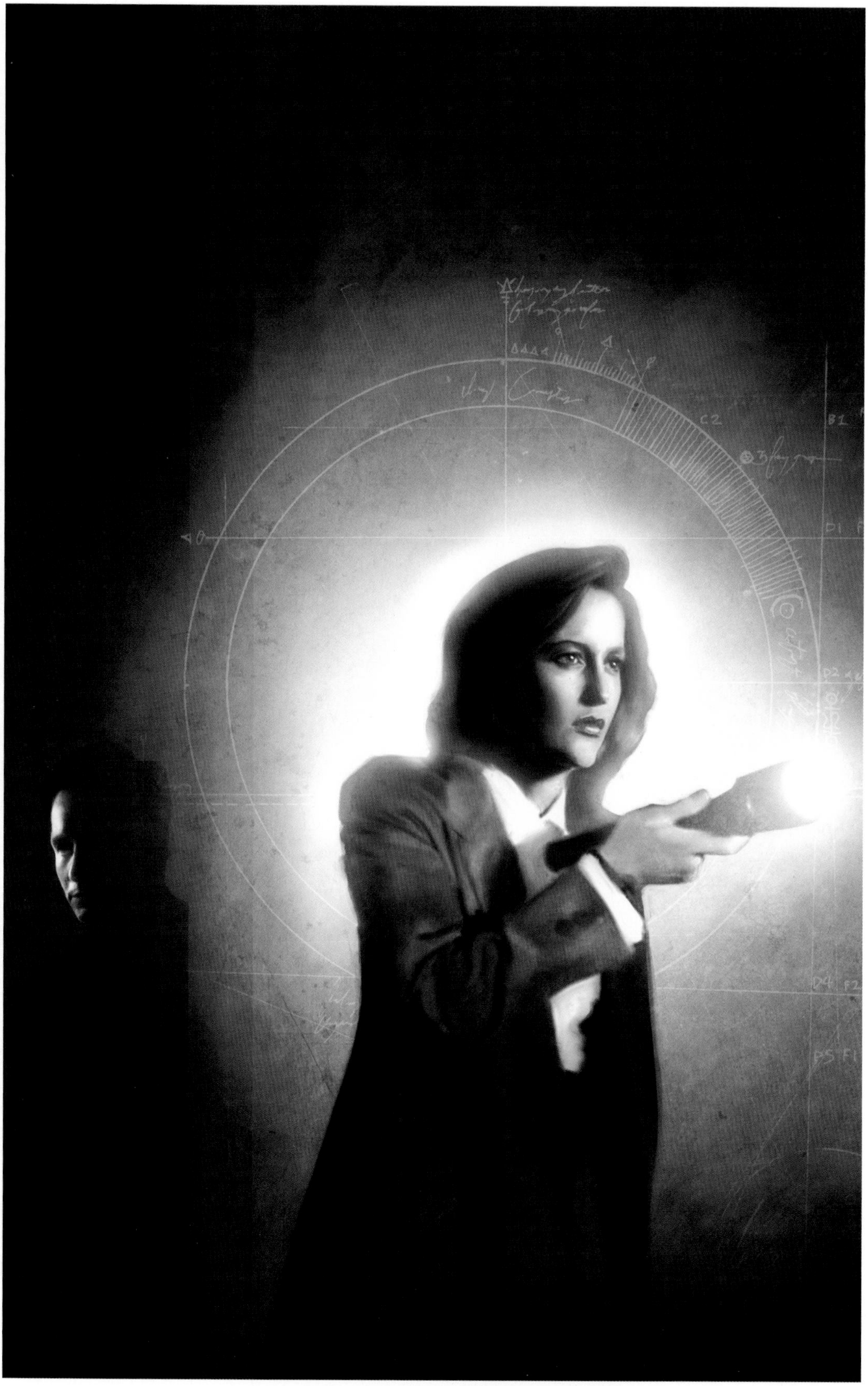

Art by Menton3

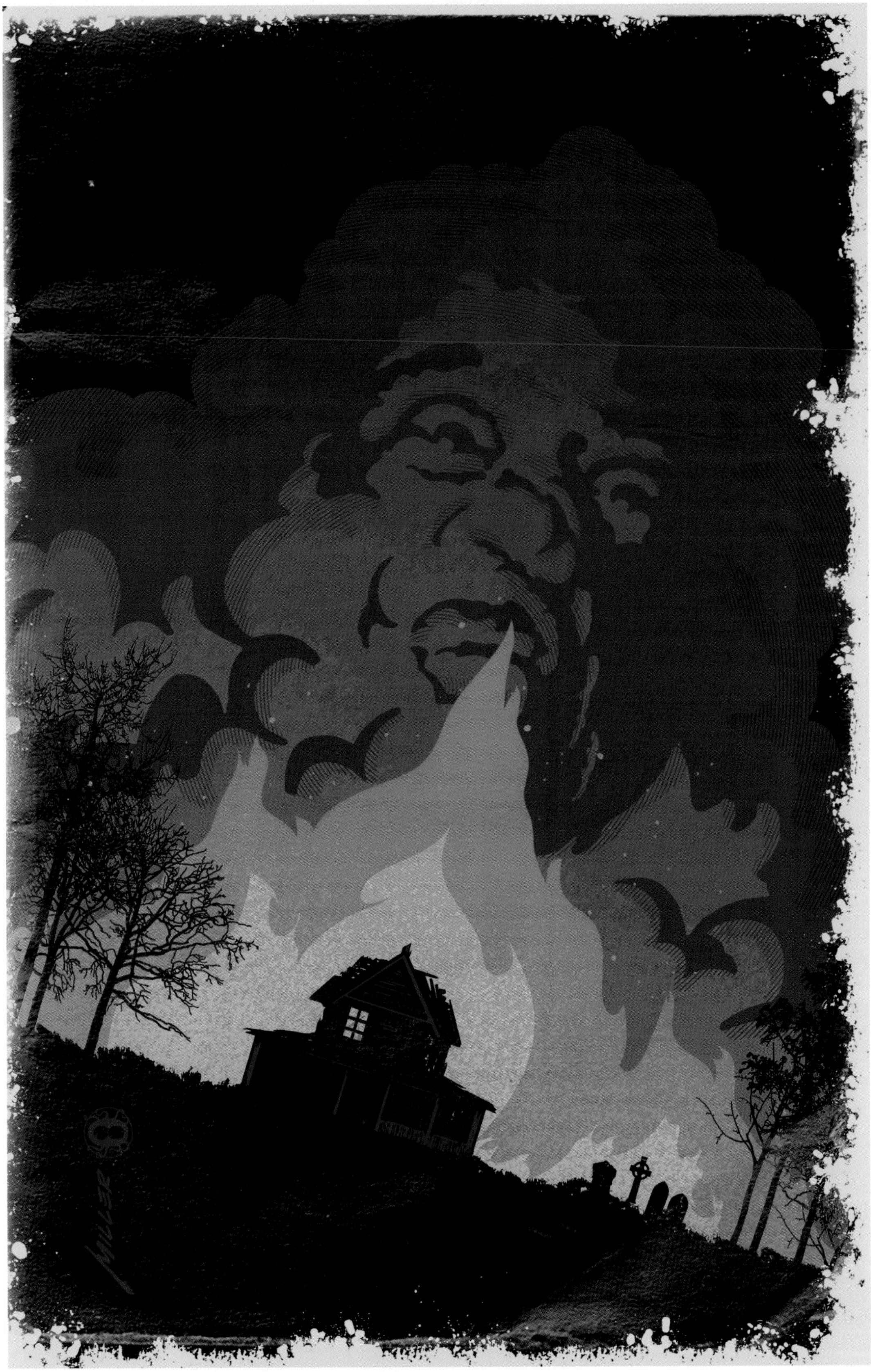

Art by Brian Miller

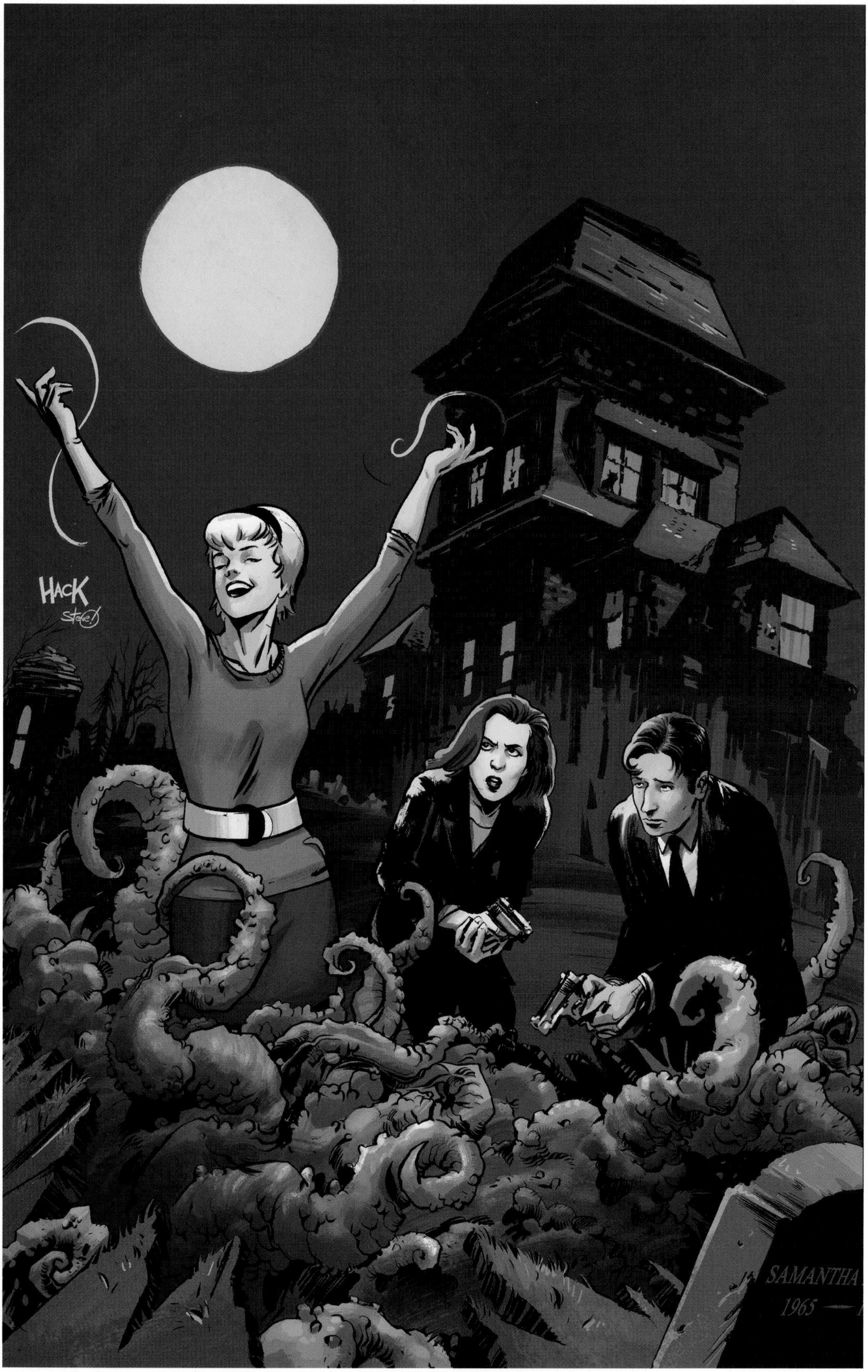
HACK
SAMANTHA
1965

Art by Robert Hack, Colors by Stephen Downer

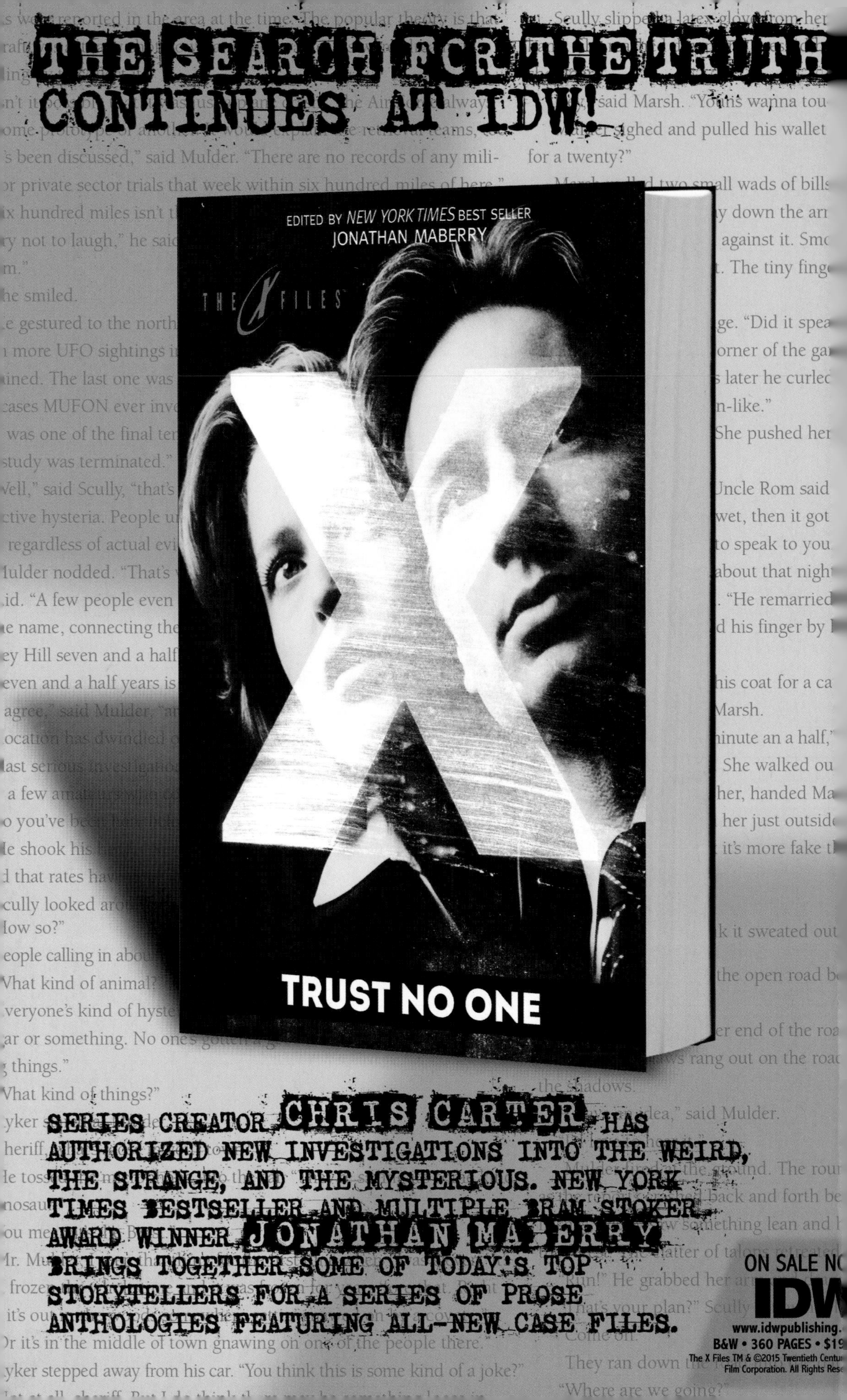
THE SEARCH FOR THE TRUTH CONTINUES AT IDW!
EDITED BY NEW YORK TIMES BEST SELLER
JONATHAN MABERRY
THE X FILES
X
TRUST NO ONE
SERIES CREATOR CHRIS CARTER HAS AUTHORIZED NEW INVESTIGATIONS INTO THE WEIRD, THE STRANGE, AND THE MYSTERIOUS. NEW YORK TIMES BESTSELLER AND MULTIPLE BRAM STOKER AWARD WINNER JONATHAN MABERRY BRINGS TOGETHER SOME OF TODAY'S TOP STORYTELLERS FOR A SERIES OF PROSE ANTHOLOGIES FEATURING ALL-NEW CASE FILES.
ON SALE NO
IDW
www.idwpublishing.
B&W • 360 PAGES • $19
The X Files TM & ©2015 Twentieth Centu
Film Corporation. All Rights Rese